FOUR
ENGLISH COMEDIES

*of the 17th and 18th
Centuries*

—

VOLPONE

THE WAY OF THE WORLD

SHE STOOPS TO CONQUER

THE SCHOOL FOR SCANDAL

—

Edited by J. M. Morrell

PENGUIN BOOKS

Penguin Books Ltd, Harmondsworth, Middlesex, England
Penguin Books Inc., 7110 Ambassador Road, Baltimore, Maryland 21207, U.S.A.
Penguin Books Australia Ltd, Ringwood, Victoria, Australia
Penguin Books Canada Ltd, 41 Steelcase Road West, Markham, Ontario, Canada
Penguin Books (N.Z.) Ltd, 182–190 Wairau Road, Auckland 10, New Zealand

—

This collection first published 1950
Reprinted 1951, 1954, 1959, 1960, 1962, 1964, 1965, 1967, 1969,
1970, 1971, 1972, 1974, 1975, 1976

—

Made and printed in Great Britain
by C. Nicholls & Company Ltd
Set in Monotype Baskerville

CONTENTS

PREFACE

English comedy would appear sufficiently rich for a choice of four representative plays to be a fairly easy task. Something by Shakespeare, naturally, Sheridan, Wilde, Shaw, and, warming to the work, a compiler could add name to name. Here the question of accessibility arises. The Importance of Being Earnest *is much easier to find than a copy of, say, Congreve's* Way of the World. *Therefore the aim of this volume is to provide a selection of plays which are established in their own right, and have the measure of universality which will ensure an audience as delighted now as when the play appeared – perhaps even more so – but which have not as yet been collected in a single volume.*

This, then, explains the omission alike of Shakespeare and more recent playwrights. Yet even now the choice is varied enough to call, perhaps, for an explanation of this particular selection. Pre-Shakespearian comedy will always be the field of the student of literature rather than the reader of plays. Shakespeare's elder contemporaries, such as Peele or Greene, have enough in common with Shakespeare to incline the general reader to dwell rather on what they lack in comparison with him than on what they possess in their own right. From the glorious summer of the seventeenth-century drama Ben Jonson chooses himself, for originality of subject, strength in treatment, and a distinctive and considered view of what he intended his comedy to achieve. Volpone *has been chosen as one of Jonson's finest plays; it reads most easily, and the weight of the satirical comedy gives the play a massive dignity and vigour.*

Restoration comedy must be represented. It is a remarkably self-contained body of social comedy, springing from the life of an urbane and leisured part of the community. Manners and attitudes provide the comedy, style and elegance adorn the language. Congreve's Way of the World *has been chosen chiefly because the dialogue moves with such exquisite grace:* 'Beauty the lover's gift? Lord, what is a lover, that it can give? Why, one makes lovers as fast as one pleases, and they live as long as one pleases, and then if one pleases one makes more.'

Moving on to the eighteenth century, a selection of writers makes itself, Sheridan and Goldsmith. Here also are plays which offer further varieties of comedy. The School for Scandal *and* She Stoops to Conquer *both show the fun that comes from a good comic plot, which includes mistaken identities, disguises, and, when Tony Lumpkin conducts the revels and leads his mother in a circumbendibus, something very near slapstick. Sheridan's* School for Scandal *has been chosen rather than* The Rivals, *as, in addition to a good plot, it offers more variety of character and, for example in the conversation of the scandal-mongers, more brilliant dialogue.* She Stoops to Conquer *is distinguished by something absent in all the other plays, a hearty good humour, an exuberant sense of fun, and characters all of whom are likeable.*

Though comedies, all four offer a different view of the comic theme. It is a pity that there is nothing to show English romantic comedy, but for this the reader must go to Shakespeare. The four plays selected are no chamber drama, but plays which have remained in the comic repertory. All have been on the stage within living memory, and, though Congreve or Jonson may be more in tune with our generation than Goldsmith, nevertheless it can safely be assumed that the wheel will come full circle and that each will have his turn.

The texts of all four plays have been carefully compared with the earliest printed editions, and are presented in each case without omissions of any kind, and with the stage directions of the original text. But, although the Prologues *and* Epilogues *have been added, it has not seemed necessary to include all those minor hors d'œuvres and savouries with which seventeenth and eighteenth century playwrights and their printers rejoiced to deck their literary dishes. Accordingly, Jonson's lengthy prose dedication of* Volpone *to 'the Two Famous Universities', Steele's prefatory verses to* The Way of the World *and Congreve's prose dedication of the play to Montague, Goldsmith's dedication to Jonson of* She Stoops to Conquer, *and Sheridan's 'Portrait' addressed to Mrs Crewe which appeared with the original edition of* The School for Scandal, *have been omitted.*

Spelling and capitalization have in general been adapted to modern practice, but the original punctuation has been followed except where it is likely to cause difficulty to a reader of the present day.

Volpone, *first acted in 1606, was first printed in the following year.* The Way of the World, *produced at the Lincoln's Inn Theatre in 1700, was first printed in the same year. The premier production of* She Stoops to Conquer *took place at Covent Garden in 1773; that of* The School for Scandal *at Drury Lane in 1777.*

VOLPONE;

or, The Fox

——

by BEN JONSON

THE PERSONS OF
THE PLAY

VOLPONE, *a Magnifico*
MOSCA, *his Parasite*
VOLTORE, *an Advocate*
CORBACCIO, *an old Gentleman*
CORVINO, *a Merchant*
BONARIO, *son to Corbaccio*
SIR POLITICK WOULD-BE, *a Knight*
PEREGRINE, *a Gentleman Traveller*
NANO, *a Dwarf*
CASTRONE, *an Eunuch*
ANDROGYNO, *an Hermaphrodite*
GREGE (*or Mob*)
Commandadori, *Officers of Justice*
Mercatori, *three Merchants*
Avocatori, *four Magistrates*
Notario, *the Register*
LADY WOULD-BE, *Sir Politick's Wife*
CELIA, *Corvino's Wife*
Servitori, Servants, *two* Waiting-women, &c.

SCENE — VENICE

VOLPONE; OR, THE FOX

—

ARGUMENT

V olpone, childless, rich, feigns sick, despairs,
O ffers his state to hopes of several heirs,
L ies languishing; his parasite receives
P resents of all, assures, deludes; then weaves
O ther cross-plots, which ope themselves, are told.
N ew tricks for safety are sought; they thrive; when, bold
E ach tempts the other again, and all are sold.

PROLOGUE

Now, luck yet send us, and a little wit
   Will serve to make our play hit;
(According to the palates of the season.)
   Here is rhyme, not empty of reason.
This we were bid to credit, from our poet,
   Whose true scope, if you would know it,
In all his poems still have been this measure,
   To mix profit with your pleasure;
And not as some, whose throats their envy failing,
   Cry hoarsely, all he writes is railing:
And when his plays come forth, think they can flout them,
   With saying, he was a year about them.
To this there needs no lie, but this his creature,
   Which was, two months since, no feature;
And though he dares give them five lives to mend it,
   'Tis known, five weeks fully penn'd it,
From his own hand, without a co-adjutor,
   Novince, journey-man, or tutor.

Yet thus much I can give you as a token
  Of his play's worth, no eggs are broken,
Nor quaking custards with fierce teeth affrighted
  Wherewith your rout are so delighted;
Nor hales he in a gull, old ends reciting,
  To stop gaps in his loose writing;
With such a deal of monstrous and forced action,
  As might make Bethlem a faction:
Nor made he his play for jests stolen from each table,
  But makes jests to fit his fable;
And so presents quick comedy, refined,
  As best critics have designed;
The laws of time, place, persons he observeth,
  From no needful rule he swerveth.
All gall and copperas from his ink he draineth,
  Only a little salt remaineth,
Wherewith he'll rub your cheeks, till, red with laughter,
  They shall look fresh a week after.

———

ACT I, SCENE 1

VOLPONE, MOSCA

Volp. Good morning to the day; and next, my gold:
  Open the shrine, that I may see my saint.
  Hail the world's soul, and mine. More glad than is
  The teeming earth to see the longed-for sun
  Peep through the horns of the celestial Ram,
  Am I, to view thy splendour darkening his;
  That lying here, amongst my other hoards,
  Showest like a flame by night; or like the day
  Struck out of chaos, when all darkness fled
  Unto the centre. O, thou son of Sol,
  But brighter than thy father, let me kiss,
  With adoration, thee, and every relic
  Of sacred treasure in this blessed room.
  Well did wise poets, by thy glorious name,

Title that age, which they would have the best;
Thou being the best of things, and far transcending
All style of joy, in children, parents, friends,
Or any other waking dream on earth.
Thy looks when they to Venus did ascribe,
They should have given her twenty thousand Cupids;
Such are thy beauties and our loves! Dear saint,
Riches, the dumb god, that givest all men tongues,
Thou canst do nought, and yet makest men do all
    things;
The price of souls; even hell, with thee to boot,
Is made worth heaven! Thou art virtue, fame,
Honour, and all things else! Who can get thee,
He shall be noble, valiant, honest, wise –
Mos. And what he will, sir. Riches are in fortune
A greater good, than wisdom is in nature.
Volp. True, my beloved Mosca. Yet I glory
More in the cunning purchase of my wealth,
Than in the glad possession, since I gain
No common way: I use no trade, no venture;
I wound no earth with plough-shares; fat no beasts,
To feed the shambles; have no mills for iron,
Oil, corn, or men, to grind them into powder;
I blow no subtle glass; expose no ships
To threatening of the furrow-faced sea;
I turn no monies in the public bank,
Nor usure private –
Mos. No, sir, nor devour
Soft prodigals. You shall have some will swallow
A melting heir as glibly as your Dutch
Will pills of butter, and ne'er purge for it;
Tear forth the fathers of poor families
Out of their beds, and coffin them, alive,
In some kind, clasping prison, where their bones
May be forthcoming, when the flesh is rotten;
But your sweet nature doth abhor these courses;
You loathe the widow's or the orphan's tears

Should wash your pavements, or their piteous cries
Ring in your roofs, and beat the air for vengeance.
Volp. Right, Mosca, I do loathe it.
Mos. And besides, sir,
You are not like the thresher that doth stand
With a huge flail, watching a heap of corn,
And, hungry, dares not taste the smallest grain,
But feeds on mallows, and such bitter herbs;
Nor like the merchant, who hath filled his vaults
With Romagnia, and rich Candian wines,
Yet drinks the lees of Lombard's vinegar:
You will lie not in straw, whilst moths and worms
Feed on your sumptuous hangings and soft beds.
You know the use of riches, and dare give now
From that bright heap, to me, your poor observer,
Or to your dwarf, or your hermaphrodite,
Your eunuch, or what other household trifle
Your pleasure allows maintenance –
Volp. Hold thee, Mosca,   [*Gives him money.*
Take of my hand; thou strik'st on truth in all,
And they are envious term thee parasite.
Call forth my dwarf, my eunuch, and my fool,
And let them make me sport.
            [*Exit Mos.*] What should I do,
But cocker up my genius, and live free
To all delights my fortune calls me to?
I have no wife, no parent, child, ally,
To give my substance to; but whom I make
Must be my heir: and this makes men observe me.
This draws new clients, daily, to my house,
Women and men of every sex and age,
That bring me presents, send me plate, coin, jewels,
With hope that when I die (which they expect
Each greedy minute) it shall then return,
Tenfold, upon them; whilst some, covetous
Above the rest, seek to engross me whole,
And counter-work the one unto the other,

Contend in gifts, as they would seem in love:
All which I suffer, playing with their hopes,
And am content to coin them into profit,
And look upon their kindness, and take more,
And look on that; still bearing them in hand,
Letting the cherry knock against their lips,
And draw it by their mouths, and back again.
How now!

———

ACT I, SCENE 2

NANO, ANDROGYNO, CASTRONE, VOLPONE, MOSCA

Nan. Now, room for fresh gamesters, who do will you to
        know
They do bring you neither play nor university show;
And therefore do intreat you, that whatsoever they
        rehearse,
    May not fare a whit the worse, for the false pace
    of the verse.
If you wonder at this, you will wonder more ere we pass,
    For know, here is inclosed the soul of Pythagoras,
That juggler divine, as hereafter shall follow;
    Which soul, fast and loose, sir, came first from Apollo,
And was breath'd into Æthalides, Mercurius his son,
    Where it had the gift to remember all that ever was
    done.
From thence it fled forth, and made quick trans-
        migration
    To goldy-lock'd Euphorbus, who was killed, in good
    fashion,
At the siege of old Troy, by the Cuckold of Sparta.
    Hermotimus was next (I find it in my charta)
To whom it did pass, where no sooner it was missing,
    But with one Pyrrhus of Delos it learn'd to go a
    fishing;

And thence did it enter the Sophist of Greece.
　　From Pythagore, she went into a beautiful piece,
　Hight Aspasia, the meretrix; and the next toss of her
　　Was again of a whore, she became a philosopher,
Crates the cynic, as itself doth relate it:
　　Since kings, knights, and beggars, knaves, lords, and
　　　fools gat it,
Besides ox and ass, camel, mule, goat, and brock.
　　In all which it hath spoke, as in the cobbler's cock.
But I come not here to discourse of that matter,
　Or his one, two, or three, or his great oath, BY
　　QUATER!
His musics, his trigon, his golden thigh,
　　Or his telling how elements shift, but I
Would ask, how of late thou hast suffered translation,
　　And shifted thy coat in these days of reformation?
And. Like one of the reformed, a fool, as you see,
　Counting all old doctrine heresy.
Nan. But not on thine own forbid meats hast thou
　ventured?
And. On fish, when first a Carthusian I enter'd.
Nan. Why, then thy dogmatical silence hath left thee?
And. Of that an obstreperous lawyer bereft me.
Nan. O wonderful change, when sir lawyer forsook thee!
　For Pythagore's sake, what body then took thee?
And. A good dull mule.
Nan. 　　　　　　　　　And how! by that means
　Thou wert brought to allow of the eating of beans?
And. Yes.
Nan. 　　　But from the mule into whom didst thou pass?
And. Into a very strange beast, by some writers call'd
　　an ass;
　By others a precise pure, illuminate brother,
　　Of those devour flesh, and sometimes one another;
　And will drop you forth a libel, or a sanctified lie,
　　Betwixt every spoonful of a nativity pie.
Nan. Now quit thee for heaven, of that profane nation,

And gently report thy next transmigration.

And. To the same that I am.

Nan.   A creature of delight?
And, what is more than a fool, an hermaphrodite?
Now pray thee, sweet soul, in all thy variation
Which body would'st thou choose to take up thy
    station?

And. Troth, this I am in, even here would I tarry.

Nan. 'Cause here, the delight of each sex thou canst vary?

And. Alas, those pleasures be stale, and forsaken;
No, 'tis your fool wherewith I am so taken,
The only one creature that I can call blessed;
For all other forms I have proved most distressed.

Nan. Spoke true, as thou wert in Pythagoras still.
This learned opinion we celebrate will,
Fellow eunuch, as behoves us, with all our wit and art,
To dignity that whereof ourselves are so great and
    special a part.

Volp. Now very, very pretty. Mosca, this
Was thy invention?

Mos. If it please my patron,
Not else.

Volp. It doth, good Mosca.

Mos. Then it was, sir.

Nano *and* Castrone *sing*

Fools, they are the only nation
Worth men's envy or admiration;
Free from care or sorrow-taking,
Selves and others merry making:
All they speak or do is sterling.
Your fool, he is your great man's darling,
And your ladies' sport and pleasure;
Tongue and bauble are his treasure.
E'en his face begetteth laughter,
And he speaks truth, free from slaughter;
He's the grace of every feast,
And sometimes the chiefest guest:
Hath his trencher and his stool,

When wit waits upon the fool.
O, who would not be
He, he, he?

[One knocks without.

Volp. Who's that? Away!　　*[Exeunt Nano and Castrone.*
Look, Mosca.
Mos. Fool. Begone!　　　　　*[Exit Androgyno.*
'Tis Signior Voltore, the advocate,
I know him by his knock.
Volp. Fetch me my gown,
My furs and nightcaps; say, my couch is changing,
And let him entertain himself awhile
Without i' the gallery. [*Exit Mosca*] Now, now, my
　clients
Begin their visitation! Vulture, kite,
Raven, and gorcrow, all my birds of prey,
That think me turning carcase, now they come;
I am not for them yet.

Re-enter MOSCA, *with the gown, etc.*

How now! The news?

Mos. A piece of plate, sir.
Volp. Of what bigness?
Mos. Huge,
Massy, and antique, with your name inscribed,
And arms engraven.
Volp. Good! and not a fox
Stretched on the earth, with fine delusive sleights,
Mocking a gaping crow? Ha, Mosca?
Mos. Sharp, sir.
Volp. Give me my furs. [*Puts on his sick dress*] Why dost
　thou laugh so, man?
Mos. I cannot choose, sir, when I apprehend
What thoughts he has without now, as he walks:
That this might be the last gift he should give;
That this would fetch you; if you died today,
And gave him all, what he should be tomorrow;
What large return would come of all his ventures;

How he should worshipped be, and reverenced;
Ride with his furs and foot-cloths; waited on
By herds of fools, and clients; have clear way
Made for his mule, as lettered as himself;
Be called the great and learned advocate:
And then concludes, there's nought impossible.

Volp. Yes, to be learned, Mosca.

Mos. O, no: rich
  Implies it. Hood an ass with reverend purple,
  So you can hide his two ambitious ears,
  And he shall pass for a cathedral doctor.

Volp. My caps, my caps, good Mosca. Fetch him in.

Mos. Stay, sir; your ointment for your eyes.

Volp. That's true;
  Dispatch, dispatch: I long to have possession
  Of my new present.

Mos. That, and thousands more,
  I hope to see you lord of.

Volp. Thanks, kind Mosca.

Mos. And that, when I am lost in blended dust,
  And hundred such, as I am, in succession –

Volp. Nay, that were too much, Mosca.

Mos. You shall live,
  Still, to delude these harpies.

Volp. Loving Mosca,
  'Tis well: my pillow now, and let him enter.

                              [*Exit Mosca.*
  Now, my feigned cough, my phthisic, and my gout,
  My apoplexy, palsy, and catarrhs,
  Help, with your forced functions, this my posture,
  Wherein, this three year, I have milked their hopes.
  He comes; I hear him – Uh! uh! uh! uh! O –

ACT I, SCENE 3

MOSCA, VOLTORE, VOLPONE

Mos. You still are what you were, sir. Only you,
   Of all the rest, are he commands his love:
   And you do wisely to preserve it, thus,
   With early visitation and kind notes
   Of your good meaning to him, which, I know,
   Cannot but come most grateful. Patron, sir,
   Here's Signior Voltore is come –

Volp. [*faintly.*] What say you?

Mos. Sir, Signior Voltore is come this morning
   To visit you.

Volp. I thank him.

Mos. And hath brought
   A piece of antique plate, bought of St Mark,
   With which he here presents you.

Volp. He is welcome.
   Pray him to come more often.

Mos. Yes.

Volt. What says he?

Mos. He thanks you, and desires you see him often.

Volp. Mosca.

Mos. My patron?

Volp. Bring him near, where is he?
   I long to feel his hand.

Mos. The plate is here, sir.

Volt. How fare you, sir?

Volp. I thank you, Signior Voltore.
   Where is the plate? Mine eyes are bad.

Volt. [*putting it into his hands.*] I'm sorry
   To see you still thus weak.

Mos. That he is not weaker.   [*Aside.*

Volp. You are too munificent.

Volt. No, sir, would to heaven,
   I could as well give health to you, as that plate.

Volp. You give, sir, what you can. I thank you. Your
   love
  Hath taste in this, and shall not be unanswered:
  I pray you see me often.
Volt. Yes, I shall, sir.
Volp. Be not far from me.
Mos. Do you observe that, sir?
Volp. Hearken unto me still; it will concern you.
Mos. You are a happy man, sir; know your good.
Volp. I cannot now last long –
Mos. You are his heir, sir.
Volt. Am I?
Volp. I feel me going; uh! uh! uh! uh!
  I am sailing to my port. Uh! uh! uh! uh!
  And I am glad I am so near my haven.
Mos. Alas, kind gentleman. Well, we must all go –
Volt. But, Mosca –
Mos. Age will conquer.
Volt. Pray thee, hear me.
  Am I inscribed his heir for certain?
Mos. Are you?
  I do beseech you, sir, you will vouchsafe
  To write me i' your family. All my hopes
  Depend upon your worship. I am lost,
  Except the rising sun do shine on me.
Volt. It shall both shine, and warm thee, Mosca.
Mos. Sir,
  I am a man that hath not done your love
  All the worst offices: here I wear your keys,
  See all your coffers and your caskets locked,
  Keep the poor inventory of your jewels,
  Your plate and monies, am your steward, sir,
  Husband your goods here.
Volt. But am I sole heir?
Mos. Without a partner, sir, confirmed this morning;
  The wax is warm yet, and the ink scarce dry
  Upon the parchment.

Volt. Happy, happy, me!
　By what good chance, sweet Mosca?
Mos. Your desert, sir;
　I know no second cause.
Volt. Thy modesty
　Is not to know it: well, we shall requite it.
Mos. He ever liked your course, sir, that first took him.
　I oft have heard him say how he admired
　Men of your large profession, that could speak
　To every cause, and things mere contraries,
　Till they were hoarse again, yet all be law;
　That, with most quick agility, could turn,
　And re-turn; make knots, and undo them;
　Give forked counsel; take provoking gold
　On either hand, and put it up; these men,
　He knew, would thrive with their humility.
　And for his part he thought he should be blest
　To have his heir of such a suffering spirit,
　So wise, so grave, of so perplex'd a tongue,
　And loud withal, that would not wag, nor scarce
　Lie still, without a fee; when every word
　Your worship but lets fall, is a *cecchine*! –
　　　　　　　　　　　　　　　[*Another knocks.*
　Who's that? One knocks, I would not have you seen,
　　sir.
　And yet – pretend you came, and went in haste:
　I'll fashion an excuse. And, gentle sir,
　When you do come to swim in golden lard,
　Up to the arms in honey, that your chin
　Is borne up stiff with fatness of the flood,
　Think on your vassal; but remember me;
　I have not been your worst of clients.
Volt. Mosca –
Mos. When will you have your inventory brought, sir?
　Or see a copy of the will? – Anon –
　I'll bring them to you, sir. Away, be gone,
　Put business i' your face.　　　　　[*Exit Voltore.*

Volp. [*springing up.*] Excellent, Mosca!
  Come hither, let me kiss thee.
Mos. Keep you still, sir.
  Here is Corbaccio.
Volp. Set the plate away:
  The vulture's gone, and the old raven's come!

———

ACT I, SCENE 4
Mosca, Corbaccio, Volpone

Mos. Betake you to your silence, and your sleep:
  Stand there and multiply. [*Putting the plate to the rest.*
    Now, shall we see
  A wretch who is indeed more impotent
  Than this can feign to be; yet hopes to hop
  Over his grave.
              Signior Corbaccio!
  You're very welcome, sir.
Corb. How does your patron?
Mos. Troth, as he did, sir; no amends.
Corb. What! mends he?
Mos. No, sir: he is rather worse.
Corb. That's well. Where is he?
Mos. Upon his couch, sir, newly fall'n asleep.
Corb. Does he sleep well?
Mos. No wink, sir, all this night,
  Nor yesterday; but slumbers.
Corb. Good! He should take
  Some counsel of physicians: I have brought him
  An opiate here, from mine own doctor.
Mos. He will not hear of drugs.
Corb. Why? I myself
  Stood by while it was made, saw all the ingredients:
  And know it cannot but most gently work.
  My life for his, 'tis but to make him sleep.
Volp. Ay, his last sleep, if he would take it.   [*Aside.*

Mos. Sir,
  He has no faith in physic.
Corb. Say you, say you?
Mos. He has no faith in physic: he does think
  Most of your doctors are the greater danger,
  And worse disease, t' escape. I often have
  Heard him protest that your physician
  Should never be his heir.
Corb. Not I his heir?
Mos. Not your physician, sir.
Corb. O, no, no, no.
  I do not mean it.
Mos. No, sir, nor their fees
  He cannot brook: he says, they flay a man
  Before they kill him.
Corb. Right, I do conceive you.
Mos. And then, they do it by experiment;
  For which the law not only doth absolve them,
  But gives them great reward: and he is loth
  To hire his death so.
Corb. It is true, they kill
  With as much license as a judge.
Mos. Nay, more:
  For he but kills, sir, where the law condemns,
  And these can kill him too.
Corb. Ay, or me;
  Or any man. How does his apoplex?
  Is that strong on him still?
Mos. Most violent.
  His speech is broken, and his eyes are set,
  His face drawn longer than 'twas wont —
Corb. How? how?
  Stronger than he was wont?
Mos. No, sir: his face
  Drawn longer than 'twas wont.
Corb. O, good!

Mos. His mouth
  Is ever gaping, and his eyelids hang.
Corb. Good.
Mos. A freezing numbness stiffens all his joints,
  And makes the colour of his flesh like lead.
Corb. 'Tis good.
Mos. His pulse beats slow and dull.
Corb. Good symptoms still.
Mos. And from his brain –
Corb. I conceive you; good.
Mos. Flows a cold sweat, with a continual rheum,
  Forth the resolved corners of his eyes.
Corb. Is it possible? Yet I am better, ha!
  How does he with the swimming of his head?
Mos. Oh, sir, 'tis past the scotomy; he now
  Hath lost his feeling, and hath left to snort!
  You hardly can perceive him, that he breathes.
Corb. Excellent, excellent, sure I shall outlast him:
  This makes me young again, a score of years.
Mos. I was a-coming for you, sir.
Corb. Has he made his will?
  What has he given me?
Mos. No, sir.
Corb. Nothing? ha?
Mos. He has not made his will, sir.
Corb. Oh, oh, oh!
  What then did Voltore, the lawyer, here?
Mos. He smelt a carcase, sir, when he but heard
  My master was about his testament;
  As I did urge him to it, for your good –
Corb. He came unto him, did he? I thought so.
Mos. Yes, and presented him this piece of plate.
Corb. To be his heir?
Mos. I do not know, sir.
Corb. True,
  I know it too.

Mos. By your own scale, sir.   [*Aside.*
Corb. Well,
    I shall prevent him yet. See, Mosca, look,
    Here, I have brought a bag of bright *cecchines*,
    Will quite weigh down his plate.
Mos. [*taking the bag.*] Yea, marry, sir.
    This is true physic, this your sacred medicine;
    No talk of opiates, to this great elixir!
Cor. 'Tis *aurum palpabile*, if not *potabile*.
Mos. It shall be ministered to him, in his bowl.
Corb. Ay, do, do, do.
Mos. Most blessed cordial!
    This will recover him.
Corb. Yes, do, do, do.
Mos. I think it were not best, sir.
Corb. What?
Mos. To recover him.
Corb. O, no, no, no; by no means.
Mos. Why, sir, this
    Will work some strange effect, if he but feel it.
Corb. 'Tis true, therefore forbear; I'll take my venture:
    Give me't again.
Mos. At no hand, pardon me;
    You shall not do yourself that wrong, sir. I
    Will so advise you, you shall have it all.
Corb. How?
Mos. All, sir, 'tis your right, your own: no man
    Can claim a part: 'tis yours, without a rival,
    Decreed by destiny.
Corb. How, how, good Mosca?
Mos. I'll tell you, sir. This fit he shall recover —
Corb. I do conceive you.
Mos. And, on first advantage
    Of his gained sense, will I re-importune him
    Unto the making of his testament:
    And show him this.   [*Pointing to the money.*
Corb. Good, good.

Mos. 'Tis better yet,
  If you will hear, sir.
Corb. Yes, with all my heart.
Mos. Now, would I counsel you, make home with speed;
  There frame a will; whereto you shall inscribe
  My master your sole heir.
Corb. And disinherit
  My son?
Mos. O, sir, the better: for that colour
  Shall make it much more taking.
Corb. O, but colour?
Mos. This will, sir, you shall send it unto me.
  Now, when I come to enforce, as I will do,
  Your cares, your watchings, and your many prayers,
  Your more than many gifts, your this day's present,
  And last, produce your will; where, without thought,
  Or least regard, unto your proper issue,
  A son so brave, and highly meriting,
  The stream of your diverted love hath thrown you
  Upon my master, and made him your heir:
  He cannot be so stupid, or stone-dead,
  But, out of conscience and mere gratitude —
Corb. He must pronounce me his?
Mos. 'Tis true.
Corb. This plot
  Did I think on before.
Mos. I do believe it.
Corb. Do you not believe it?
Mos. Yes, sir.
Corb. Mine own project.
Mos. Which when he hath done, sir —
Corb. Published me his heir?
Mos. And you so certain to survive him —
Corb. Ay.
Mos. Being so lusty a man —
Corb. 'Tis true.
Mos. Yes, sir —

Corb. I thought on that too. See how he should be
  The very organ to express my thoughts!
Mos. You have not only done yourself a good –
Corb. But multiplied it on my son?
Mos. 'Tis right, sir.
Corb. Still, my invention.
Mos. 'Las, sir, heaven knows,
  It hath been all my study, all my care,
  (I e'en grow grey withal), how to work things –
Corb. I do conceive, sweet Mosca.
Mos. You are he
  For whom I labour here.
Corb. Ay, do, do, do:
  I'll straight about it.   [*Going.*
Mos. Rook go with you, raven.
Corb. I know thee honest.
Mos. You do lie, sir –   [*Aside.*
Corb. And –
Mos. Your knowledge is no better than your ears, sir.
Corb. I do not doubt to be a father to thee.
Mos. Nor I to gull my brother of his blessing.
Corb. I may have my youth restored to me, why not?
Mos. Your worship is a precious ass –
Corb. What say'st thou?
Mos. I do desire your worship to make haste, sir.
Corb. 'Tis done, 'tis done, I go.   [*Exit.*
Volp. [*leaping from his couch.*] O, I shall burst;
  Let out my sides, let out my sides –
Mos. Contain
  Your flux of laughter, sir: you know this hope
  Is such a bait, it covers any hook.
Volp. O, but thy working and thy placing it!
  I cannot hold; good rascal, let me kiss thee:
  I never knew thee in so rare a humour.
Mos. Alas, sir, I but do as I am taught;
  Follow your grave instructions; give them words;
  Pour oil into their ears: and send them hence.

Volp. 'Tis true, 'tis true. What a rare punishment
  Is avarice to itself!
Mos. Ay, with our help, sir.
Volp. So many cares, so many maladies,
  So many fears attending on old age,
  Yea, death so often called on, as no wish
  Can be more frequent with them, their limbs faint,
  Their senses dull, their seeing, hearing, going,
  All dead before them; yea, their very teeth,
  Their instruments of eating, failing them:
  Yet this is reckoned life! Nay, here was one,
  Is now gone home, that wishes to live longer!
  Feels not his gout, nor palsy; feigns himself
  Younger by scores of years, flatters his age
  With confident belying it, hopes he may,
  With charms, like Æson, have his youth restored:
  And with these thoughts so battens, as if fate
  Would be as easily cheated on, as he,
  And all turns air! [*Knocking within.*] Who's that there,
    now? a third!
Mos. Close, to your couch again; I hear his voice:
  It is Corvino, our spruce merchant.
Volp. [*lies down as before.*] Dead.
Mos. Another bout, sir, with your eyes. [*Anointing them.*]
  Who's there?

———

ACT I, SCENE 5

Mosca, Corvino, Volpone

Mos. Signor Corvino! come most wish'd for! O,
  How happy were you, if you knew it, now!
Corv. Why? what? wherein?
Mos. The tardy hour is come, sir.
Corv. He is not dead?
Mos. Not dead, sir, but as good;
  He knows no man.

Corv. How shall I do then?

Mos. Why, sir?

Corv. I have brought him here a pearl.

Mos. Perhaps he has
　　So much remembrance left as to know you, sir;
　　He still calls on you; nothing but your name
　　Is in his mouth. Is your pearl orient, sir?

Corv. Venice was never owner of the like.

Volp. [*faintly.*] Signor Corvino.

Mos. Hark.

Volp. Signor Corvino.

Mos. He calls you, step and give it him. He's here, sir,
　　And he has brought you a rich pearl.

Corv. How do you, sir?
　　Tell him it doubles the twelfth carat.

Mos. Sir,
　　He cannot understand, his hearing's gone;
　　And yet it comforts him to see you —

Corv. Say,
　　I have a diamond for him, too.

Mos. Best show 't, sir;
　　Put it into his hand; 'tis only there
　　He apprehends: he has his feeling yet.
　　See, how he grasps it!

Corv. 'Las, good gentleman!
　　How pitiful the sight is!

Mos. Tut! forget, sir.
　　The weeping of an heir should still be laughter
　　Under a visor.

Corv. Why, am I his heir?

Mos. Sir, I am sworn, I may not show the will
　　Till he be dead; but here has been Corbaccio,
　　Here has been Voltore, here were others too,
　　I cannot number 'em, they were so many,
　　All gaping here for legacies; but I,
　　Taking the vantage of his naming you,
　　Signor Corvino, Signor Corvino, took

Paper and pen and ink, and there I asked him,
Whom he would have his heir? Corvino. Who
Should be executor? Corvino. And,
To any question he was silent to,
I still interpreted the nods he made,
Through weakness, for consent: and sent home the
    others,
Nothing bequeathed them, but to cry and curse.

Corv. Oh, my dear Mosca! [*They embrace.*] Does he not
    perceive us?

Mos. No more than a blind harper. He knows no man,
No face of friend, nor name of any servant,
Who 'twas that fed him last, or gave him drink:
Not those he hath begotten, or brought up,
Can he remember.

Corv. Has he children?

Mos. Bastards,
Some dozen, or more, that he begot on beggars,
Gipsies, and Jews, and blackmoors, when he was
    drunk.
Knew you not that, sir? 'Tis the common fable.
The dwarf, the fool, the eunuch, are all his;
He's the true father of his family,
In all, save me: but he has given them nothing.

Corv. That's well, that's well. Art sure he does not hear
    us?

Mos. Sure, sir? Why, look you, credit your own sense.
                              [*Shouts in Vol.'s ear.*
The pox approach, and add to your diseases,
If it would send you hence the sooner, sir,
For your incontinence, it hath deserved it
Throughly, and throughly, and the plague to boot.
You may come near, sir. Would you would once close
Those filthy eyes of yours, that flow with slime,
Like two frog-pits; and those same hanging cheeks,
Covered with hide instead of skin – nay, help, sir –
That look like frozen dish-clouts set on end!

Corv. [*aloud.*] Or like an old smoked wall, on which the rain

Ran down in streaks!

Mos. Excellent, sir, speak out:

You may be louder yet; a culverin

Discharged in his ear would hardly bore it.

Corv. His nose is like a common sewer, still running,

Mos. 'Tis good! And what his mouth?

Corv. A very draught.

Mos. Oh, stop it up –

Corv. By no means.

Mos. Pray you, let me:

Faith, I could stifle him rarely with a pillow,

As well as any woman that should keep him.

Corv. Do as you will, but I'll begone.

Mos. Be so:

It is your presence makes him last so long.

Corv. I pray you, use no violence.

Mos. No, sir? Why?

Why should you be thus scrupulous, pray you, sir?

Corv. Nay, at your discretion.

Mos. Well, good sir, begone.

Corv. I will not trouble him now, to take my pearl.

Mos. Puh! nor your diamond. What a needless care

Is this afflicts you? Is not all here yours?

Am not I here, whom you have made your creature?

That owe my being to you?

Corv. Grateful Mosca!

Thou art my friend, my fellow, my companion,

My partner, and shalt share in all my fortunes.

Mos. Excepting one.

Corv. What's that?

Mos. Your gallant wife, sir. [*Exit Corv.*

Now is he gone: we had no other means

To shoot him hence, but this.

Volp. My divine Mosca!

Thou hast today outgone thyself. [*Another knocks.*

Who's there?
I will be troubled with no more. Prepare
Me music, dances, banquet, all delights;
The Turk is not more sensual in his pleasures,
Than will Volpone. [*Exit Mos.*] Let me see, a pearl!
A diamond! plate! *cecchines*! Good morning's purchase!
Why, this is better than rob churches, yet;
Or fat, by eating, once a month, a man –

Re-enter MOSCA

Who is 't?
Mos. The beauteous Lady Would-be, sir,
    Wife to the English knight, Sir Politick Would-be
    (This is the style, sir, is directed me),
    Hath sent to know how you have slept tonight,
    And if you would be visited.
Volp. Not now;
    Some three hours hence –
Mos. I told the squire so much.
Volp. When I am high with mirth and wine; then, then:
    'Fore heaven, I wonder at the desperate valour
    Of the bold English, that they dare let loose
    Their wives to all encounters!
Mos. Sir, this knight
    Had not his name for nothing, he is *politick*,
    And knows, howe'er his wife affect strange airs,
    She hath not yet the face to be dishonest:
    But had she Signor Corvino's wife's face –
Volp. Has she so rare a face?
Mos. Oh, sir, the wonder,
    The blazing star of Italy! a wench
    Of the first year! a beauty ripe as harvest!
    Whose skin is whiter than a swan all over,
    Than silver, snow, or lilies! a soft lip,
    Would tempt you to eternity of kissing!
    And flesh that melteth in the touch to blood!
    Bright as your gold, and lovely as your gold.
Volp. Why had not I known this before?

Mos. Alas, sir,
  Myself but yesterday discovered it.
Volp. How might I see her?
Mos. Oh, not possible;
  She's kept as warily as is your gold;
  Never does come abroad, never takes air
  But at a window. All her looks are sweet
  As the first grapes or cherries, and are watched
  As near as they are.
Volp. I must see her –
Mos. Sir,
  There is a guard of spies ten thick upon her;
  All this whole household; each of which is set
  Upon his fellow, and have all their charge
  When he goes out, when he comes in, examined.
Volp. I will go see her, though but at her window.
Mos. In some disguise, then.
Volp. That is true; I must
  Maintain mine own shape still the same: we'll think.
                       [Exeunt.

ACT II, SCENE 1

Politick Would-be, Peregrine

Sir P. Sir, to a wise man, all the world's his soil.
  It is not Italy, nor France, nor Europe,
  That must bound me, if my fates call me forth.
  Yet, I protest, it is no salt desire
  Of seeing countries, shifting a religion,
  Nor any disaffection to the state
  Where I was bred, and unto which I owe
  My dearest plots, hath brought me out; much less,
  That idle, antique, stale, grey-headed project
  Of knowing men's minds and manners, with Ulysses:
  But a peculiar humour of my wife's,
  Laid for this height of Venice, to observe,
  To quote, to learn the language, and so forth —
  I hope you travel, sir, with licence?
Per. Yes.
Sir P. I dare the safelier converse. How long, sir,
  Since you left England?
Per. Seven weeks.
Sir P. So lately!
  You ha' not been with my Lord Ambassador?
Per. Not yet, sir.
Sir P. Pray you, what news, sir, vents our climate?
  I heard last night a most strange thing reported
  By some of my lord's followers, and I long
  To hear how 'twill be seconded.
Per. What was't, sir?
Sir P. Marry, sir, of a raven that should build
  In a ship royal of the king's.
Per. This fellow,
  Does he gull me, trow? or is gulled? Your name, sir?
Sir P. My name is Politick Would-be.
Per. Oh, that speaks him.
  A knight, sir!

Sir P. A poor knight, sir.

Per. Your lady
Lies here in Venice, for intelligence
Of tires, and fashions, and behaviour,
Among the courtezans? the fine Lady Would-be?

Sir P. Yes, sir, the spider and the bee oft-times
Suck from one flower.

Per. Good Sir Politick!
I cry you mercy; I have heard much of you:
'Tis true, sir, of your raven.

Sir P. On your knowledge?

Per. Yes, and your lion's whelping in the Tower.

Sir P. Another whelp!

Per. Another, sir.

Sir P. Now heaven!
What prodigies be these? The fires at Berwick!
And the new star! these things concurring, strange!
And full of omen! Saw you those meteors?

Per. I did, sir.

Sir P. Fearful! Pray you, sir, confirm me,
Were there three porpoises seen above the bridge,
As they give out?

Per. Six, and a sturgeon, sir.

Sir P. I am astonished.

Per. Nay, sir, be not so;
I'll tell you a greater prodigy than these —

Sir P. What should these things portend!

Per. The very day
(Let me be sure) that I put forth from London,
There was a whale discover'd in the river,
As high as Woolwich, that had waited there,
Few know how many months, for the subversion
Of the Stode Fleet.

Sir P. Is't possible? believe it,
'Twas either sent from Spain, or the Archdukes:
Spinola's whale, upon my life, my credit!
Will they not leave these projects? Worthy sir,

Some other news.

Per. Faith, Stone the fool is dead,
And they do lack a tavern-fool extremely.

Sir P. Is Mas' Stone dead?

Per. He's dead, sir; why, I hope
You thought him not immortal? O, this knight,
Were he well known, would be a precious thing
To fit our English stage: he that should write
But such a fellow, should be thought to feign
Extremely, if not maliciously.

Sir P. Stone dead!

Per. Dead. Lord! how deeply, sir, you apprehend it?
He was no kinsman to you –

Sir P. That I know of.
Well! that same fellow was an unknown fool.

Per. And yet you knew him, it seems?

Sir P. I did so. Sir,
I knew him one of the most dangerous heads
Living within the state, and so I held him.

Per. Indeed, sir?

Sir P. While he lived, in action.
He has received weekly intelligence,
Upon my knowledge, out of the Low Countries,
For all parts of the world, in cabbages;
And those dispensed again to ambassadors,
In oranges, musk-melons, apricots,
Lemons, pome-citrons, and such like; sometimes
In Colchester oysters, and your Selsey cockles.

Per. You make me wonder!

Sir P. Sir, upon my knowledge.
Nay, I have observed him, at your public ordinary
Take his advertisement from a traveller,
A conceal'd statesman, in a trencher of meat:
And instantly, before the meal was done,
Convey an answer in a toothpick.

Per. Strange!
How could this be, sir?

Sir P. Why, the meat was cut
  So like his character, and so laid, as he
  Must easily read the cipher.
Per. I have heard,
  He could not read, sir.
Sir P. So 'twas given out,
  In policy, by those that did employ him:
  But he could read, and had your languages,
  And to't, as sound a noddle –
Per. I have heard, sir,
  That your baboons were spies, and that they were
  A kind of subtle nation, near to China.
Sir P. Ay, ay, your Mamaluchi. Faith, they had
  Their hand in a French plot or two; but they
  Were so extremely given to women, as
  They made discovery of all: yet I
  Had my advices here, on Wednesday last,
  From one of their own coat, they were return'd,
  Made their relations, as the fashion is,
  And now stand fair for fresh employment.
Per. Heart!
  This Sir Pol will be ignorant of nothing.
  It seems, sir, you know all.
Sir P. Not all, sir. But
  I have some general notions: I do love
  To note and to observe: though I live out,
  Free from the active torrent, yet I'd mark
  The currents and the passages of things,
  For mine own private use; and know the ebbs
  And flows of state.
Per. Believe it, sir, I hold
  Myself in no small tie unto my fortunes,
  For casting me thus luckily upon you,
  Whose knowledge, if your bounty equal it,
  May do me great assistance, in instruction
  For my behaviour, and my bearing, which
  Is yet so rude and raw –

Sir P. Why, came you forth
  Empty of rules for travel?
Per. Faith, I had
  Some common ones, from out that vulgar grammar,
  Which he that cried Italian to me, taught me.
Sir P. Why this it is that spoils all our brave bloods,
  Trusting our hopeful gentry unto pedants,
  Fellows of outside, and mere bark. You seem
  To be a gentleman, of ingenuous race –
  I not profess it, but my fate hath been
  To be, where I have been consulted with,
  In this high kind, touching some great men's sons,
  Persons of blood and honour. –
Per. Who be these, sir?

———

ACT II, SCENE 2

Mosca, Politick, Peregrine, Volpone, Nano, Grege

Mos. Under that window, there't must be. The same.
Sir P. Fellows, to mount a bank. Did your instructor
  In the dear tongues, never discourse to you
  Of the Italian mountebanks?
Per. Yes, sir.
Sir P. Why,
  Here you shall see one.
Per. They are quacksalvers,
  Fellows that live by vending oils and drugs.
Sir P. Was that the character he gave you of them?
Per. As I remember.
Sir P. Pity his ignorance.
  They are the only knowing men of Europe!
  Great general scholars, excellent physicians,
  Most admired statesmen, professed favourites,
  And cabinet counsellors to the greatest princes;
  The only languaged-men of all the world!

Per. And, I have heard, they are most lewd impostors;
　　Made of all terms and shreds; no less beliers
　　Of great men's favours, than their own vile med'cines;
　　Which they will utter upon monstrous oaths:
　　Selling that drug for twopence, ere they part,
　　Which they have valued at twelve crowns before.

Sir P. Sir, calumnies are answered best with silence.
　　Yourself shall judge. Who is it mounts, my friends?

Mos. Scoto of Mantua, sir.

Sir P. Is't he? Nay, then
　　I'll proudly promise, sir, you shall behold
　　Another man that has been fant'sied to you.
　　I wonder, yet, that he should mount his bank,
　　Here in this nook, that has been wont t' appear
　　In face of the Piazza! Here, he comes.

Volp. Mount, zany.

Greg. Follow, follow, follow, follow, follow.

Sir P. See how the people follow him! He's a man
　　May write ten thousand crowns in bank here. Note,
　　Mark but his gesture: I do use to observe
　　The state he keeps in getting up.

Per. 'Tis worth it, sir.

Volp. Most noble gentlemen, and my worthy patrons, it
　　may seem strange that I, your Scoto Mantuano, who
　　was ever wont to fix my bank in face of the public
　　Piazza, near the shelter of the Portico to the Pro-
　　curatìa, should now, after eight months' absence from
　　this illustrious city of Venice, humbly retire myself
　　into an obscure nook of the Piazza.

Sir P. Did not I now object the same?

Per. Peace, sir.

Volp. Let me tell you: I am not, as your Lombard
　　proverb saith, cold on my feet; or content to part with
　　my commodities at a cheaper rate than I accustomed:
　　look not for it. Nor that the calumnious reports of that
　　impudent detractor and shame to our profession
　　(Alessandro Buttone, I mean), who gave out in public

I was condemned a Sforzato to the galleys, for poisoning the Cardinal Bembo's – cook, hath at all attached,
much less dejected me. No, no, worthy gentlemen;
to tell you true, I cannot endure to see the rabble of
these ground ciarlitani, that spread their cloaks on
the pavement, as if they meant to do feats of activity,
and then come in lamely, with their mouldy tales out
of Boccacio, like stale Tabarine, the fabulist: some of
them discoursing their travels, and of their tedious
captivity in the Turks' galleys, when, indeed, were the
truth known, they were the Christians' galleys, where
very temperately they ate bread and drank water, as a
wholesome penance, enjoined them by their confes-
sors, for base pilferies.

Sir P. Note but his bearing, and contempt of these.

Volp. These turdy-facy-nasty-paty-fartical rogues, with
one poor groat's worth of unprepared antimony,
finely wrapped up in several cartoccios, are able,
very well, to kill their twenty a week, and play; yet
these meagre, starved spirits, who have half stopped
the organs of their minds with earthy appilations,
want not their favourers among your shrivelled, salad-
eating artisans, who are overjoyed that they may
have their ha'porth of physic, though it purge them
into another world, it makes no matter.

Sir P. Excellent! Ha' you heard better language, sir?

Volp. Well, let them go. And, gentlemen, honourable
gentlemen, know that for this time our bank, being
thus removed from the clamours of the canaglia, shall
be the scene of pleasure and delight; for I have
nothing to sell, little or nothing to sell.

Sir P. I told you, sir, his end.

Per. You did so, sir.

Volp. I protest, I and my six servants, are not able to
make of this precious liquor, so fast as it is fetched
away from my lodging by gentlemen of your city,
strangers of the terra-firma, worshipful merchants;

ay, and senators too; who, ever since my arrival, have detained me to their uses, by their splendidous liberalities. And worthily. For what avails your rich man to have his magazines stuffed with moscadelli, or of the purest grape, when his physicians prescribe him, on pain of death, to drink nothing but water cocted with aniseeds? Oh, health, health! the blessing of the rich! the riches of the poor! who can buy thee at too dear a rate, since there is no enjoying this world without thee? Be not then so sparing of your purses, honourable gentlemen, as to abridge the natural course of life –

Per. You see his end.

Sir P. Ay, is't not good?

Volp. For when a humid flux or catarrh, by the mutability of air, falls from your head into an arm or shoulder, or any other part, take you a ducat, or your *cecchine* of gold, and apply to the place affected: see what good effect it can work. No, no; 'tis this blessed unguento, this rare extraction, that hath only power to disperse all malignant humours, that proceed either of hot, cold, moist, or windy causes –

Per. I would he had put in dry too.

Sir P. Pray you, observe.

Volp. To fortify the most indigest and crude stomach, ay, were it of one that, through extreme weakness, vomited blood, applying only a warm napkin to the place, after the unction and fricace; for the vertigine in the head, putting but a drop into your nostrils, likewise behind the ears; a most sovereign and approved remedy: the mal-caduco, cramps, convulsions, paralysies, epilepsies, tremor-cordia, retired nerves, ill vapours of the spleen, stoppings of the liver, the stone, the strangury, hernia ventosa, iliaca passio; stops the dysenteria immediately; easeth the torsion of the small guts; and cures melancholia hypocondriaca, being taken and applied, according to my printed receipt. [*Pointing to his bill and his glass.*] For this is the physician, this the medicine; this counsels, this cures; this gives the direction, this works the effect; and, in sum, both together may be termed an abstract of the theorick and practick in the Aesculapian art. 'Twill cost you eight crowns. And, pray thee Zan Fritada, sing a verse extempore in honour of it.

Sir P. How do you like him, sir?

Per. Most strangely, I!

Sir P. Is not his language rare?

Per. But Alchemy,
   I never heard the like; or Broughton's books.

Song

> Had old Hippocrates, or Galen,
> That to their books put med'cines all in,
> But known this secret, they had never
> (Of which they will be guilty ever)
> Been murderers of so much paper,
> Or wasted many a hurtless taper:
> No Indian drug had e'er been famed,
> Tobacco, sassafras not named;
> Ne yet, of guacum one small stick, sir,
> Nor Raymund Lully's great elixir.
> Ne had been known the Danish Gonswart,
> Or Paracelsus, with his long sword.

Per. All this, yet, will not do; eight crowns is high.

Volp. No more. Gentlemen, if I had but time to discourse to you the miraculous effects of this my oil, surnamed Oglio del Scoto; with the countless catalogue of those I have cured of the aforesaid and many more diseases: the patents and privileges of all the Princes and commonwealths of Christendom; or but the depositions of those that appeared on my part before the signiory of the Sanita and most learned College of Physicians; where I was authorized, upon notice taken of the admirable virtues of my medicaments, and mine own excellency in matter of rare and unknown secrets, not only to disperse them publicly in this famous city, but in all the territories, that happily joy under the

government of the most pious and magnificent states of
Italy. But may some other gallant fellow say, O,
there be divers that make profession to have as good
and as experimented receipts as yours; indeed, very
many have assayed, like apes in imitation of that,
which is really and essentially in me, to make of this
oil; bestowed great cost in furnaces, stills, alembecks,
continual fires, and preparation of the ingredients
(as indeed there goes to it six hundred several simples,
besides some quantity of human fat for the conglu-
tination, which we buy of the anatomists) but, when
these practitioners come to the last decoction, blow,
blow, puff, puff, and all flies in fumo: ha, ha, ha.
Poor wretches! I rather pity their folly and indiscretion, than their loss of time and money; for those may
be recovered by industry: but to be a fool born is a
disease incurable. For myself, I always from my youth
have endeavoured to get the rarest secrets, and book
them, either in exchange or for money: I spared not
cost nor labour where anything was worthy to be
learned. And, gentlemen, honourable gentlemen, I will
undertake, by virtue of chemical art, out of the honourable hat that covers your head, to extract the four
elements; that is to say, the fire, air, water and earth,
and return you your felt without burn or stain. For,
whilst others have been at the Balloo, I have been at
my book; and am now past the craggy paths of study,
and come to the flowery plains of honour and reputation.

Sir P. I do assure you, sir, that is his aim.

Volp. But to our price.

Per. And that withal, Sir Pol.

Volp. You all know, honourable gentlemen, I never
valued this ampulla, or vial, at less than eight crowns,
but for this time I am content to be deprived of it for
six: six crowns is the price, and less in courtesy I know
you cannot offer me; take it or leave it, howsoever,
both it and I am at your service. I ask you not as the

value of the thing, for then I should demand of you a
thousand crowns, so the Cardinals Montalto, Fernese,
the great Duke of Tuscany, my gossip, with divers
other Princes have given me, but I despise money.
Only to show my affection to you, honourable gentlemen, and your illustrious State here, I have neglected
the messages of these Princes, mine own offices, framed
my journey hither only to present you with the fruits
of my travels. Tune your voices once more to the touch
of your instruments, and give the honourable assembly
some delightful recreation.

Per. What monstrous and most painful circumstance
    Is here, to get some three or four gazettes,
    Some three-pence in the whole! for that 'twill come to.

Song

You that would last long, list to my song,
Make no more coil, but buy of this oil,
Would you be ever fair? and young?
Stout of teeth? and strong of tongue?
Tart of palate? quick of ear?
Sharp of sight? of nostril clear?
Moist of hand? and light of foot?
Or, I will come nearer to 't,
Would you live free from all diseases?
Do the act your mistress pleases,
Yet fright all aches from your bones?
Here's a med'cine, for the nones.

Volp. Well, I am in a humour at this time to make a
present of the small quantity my coffer contains: to the
rich in courtesy, and to the poor for God's sake.
Wherefore, now mark: I asked you six crowns, and
six crowns at other times you have paid me; you shall
not give me six crowns, nor five, nor four, nor three,
nor two, nor one; nor half a ducat; no, nor a muc-
cinigo. Sixpence it will cost you, or six hundred
pound – expect no lower price, for, by the banner of
my front, I will not bate a bagatine, that I will have
only a pledge of your loves, to carry something
from amongst you, to show I am not condemned by

you. Therefore now toss your handkerchiefs cheerfully, cheerfully; and be advertised that the first heroic spirit that deigns to grace me with an handkerchief, I will give it a little remembrance of something beside, shall please it better than if I had presented it with a double pistolet.

Per. Will you be that heroic spark, Sir Pol?

Oh, see! the window has prevented you.

Volp. Lady, I kiss your bounty and for this timely grace you have done your poor Scoto of Mantua, I will return you, over and above my oil, a secret of that high and inestimable nature, shall make you for ever enamoured on that minute, wherein your eye first descended on so mean, yet not altogether to be despised, an object. Here is a powder concealed in this paper, of which, if I should speak to the worth, nine thousand volumes were but as one page, that page as a line, that line as a word; so short is this pilgrimage of man (which some call life) to the expressing of it. Would I reflect on the price? Why, the whole world is but as an empire, that empire as a province, that province as a bank, that bank as a private purse, to the purchase of it. I will only tell you, it is the powder that made Venus a goddess, (given her by Apollo) that kept her perpetually young, cleared her wrinkles, firmed her gums, filled her skin, coloured her hair; from her derived to Helen, and at the sack of Troy unfortunately lost: till now, in this our age, it was as happily recovered, by a studious antiquary, out of some ruins of Asia, who sent a moiety of it to the Court of France (but much sophisticated) wherewith the ladies there now colour their hair. The rest, at this present, remains with me; extracted to a quintessence: so that, wherever it but touches, in youth it perpetually preserves, in age restores the complexion; seats your teeth, did they dance like virginal jacks, firm as a wall; makes them white as ivory, that were black as –

ACT II, SCENE 3

Corvino, Politick, Peregrine

Corv. Spite o' the devil, and my shame! come down here;

           [He beats away the mountebank etc.

  Come down. No house but mine to make your scene?

  Signor Flamino, will you down, sir? down?

  What, is my wife your Franciscina, sir?

  No windows on the whole piazza, here,

  To make your properties, but mine? but mine?

  Heart! ere tomorrow I shall be new-christened,

  And called the Pantalone di besogniosi,

  About the town.

Per. What should this mean, Sir Pol?

Sir P. Some trick of state, believe it. I will home.

Per. It may be some design on you.

Sir P. I know not.

  I'll stand upon my guard.

Per. It is your best, sir.

Sir P. This three weeks, all my advices, all my letters,

  They have been intercepted.

Per. Indeed, sir?

  Best have a care.

Sir P. Nay, so I will.

Per. This knight,

  I may not lose him, for my mirth, till night.

———

ACT II, SCENE 4

Volpone, Mosca

Volp. O, I am wounded!

Mos. Where, sir?

Volp. Not without;

  Those blows were nothing: I could bear them ever.

  But angry Cupid, bolting from her eyes,

Hath shot himself into me, like a flame;
Where, now, he flings about his burning heat,
As in a furnace, an ambitious fire,
Whose vent is stopt. The fight is all within me.
I cannot live, except thou help me, Mosca;
My liver melts, and I, without the hope
Of some soft air, from her refreshing breath,
Am but a heap of cinders.

Mos. 'Las, good sir!
  Would you had never seen her.

Volp. Nay, would thou
  Had'st never told me of her.

Mos. Sir, 'tis true;
  I do confess, I was unfortunate,
  And you unhappy: but I'm bound in conscience,
  No less than duty, to effect my best
  To your release of torment, and I will, sir.

Volp. Dear Mosca, shall I hope?

Mos. Sir, more than dear,
  I will not bid you to despair of aught
  Within a human compass.

Volp. Oh, there spoke
  My better angel. Mosca, take my keys,
  Gold, plate, and jewels, all 's at thy devotion;
  Employ them how thou wilt; nay, coin me, too:
  So thou, in this, but crown my longings, Mosca.

Mos. Use but your patience.

Volp. So I have.

Mos. I doubt not
  To bring success to your desires.

Volp. Nay, then,
  I not repent me of my late disguise.

Mos. If you can horn him, sir, you need not.

Volp. True:
  Besides, I never meant him for my heir.
  Is not the colour o' my beard and eyebrows
  To make me known?

Mos. No jot.
Volp. I did it well.
Mos. So well, would I could follow you in mine,
   With half the happiness; and yet I would
   Escape your epilogue.
Volp. But, were they gulled
   With a belief that I was Scoto?
Mos. Sir,
   Scoto himself could hardly have distinguished!
   I have not time to flatter you now; we'll part;
   And as I prosper, so applaud my art.

———

ACT II, SCENE 5
CORVINO, CELIA, SERVITORE

Corv. Death of mine honour, with the city's fool?
   A juggling, tooth-drawing, prating mountebank?
   And at a public window! where, whilst he,
   With his strained action, and his dole of faces,
   To his drug-lecture draws your itching ears,
   A crew of old, unmarried, noted lechers,
   Stood leering up like satyrs: and you smile
   Most graciously, and fan your favours forth,
   To give your hot spectators satisfaction!
   What, was your mountebank their call? their
     whistle?
   Or were you enamoured on his copper rings,
   His saffron jewel, with the toad-stone in't,
   Or his embroidered suit, with the cope-stitch,
   Made of a hearse-cloth? or his old tilt-feather?
   Or his starched beard? Well, you shall have him, yes.
   He shall come home, and minister unto you
   The fricace for the mother. Or, let me see,
   I think you had rather mount; would you not mount?
   Why, if you'll mount, you may; yes truly, you may.
   And so you may be seen, down to the foot.

Get you a cittern, lady Vanity,
And be a dealer with the virtuous man;
Make one: I'll but protest myself a cuckold,
And save your dowry. I'm a Dutchman, I!
For, if you thought me an Italian,
You would be damned, ere you did this, you whore:
Thou 'dst tremble to imagine, that the murder
Of a father, mother, brother, all thy race,
Should follow, as the subject of my justice!

Cel. Good, sir, have patience.

Corv. What couldst thou propose
Less to thyself, than, in this heat of wrath,
And stung with my dishonour, I should strike
This steel into thee, with as many stabs,
As thou wert gazed upon with goatish eyes?

Cel. Alas sir, be appeased! I could not think
My being at the window should more now
Move your impatience than at other times.

Corv. No? not to seek and entertain a parley
With a known knave, before a multitude?
You were an actor with your handkerchief,
Which he most sweetly kissed in the receipt,
And might, no doubt, return it with a letter,
And point the place where you might meet; your
    sister's,
Your mother's, or your aunt's might serve the turn.

Cel. Why, dear sir, when do I make these excuses,
Or ever stir abroad, but to the church?
And that so seldom –

Corv. Well, it shall be less;
And thy restraint before was liberty
To what I now decree: and therefore, mark me.
First, I will have this bawdy light damned up;
And till 't be done, some two or three yards off
I'll chalk a line: o'er which, if thou but chance
To set thy desperate foot, more hell, more horror,
More wild, remorseless rage shall seize on thee,

Than on a conjurer that had heedless left
His circle's safety ere his devil was laid.
Then here's a lock which I will hang upon thee;
And, now I think on 't, I will keep thee backwards;
Thy lodging shall be backwards; thy walks backwards;
Thy prospect – all be backwards; and no pleasure,
That thou shalt know but backwards; nay, since you force
    force
My honest nature, know it is your own,
Being too open, makes me use you thus:
Since you will not contain your subtile nostrils
In a sweet room, but they must snuff the air
Of rank and sweaty passengers. One knocks.
Away, and be not seen, pain of thy life;
Nor look toward the window: if thou dost –
Nay, stay, hear this – let me not prosper, whore,
But I will make thee an anatomy,
Dissect thee mine own self, and read a lecture
Upon thee to the city, and in public.
Away. Who's there?
Serv. 'Tis Signor Mosca, sir.

———

ACT II, SCENE 6

CORVINO, MOSCA

Corv. Let him come in, his master's dead: there's yet
    Some good to help the bad. My Mosca, welcome!
    I guess your news.
Mos. I fear you cannot, sir.
Corv. Is 't not his death?
Mos. Rather the contrary.
Corv. Not his recovery?
Mos. Yes, sir.
Corv. I am cursed,
    I am bewitched, my crosses meet to vex me.
    How? how? how? how?

Mos. Why, sir, with Scoto's oil;
    Corbaccio and Voltore brought of it,
    Whilst I was busy in an inner room –
Corv. Death! that damned mountebank; but for the law
    Now, I could kill the rascal: it cannot be
    His oils should have that virtue. Have not I
    Known him a common rogue, come fiddling in
    To the osteria with a tumbling whore,
    And, when he has done all his forced tricks, been glad
    Of a poor spoonful of dead wine with flies in 't?
    It cannot be. All his ingredients
    Are a sheep's gall, a roasted bitch's marrow,
    Some few sod earwigs, pounded caterpillars,
    A little capon's grease, and fasting spittle:
    I know them to a dram.
Mos. I know not, sir;
    But some on 't there, they poured into his ears,
    Some in his nostrils, and recovered him;
    Applying but the fricace.
Corv. Pox o' that fricace!
Mos. And since, to seem the more officious
    And flattering of his health, there they have had
    At extreme fees, the college of physicians
    Consulting on him, how they might restore him;
    Where one would have a cataplasm of spices,
    Another a flayed ape clapped to his breast,
    A third would have it a dog, a fourth an oil,
    With wild cats' skins: at last they all resolved
    That to preserve him was no other means
    But some young woman must be straight sought out,
    Lusty, and full of juice, to sleep by him;
    And to this service, most unhappily,
    And most unwillingly am I now employed,
    Which here I thought to pre-acquaint you with,
    For your advice, since it concerns you most;
    Because I would not do that thing might cross
    Your ends, on whom I have my sole dependence, sir.

Yet, if I do it not, they may delate
My slackness to my patron, work me out
Of his opinion; and there all your hopes,
Ventures, or whatsoever, are all frustrate!
I do but tell you, sir. Besides, they are all
Now striving who shall first present him. Therefore –
I could entreat you, briefly, conclude somewhat;
Prevent them if you can.

Corv. Death to my hopes,
This is my villainous fortune! Best to hire
Some common courtezan.

Mos. Ay, I thought on that, sir;
But they are all so subtle, full of art –
And age again doting and flexible,
So as – I cannot tell – we may, perchance,
Light on a quean may cheat us all.

Corv. 'Tis true.

Mos. No, no: it must be one that has no tricks, sir,
Some simple thing, a creature made unto it;
Some girl you may command. Have you no kins-
woman?
God's so – Think, think, think, think, think, think,
think, sir.
One o' the doctors offered there his daughter.

Corv. How!

Mos. Yes, Signor Lupo, the physician.

Corv. His daughter!

Mos. And a virgin, sir. Why, alas,
He knows the state of 's body, what it is;
That nought can warm his blood, sir, but a fever;
Nor any incantation raise his spirit;
A long forgetfulness hath seized that part.
Besides, sir, who shall know it? some one or two –

Corv. I pray thee give me leave. If any man
But I had had this luck – The thing in 't self,
I know, is nothing – Wherefore should not I
As well command my blood and my affections

As this dull doctor? In the point of honour
The cases are all one of wife and daughter.

Mos. I hear him coming.

Corv. She shall do 't: 'tis done.
  'Slight, if this doctor, who is not engaged,
  Unless 't be for his counsel, which is nothing,
  Offer his daughter, what should I, that am
  So deeply in? I will prevent him: wretch!
  Covetous wretch! Mosca, I have determined.

Mos. How, sir?

Corv. We'll make all sure. The party you wot of
  Shall be mine own wife, Mosca.

Mos. Sir, the thing,
  But that I would not seem to counsel you,
  I should have motioned to you, at the first:
  And make your count, you have cut all their throats,
  Why, 'tis directly taking a possession!
  And in his next fit we may let him go.
  'Tis but to pull the pillow from his head,
  And he is throttled: it had been done before,
  But for your scrupulous doubts.

Corv. Ay, a plague on't,
  My conscience fools my wit. Well, I'll be brief,
  And so be thou, lest they should be before us:
  Go home, prepare him, tell him with what zeal
  And willingness I do it; swear it was
  On the first hearing, as thou may'st do, truly,
  Mine own free motion.

Mos. Sir, I warrant you,
  I'll so possess him with it, that the rest
  Of his starved clients shall be banished all;
  And only you received. But come not, sir,
  Until I send, for I have something else
  To ripen for your good, you must not know 't.

Corv. But do not you forget to send now.

Mos. Fear not.

ACT II, SCENE 7
CORVINO, CELIA

Corv. Where are you, wife? My Celia! Wife! What!
   blubbering?
   Come, dry those tears. I think thou thoughtst me in
      earnest.
   Ha? by this light I talked so but to try thee.
   Methinks the lightness of the occasion
   Should have confirmed thee. Come, I am not jealous.
Cel. No?
Corv. Faith, I am not, I, nor never was:
   It is a poor unprofitable humour.
   Do not I know, if women have a will,
   They'll do 'gainst all the watches of the world,
   And that the fiercest spies are tamed with gold?
   Tut, I am confident in thee, thou shalt see 't;
   And see, I'll give thee cause, too, to believe it.
   Come, kiss me. Go, and make thee ready, straight,
   In all thy best attire, thy choicest jewels,
   Put them all on, and, with them, thy best looks:
   We are invited to a solemn feast,
   At old Volpone's, where it shall appear
   How far I am free from jealousy or fear.

ACT III, SCENE 1

MOSCA

Mos. I fear I shall begin to grow in love
  With my dear self, and my most prosperous parts,
  They do so spring and burgeon; I can feel
  A whimsy in my blood: I know not how,
  Success hath made me wanton. I could skip
  Out of my skin, now, like a subtle snake,
  I am so limber. O! your parasite
  Is a most precious thing, dropt from above,
  Not bred 'mongst clods and clodpoles, here on earth.
  I muse the mystery was not made a science,
  It is so liberally professed! Almost
  All the wise world is little else, in nature,
  But parasites or sub-parasites. And yet,
  I mean not those that have your bare town-art,
  To know who 's fit to feed them; have no house,
  No family, no care, and therefore mould
  Tales for men's ears, to bait that sense; or get
  Kitchen-invention, and some stale receipts
  To please the belly and the groin; nor those,
  With their court-dog tricks, that can fawn and fleer,
  Make their revenue out of legs and faces,
  Echo my lord, and lick away a mote:
  But your fine elegant rascal, that can rise,
  And stoop, almost together, like an arrow;
  Shoot through the air as nimbly as a star;
  Turn short as doth a swallow; and be here,
  And there, and here, and yonder, all at once;
  Present to any humour, all occasion;
  And change a visor, swifter than a thought!
  This is the creature had the art born with him;
  Toils not to learn it, but doth practise it
  Out of most excellent nature; and such sparks
  Are the true parasites, others but their zanies.

ACT III, SCENE 2

MOSCA, BONARIO

Mos. Who's this? Bonario, old Corbaccio's son?
   The person I was bound to seek. Fair sir,
   You are happily met.
Bon. That cannot be by thee.
Mos. Why, sir?
Bon. Nay, pray thee, know thy way, and leave me:
   I would be loth to interchange discourse
   With such a mate as thou art.
Mos. Courteous sir,
   Scorn not my poverty.
Bon. Not I, by heaven;
   But thou shalt give me leave to hate thy baseness.
Mos. Baseness?
Bon. Ay, answer me, is not thy sloth
   Sufficient argument? thy flattery?
   Thy means of feeding?
Mos. Heaven be good to me –
   These imputations are too common, sir,
   And easily stuck on virtue when she 's poor;
   You are unequal to me, and however
   Your sentence may be righteous, yet you are not,
   That ere you know me, thus proceed in censure:
   St Mark bear witness 'gainst you, 'tis inhuman.
Bon. What! does he weep? the sign is soft and good!
   I do repent me that I was so harsh.
Mos. 'Tis true, that, swayed by strong necessity,
   I am enforced to eat my careful bread
   With too much obsequy; 'tis true, beside,
   That I am fain to spin mine own poor raiment
   Out of my mere observance, being not born
   To a free fortune: but that I have done
   Base offices, in rending friends asunder,
   Dividing families, betraying counsels,

Whispering false lies, or mining men with praises,
Trained their credulity with perjuries,
Corrupted chastity, or am in love
With mine own tender ease, but would not rather
Prove the most rugged and laborious course,
That might redeem my present estimation;
Let me here perish, in all hope of goodness.

Bon. This cannot be a personated passion!
I was to blame, so to mistake thy nature;
Pray thee, forgive me, and speak out thy business.

Mos. Sir, it concerns you; and though I may seem,
At first, to make a main offence in manners,
And in my gratitude unto my master,
Yet, for the pure love which I bear all right,
And hatred of the wrong, I must reveal it.
This very hour your father is in purpose
To disinherit you –

Bon. How!

Mos. And thrust you forth,
As a mere stranger to his blood; 'tis true, sir,
The work no way engageth me, but, as
I claim an interest in the general state
Of goodness and true virtue, which I hear
To abound in you: and, for which mere respect,
Without a second aim, sir, I have done it.

Bon. This tale hath lost thee much of the late trust
Thou hadst with me; it is impossible;
I know not how to lend it any thought,
My father should be so unnatural.

Mos. It is a confidence that well becomes
Your piety; and formed, no doubt, it is
From your own simple innocence: which makes
Your wrong monstrous and abhorred. But, sir,
I now will tell you more. This very minute,
It is, or will be doing; and, if you
Shall be but pleased to go with me, I'll bring you,
I dare not say where you shall see, but where

Your ear shall be a witness of the deed;
Hear yourself written bastard, and professed
The common issue of the earth.

Bon. I'm mazed!

Mos. Sir, if I do it not, draw your just sword,
And score your vengeance on my front and face:
Mark me your villain: you have too much wrong,
And I do suffer for you, sir. My heart
Weeps blood in anguish –

Bon. Lead; I follow thee.

——

ACT III, SCENE 3

Volpone, Nano, Androgyno, Castrone

Volp. Mosca stays long, methinks. Bring forth your sports,
And help to make the wretched time more sweet.

Nan. Dwarf, fool, and eunuch, well met here we be.
A question it were now, whether of us three,
Being, all, the known delicates of a rich man,
In pleasing him, claim the precedency can?

Cas. I claim for myself.

And. And so doth the fool.

Nan. 'Tis foolish indeed: let me set you both to school.
First for your dwarf, he's little and witty,
And everything, as it is little, is pretty;
Else why do men say to a creature of my shape,
So soon as they see him, it's a pretty little ape?
And why a pretty ape, but for pleasing imitation
Of greater men's actions, in a ridiculous fashion?
Beside, this feat body of mine doth not crave
Half the meat, drink, and cloth, one of your bulks
  will have.
Admit your fool's face be the mother of laughter,
Yet, for his brain, it must always come after:
And though that do feed him, it's a pitiful case,
His body is beholding to such a bad face.

Volp. Who's there? my couch; away; look Nano, see.
　　　　　　　　　　　　　　　　[*Exit And. and Cas.*
　　Give me my caps, first – go, inquire. Now, Cupid
　　Send it be Mosca, and with fair return!
Nan. It is the beauteous madam –
Volp. Would-be – is it?
Nan. The same.
Volp. Now, torment on me; squire her in;
　　For she will enter, or dwell here for ever:
　　Nay, quickly. – That my fit were past. I fear
　　A second hell, too, that my loathing this
　　Will quite expel my appetite to the other:
　　Would she were taking now her tedious leave.
　　Lord, how it threats, what I am to suffer!

　　　　　　　　　　————

ACT III, SCENE 4

Lady Politick Would-be, Volpone, Nano,
2 Women

Lady P. I thank you, good sir, 'Pray you signify
　　Unto your patron, I am here. This band
　　Shows not my neck enough. I trouble you, sir,
　　Let me request you, bid one of my women
　　Come hither to me. In good faith, I am drest
　　Most favourably today. It is no matter,
　　'Tis well enough. – Look, see, these petulant things,
　　How they have done this!
Volp. I do feel the fever
　　Entering in at mine ears. O, for a charm,
　　To fright it hence!
Lady P. Come nearer: is this curl
　　In his right place? or this? why is this higher
　　Than all the rest? You have not washed your eyes, yet!
　　Or do they not stand even in your head?
　　Where is your fellow? Call her.
Nan. Now, St Mark

    Deliver us: anon, she'll beat her women,
    Because her nose is red.
Lady P. I pray you, view
    This tire, forsooth: are all things apt, or no?
First Wom. One hair a little, here, sticks out, forsooth.
Lady P. Does't so, forsooth? and where was your dear
      sight,
    When it did so, forsooth! What now! bird-eyed?
    And you, too? 'Pray you, both approach and mend it.
    Now, by that light, I muse you are not ashamed!
    I, that have preach'd these things so oft unto you,
    Read you the principles, argued all the grounds,
    Disputed every fitness, every grace,
    Call'd you to counsel of so frequent dressings –
Nan. More carefully than of your fame or honour.
Lady P. Made you acquainted, what an ample dowry
    The knowledge of these things would be unto you,
    Able, alone, to get you noble husbands
    At your return: and you thus to neglect it!
    Beside, you seeing what a curious nation
    The Italians are, what will they say of me?
    The English lady cannot dress herself.
    Here's a fine imputation to our country!
    Well, go your ways, and stay i' the next room.
    This fucus was too coarse too; it 's no matter.
    Good sir, you'll give them entertainment?
Volp. The storm comes toward me.
Lady P. How does my Volpone?
Volp. Troubled with noise, I cannot sleep; I dreamt
    That a strange fury entered, now, my house,
    And, with the dreadful tempest of her breath,
    Did cleave my roof asunder.
Lady P. Believe me, and I
    Had the most fearful dream, could I remember 't –
Volp. Out on my fate! I have given her the occasion
    How to torment me: she will tell me hers.
Lady P. Methought, the golden mediocrity,

Polite and delicate –

Volp. Oh, if you do love me,
  No more: I sweat and suffer at the mention
  Of any dream; feel how I tremble yet.

Lady P. Alas, good soul! the passion of the heart.
  Seed-pearl were good now, boiled with syrup of
    apples,
  Tincture of gold, and coral, citron-pills,
  Your elicampane root, myrobalanes –

Volp. Ah, me, I have ta'en a grasshopper by the wing.

Lady P. Burnt silk and amber: you have muscadel
  Good i' the house –

Volp. You will not drink, and part?

Lady P. No, fear not that. I doubt, we shall not get
  Some English saffron, half a dram would serve,
  Your sixteen cloves, a little musk, dried mints,
  Bugloss, and barley-meal –

Volp. She's in again.
  Before I feigned diseases, now I have one.

Lady P. And these applied with a right scarlet cloth –

Volp. Another flood of words! a very torrent!

Lady P. Shall I, sir, make you a poultice?

Volp. No, no no,
  I'm very well, you need prescribe no more.

Lady P. I have a little studied physic; but now,
  I'm all for music, save, in the forenoons,
  An hour or two for painting. I would have
  A lady, indeed, to have all, letters and arts,
  Be able to discourse, to write, to paint,
  But principal, as Plato holds, your music,
  And so does wise Pythagoras, I take it,
  Is your true rapture: when there is consent,
  In face, in voice, and clothes: and is, indeed,
  Our sex's chiefest ornament.

Volp. The poet
  As old in time as Plato, and as knowing,
  Says, that your highest female grace is silence.

Lady P. Which of your poets? Petrarch, or Tasso, or
    Dante?
  Guarini? Ariosto? Aretine?
  Cieco di Hadria? I have read them all.
Volp. Is everything a cause to my destruction?
Lady P. I think I have two or three of them about me.
Volp. The sun, the sea, will sooner both stand still
  Than her eternal tongue! nothing can escape it.
Lady P. Here's Pastor Fido –
Volp. Profess obstinate silence;
  That's now my safest.
Lady P. All our English writers,
  I mean such as are happy in the Italian,
  Will deign to steal out of this author, mainly,
  Almost as much as from Montagnié:
  He has so modern and facile a vein,
  Fitting the time and catching the court-ear.
  Your Petrarch is more passionate, yet he,
  In days of sonnetting, trusted them with much:
  Dante is hard, and few can understand him.
  But, for a desperate wit, there's Aretine;
  Only his pictures are a little obscene –
  You mark me not?
Volp. Alas, my mind's perturbed.
Lady P. Why, in such cases, we must cure ourselves,
  Make use of our philosophy –
Volp. O me!
Lady P. And as we find our passions do rebel,
  Encounter them with reason, or divert them,
  By giving scope unto some other humour
  Of lesser danger: as, in politic bodies,
  There's nothing more doth overwhelm the judgement
  And cloud the understanding than too much
  Settling and fixing, and, as 'twere, subsiding
  Upon one object. For the incorporating
  Of these same outward things into that part
  Which we call mental, leaves some certain faeces

That stop the organs, and, as Plato says,
Assassinate our knowledge.
Volp. Now, the spirit
Of patience help me.
Lady P. Come, in faith, I must
Visit you more a-days; and make you well:
Laugh and be lusty.
Volp. My good angel, save me.
Lady P. There was but one sole man in all the world
With whom I e'er could sympathize; and he
Would lie you often three, four hours together
To hear me speak; and be sometime so rapt
As he would answer me quite from the purpose,
Like you, and you are like him, just. I'll discourse,
An't be but only, sir, to bring you asleep,
How we did spend our time and loves together
For some six years.
Volp. Oh, oh, oh, oh, oh, oh!
Lady P. For we were coaetanei, and brought up –
Volp. Some power, some fate, some fortune, rescue me.

———

ACT III, SCENE 5

MOSCA, LADY POLITICK WOULD-BE, VOLPONE

Mos. God save you, madam.
Lady P. Good sir.
Volp. Mosca? welcome,
Welcome to my redemption.
Mos. Why, sir?
Volp. Oh,
Rid me of this my torture, quickly, there;
My madam, with the everlasting voice:
The bells, in time of pestilence, ne'er made
Like noise, or were in that perpetual motion;
The cock-pit comes not near it. All my house,
But now, steamed like a bath with her thick breath,

A lawyer could not have been heard; nor scarce
Another woman, such a hail of words
She has let fall. For hell's sake, rid her hence.

Mos. Has she presented?

Volp. Oh, I do not care;
I'll take her absence, upon any price,
With any loss.

Mos. Madam –

Lady P. I have brought your patron
A toy, a cap here, of mine own work.

Mos. 'Tis well.
I had forgot to tell you, I saw your knight,
Where you would little think it –

Lady P. Where?

Mos. Marry,
Where yet, if you make haste, you may apprehend him;
Rowing upon the water in a gondole
With the most cunning courtezan of Venice.

Lady P. Is't true?

Mos. Pursue them, and believe your eyes:
Leave me to make your gift. I knew 'twould take:
For lightly, they that use themselves most licence,
Are still most jealous.

Volp. Mosca, hearty thanks,
For thy quick fiction, and delivery of me.
Now to my hopes, what sayest thou?

Lady P. But do you hear, sir? –

Volp. Again! I fear a paroxysm.

Lady P. Which way
Rowed they together?

Mos. Toward the Rialto.

Lady P. I pray you lend me your dwarf.

Mos. I pray you take him.
Your hopes, sir, are like happy blossoms, fair,
And promise timely fruit, if you will stay
But the maturing; keep you at your couch,
Corbaccio will arrive straight with the will;

When he is gone I'll tell you more.
Volp. My blood,
    My spirits are returned; I am alive:
    And like your wanton gamester at primero,
    Whose thought had whispered to him, not go less,
    Methinks I lie and draw – for an encounter.

———

ACT III, SCENE 6
Mosca, Bonario

Mos. Sir, here concealed you may hear all. But, pray you
    Have patience, sir; the same's your father knocks:
    I am compelled to leave you.
Bon. Do so. Yet
    Cannot my thought imagine this a truth.

———

ACT III, SCENE 7
Mosca, Corvino, Celia, Bonario, Volpon

Mos. Death on me! you are come too soon, what meant
    you?
    Did not I say I would send?
Corv. Yes, but I feared
    You might forget it, and then they prevent us.
Mos. Prevent? Did e'er man haste so for his horns?
    A courtier would not ply it so for a place.
    Well, now there is no helping it, stay here;
    I'll presently return.
Corv. Where are you, Celia?
    You know not wherefore I have brought you hither?
Cel. Not well, except you told me.
Corv. Now I will:
    Hark hither.
Mos. Sir, your father hath sent word,   *[to Bonario.*
    It will be half-an-hour ere he come;

And therefore, if you please to walk the **while**
Into that gallery – at the upper end,
There are some books to entertain the time:
And I'll take care no man shall come unto you, sir.
Bon. Yes, I will stay there, I do doubt this fellow.
Mos. There, he is far enough; he can hear nothing:
And, for his father, I can keep him off.
Corv. Nay, now, there is no starting back; and therefore,
Resolve upon it: I have so decreed.
It must be done. Nor would I move 't afore,
Because I would avoid all shifts and tricks,
That might deny me.
Cel. Sir, let me beseech you,
Affect not these strange trials; if you doubt
My chastity, why, lock me up for ever;
Make me the heir of darkness. Let me live
Where I may please your fears, if not your trust.
Corv. Believe it, I have no such humour, I.
All that I speak I mean; yet I am not mad;
Nor horn-mad, see you? Go to, show yourself
Obedient and a wife.
Cel. O heaven!
Corv. I say it,
Do so.
Cel. Was this the train?
Corv. I've told you reasons;
What the physicians have set down: how much
It may concern me; what my engagements are;
My means; and the necessity of those means,
For my recovery: wherefore, if you be
Loyal, and mine, be won, respect my venture.
Cel. Before your honour?
Corv. Honour! tut, a breath;
There's no such thing in nature: a mere term
Invented to awe fools. What is my gold
The worse for touching? clothes for being looked on?
Why, this is no more. An old, decrepit wretch,

That has no sense, no sinew; takes his meat
With others' fingers; only knows to gape
When you do scald his gums; a voice; a shadow;
And what can this man hurt you?
Cel. Lord! what spirit
  Is this hath entered him?
Corv. And for your fame,
  That's such a jig; as if I would go tell it,
  Cry it on the Piazza! who shall know it,
  But he that cannot speak it, and this fellow,
  Whose lips are in my pocket? Save yourself,
  If you'll proclaim it you may, I know no other
  Shall come to know it.
Cel. Are heaven and saints then nothing?
  Will they be blind or stupid?
Corv. How?
Cel. Good sir,
  Be jealous still, emulate them; and think
  What hate they burn with toward every sin.
Corv. I grant you: if I thought it were a sin,
  I would not urge you. Should I offer this
  To some young Frenchman, or hot Tuscan blood
  That had read Aretine, conned all his prints,
  Knew every quirk within lust's labyrinth,
  And were professed critic in lechery;
  And I would look upon him, and applaud him,
  This were a sin; but here, 'tis contrary,
  A pious work, mere charity for physic,
  And honest policy, to assure mine own.
Cel. O heaven! canst thou suffer such a change?
Volp. Thou art mine honour, Mosca, and my pride,
  My joy, my tickling, my delight! Go, bring them.
Mos. Please you, draw near, sir.
Corv. Come on, what —
  You will not be rebellious? By that light —
Mos. Sir,
  Signor Corvino, here, is come to see you.

Volp. Oh!

Mos. And hearing of the consultation had,
So lately, for your health, is come to offer,
Or rather, sir, to prostitute –

Corv. Thanks, sweet Mosca.

Mos. Freely, unasked or unentreated –

Corv. Well.

Mos. As the true fervent instance of his love –
His own most fair and proper wife; the beauty
Only of price in Venice –

Corv. 'Tis well urged.

Mos. To be your comfortress, and to preserve you.

Volp. Alas, I am past already! Pray you, thank him
For his good care and promptness; but for that,
'Tis a vain labour e'en to fight 'gainst heaven;
Applying fire to a stone; uh, uh, uh, uh!
Making a dead leaf grow again. I take
His wishes gently, though; and you may tell him
What I have done for him; marry, my state is hopeless.
Will him to pray for me; and to use his fortune
With reverence, when he comes to it.

Mos. Do you hear, sir?
Go to him with your wife.

Corv. Heart of my father!
Wilt thou persist thus? Come, I pray thee, come.
Thou seest 'tis nothing, Celia. By this hand,
I shall grow violent. Come, do 't, I say.

Cel. Sir, kill me, rather. I will take down poison,
Eat burning coals, do anything –

Corv. Be damned!
Heart, I will drag thee hence, home, by the hair;
Cry thee a strumpet through the streets; rip up
Thy mouth unto thine ears; and slit thy nose
Like a raw rochet – Do not tempt me; come,
Yield, I am loth – Death! I will buy some slave
Whom I will kill, and bind thee to him alive;
And at my window hang you forth, devising

Some monstrous crime, which I, in capital letters,
Will eat into thy flesh with aquafortis,
And burning corrosives, on this stubborn breast.
Now, by the blood thou hast incensed, I 'll do it!
Cel. Sir, what you please, you may, I am your martyr.
Corv. Be not thus obstinate, I have not deserved it:
Think who it is entreats you. Pray thee, sweet;
Good faith, thou shalt have jewels, gowns, attires,
What thou wilt think, and ask. Do but go kiss him.
Or touch him, but. For my sake. At my suit.
This once. No? not? I shall remember this.
Will you disgrace me thus? Do you thirst my
    undoing?
Mos. Nay, gentle lady, be advised.
Corv. No, no.
She has watched her time. God's precious, this is
    scurvy,
'Tis very scurvy; and you are –
Mos. Nay, good sir.
Corv. An arrant locust, by heaven, a locust.
Whore, crocodile, that hast thy tears prepared,
Expecting how thou 'lt bid them flow.
Mos. Nay, 'pray you, sir!
She will consider.
Cel. Would my life would serve
To satisfy.
Corv. 'Sdeath! If she would but speak to him,
And save my reputation, it were somewhat;
But spitefully to affect my utter ruin!
Mos. Ay, now you have put your fortune in her
    hands.
Why i' faith, it is her modesty, I must quit her;
If you were absent, she would be more coming;
I know it: and dare undertake for her.
What woman can, before her husband? 'pray you,
Let us depart, and leave her here.
Corv. Sweet Celia,

Thou may'st redeem all, yet; I 'll say no more:
If not, esteem yourself as lost. Nay, stay there.

Cel. Oh, God, and his good angels! Whether, whether,
Is shame fled human breasts? that with such ease,
Men dare put off your honours and their own?
Is that, which ever was a cause of life,
Now placed beneath the basest circumstance?
And modesty an exile made, for money?

Volp. Ay, in Corvino, and such earth-fed minds,

> [*He leaps off from his couch.*

That never tasted the true heaven of love.
Assure thee, Celia, he that would sell thee,
Only for hope of gain, and that uncertain,
He would have sold his part of Paradise
For ready money, had he met a cope-man.
Why art thou mazed to see me thus revived?
Rather applaud thy beauty's miracle;
'Tis thy great work: that hath, not now, alone,
But sundry times raised me, in several shapes,
And, but this morning, like a mountebank,
To see thee at thy window. Ay, before
I would have left my practice for thy love,
In varying figures, I would have contended
With the blue Proteus, or the horned flood.
Now art thou welcome.

Cel. Sir!

Volp. Nay, fly me not.
Nor let thy false imagination
That I was bed-rid, make thee think I am so:
Thou shalt not find it. I am, now, as fresh,
As hot, as high, and in as jovial plight,
As when, in that so celebrated scene,
At recitation of our comedy,
For entertainment of the great Valois,
I acted young Antinous; and attracted
The eyes and ears of all the ladies present,
To admire each graceful gesture, note, and footing.

Song

Come, my Celia, let us prove,
While we can, the sports of love.
Time will not be ours for ever,
He, at length, our good will sever;
Spend not then his gifts in vain.
Suns that set may rise again:
But if once we lose this light,
'Tis with us perpetual night.
Why should we defer our joys?
Fame and rumour are but toys.
Cannot we delude the eyes
Of a few poor household spies?
Or his easier ears beguile,
Thus removed by our wile?
'Tis no sin love's fruits to steal;
But the sweet thefts to reveal;
To be taken, to be seen,
These have crimes accounted been.

Cel. Some serene blast me, or dire lightning strike
   This my offending face.
Volp. Why droops my Celia?
   Thou hast, in place of a base husband, found
   A worthy lover: use thy fortune well,
   With secrecy and pleasure. See, behold,
   What thou art queen of; not in expectation,
   As I feed others; but possessed and crown'd.
   See, here, a rope of pearl; and each more orient
   Than that the brave Egyptian queen caroused:
   Dissolve and drink them. See, a carbuncle,
   May put out both the eyes of our St. Mark;
   A diamond would have bought Lollia Paulina,
   When she came in, like star-light, hid with jewels
   That were the spoils of provinces; take these,
   And wear, and lose them: yet remains an ear-ring
   To purchase them again, and this whole state.
   A gem but worth a private patrimony
   Is nothing: we will eat such at a meal.
   The heads of parrots, tongues of nightingales,
   The brains of peacocks and of ostriches,

Shall be our food; and could we get the phoenix,
Though nature lost her kind, she were our dish.
Cel. Good sir, these things might move a mind affected
With such delights; but I, whose innocence
Is all I can think wealthy or worth th' enjoying,
And which, once lost, I have nought to lose beyond it,
Cannot be taken with these sensual baits:
If you have conscience –
Volp. 'Tis the beggar's virtue;
If thou hast wisdom, hear me, Celia.
Thy baths shall be the juice of July-flowers,
Spirit of roses and of violets,
The milk of unicorns, and panthers' breath
Gather'd in bags and mixt with Cretan wines.
Our drink shall be prepared gold and amber;
Which we will take until my roof whirl round
With the vertigo; and my dwarf shall dance,
My eunuch sing, my fool make up the antic,
Whilst we, in changed shapes, act Ovid's tales;
Thou like Europa now, and I like Jove,
Then I like Mars, and thou like Erycine:
So of the rest, till we have quite run through
And wearied all the fables of the gods.
Then will I have thee in more modern forms,
Attired like some sprightly dame of France,
Brave Tuscan lady, or proud Spanish beauty;
Sometimes unto the Persian sophy's wife,
Or the grand Signior's mistress; and, for change,
To one of our most artful courtezans,
Or some quick negro, or cold Russian;
And I will meet thee in as many shapes
Where we may so transfuse our wandering souls
Out at our lips, and score up sums of pleasures,

> That the curious shall not know
> How to tell them as they flow;
> And the envious, when they find
> What their number is, be pined.

Cel. If you have ears that will be pierced; or eyes
    That can be opened; a heart that may be touched;
    Or **any** part that yet sounds man about you:
    If you have touch of holy saints, or heaven,
    Do me the grace to let me 'scape. If not,
    Be bountiful, and kill me. You do know
    I am a creature hither ill-betrayed
    By one whose shame I would forget it were.
    If you will deign me neither of these graces,
    Yet feed your wrath, sir, rather than your lust
    (It is a vice comes nearer manliness)
    And punish that unhappy crime of Nature
    Which you miscall my beauty: flay my face,
    Or poison it with ointments, for seducing
    Your blood to this rebellion. Rub these hands
    With what may cause an eating leprosy
    E'en to my bones and marrow; anything
    That may disfavour me, save in my honour.
    And I will kneel to you, pray for you, pay down
    A thousand hourly vows, sir, for your health;
    Report and think you virtuous –
Volp. Think me cold,
    Frozen, and impotent, and so report me;
    That I had Nestor's hernia thou wouldst think.
    I do degenerate and abuse my nation
    To play with opportunity thus long;
    I should have done the act, and then have parleyed.
    Yield, or I 'll force thee.
Cel. Oh! Just God!
Volp. In vain –
Bon. [*He leaps out from where Mosca had placed him*] Forbear,
    foul ravisher, libidinous swine!
    Free the forced lady, or thou diest, impostor.
    But that I am loth to snatch thy punishment
    Out of the hand of justice, thou shouldst yet
    Be made the timely sacrifice of vengeance
    Before this altar and this dross, thy idol.

Lady, let's quit the place, it is the den
Of villainy; fear nought, you have a guard:
And he, ere long, shall meet his just reward.

Volp. Fall on me, roof, and bury me in ruin!
Become my grave that wert my shelter! O!
I am unmask'd, unspirited, undone,
Betrayed to beggary, to infamy –

———

ACT III, SCENE 8

Mosca, Volpone

Mos. Where shall I run, most wretched shame of men,
To beat out my unlucky brains?

Volp. Here, here.
What! dost thou bleed?

Mos. Oh! that his well-driv'n sword
Had been so courteous to have cleft me down
Unto the navel ere I lived to see
My life, my hopes, my spirits, my patron, all
Thus desperately engaged by my error.

Volp. Woe on thy fortune.

Mos. And my follies, sir.

Volp. Thou hast made me miserable.

Mos. And myself, sir.
Who would have thought he would have hearkened
so?

Volp. What shall we do?

Mos. I know not; if my heart
Could expiate the mischance, I'd pluck it out.
Will you be pleased to hang me, or cut my throat?
And I 'll requite you, sir. Let 's die like Romans,
Since we have lived like Grecians.

[They knock without.

Volp. Hark! Who's there?
I hear some footing, officers, the saffi,
Come to apprehend us! I do feel the brand

Hissing already at my forehead; now,
Mine ears are boring.
Mos. To your couch, sir, you
Make that place good, however. Guilty men
Suspect what they deserve still. Signior Corbaccio!

———

ACT III, SCENE 9
CORBACCIO, MOSCA, VOLTORE, VOLPONE

Corb. Why, how now, Mosca?
Mos. Oh, undone, amazed, sir.
Your son, I know not by what accident,
Acquainted with your purpose to my patron,
Touching your will, and making him your heir,
Entered our house with violence, his sword drawn,
Sought for you, called you wretch, unnatural,
Vowed he would kill you.
Corb. Me?
Mos. Yes, and my patron.
Corb. This act shall disinherit him, indeed:
Here is the will.
Mos. 'Tis well, sir.
Corb. Right and well:
Be you as careful now for me.
Mos. My life, sir,
Is not more tendered, I am only yours.
Corb. How does he? Will he die shortly, thinkest thou?
Mos. I fear
He 'll outlast May.
Corb. To-day?
Mos. No, last out May, sir.
Corb. Couldst thou not give him a dram?
Mos. Oh, by no means, sir.
Corb. Nay, I 'll not bid you.
Volt. This is a knave, I see.
Mos. How! Signor Voltore! Did he hear me?

Volt. Parasite!

Mos. Who's that? Oh, sir, most timely welcome –

Volt. Scarce,
   To the discovery of your tricks, I fear.
   You are his, *only*? and mine also, are you not?

Mos. Who? I, sir?

Volt. You, sir. What device is this
   About a will?

Mos. A plot for you, sir.

Volt. Come,
   Put not your foists upon me, I shall scent them.

Mos. Did you not hear it?

Volt. Yes, I hear Corbaccio
   Hath made your patron there his heir.

Mos. 'Tis true,
   By my device, drawn to it by my plot,
   With hope –

Volt. Your patron should reciprocate?
   And you have promised?

Mos. For your good, I did, sir.
   Nay, more, I told his son, brought, hid him here.
   Where he might hear his father pass the deed:
   Being persuaded to it by this thought, sir,
   That the unnaturalness, first, of the act,
   And then his father's oft disclaiming on him
   (Which I did mean t' help on) would sure enrage
      him
   To do some violence upon his parent,
   On which the law should take sufficient hold,
   And you be stated in a double hope:
   Truth be my comfort and my conscience,
   My only aim was to dig you a fortune
   Out of these two old rotten sepulchres –

Volt. I cry thee mercy, Mosca.

Mos. Worth your patience
   And your great merit, sir. And see the change!

Volt. Why, what success?

Mos. Most hapless! you must help, sir.
    Whilst we expected the old raven, in comes
    Corvino's wife, sent hither by her husband —
Volt. What, with a present?
Mos. No, sir, on visitation:
    (I 'll tell you how, anon) and staying long,
    The youth he grows impatient, rushes forth,
    Seizeth the lady, wounds me, makes her swear
    (Or he would murder her, that was his vow)
    To affirm my patron to have done her rape:
    Which how unlike it is, you see! and hence,
    With that pretext, he's gone to accuse his father,
    Defame my patron; defeat you —
Volt. Where 's her husband?
    Let him be sent for, straight.
Mos. Sir, I 'll go fetch him.
Volt. Bring him to the Scrutineo.
Mos. Sir, I will.
Volt. This must be stopped.
Mos. Oh, you do nobly, sir.
    Alas, 'twas laboured all, sir, for your good;
    Nor was there want of counsel in the plot:
    But fortune can, at any time, o'erthrow
    The projects of a hundred learned clerks, sir.
Corb. What 's that?
Volt. Will 't please you, sir, to go along?
Mos. Patron, go in, and pray for our success.
Volp. Need makes devotion! Heaven your labour bless!

ACT IV, SCENE 1

Sir Politick Would-be, Peregrine

Sir P. I told you, sir, it was a plot; you see
  What observation is! You mentioned me
  For some instructions: I will tell you, sir,
  (Since we are met here in this height of Venice)
  Some few particulars I have set down,
  Only for this meridian; fit to be known
  Of your crude traveller, and they are these.
  I will not touch, sir, at your phrase, or clothes,
  For they are old.
Per. Sir, I have better.
Sir P. Pardon,
  I meant, as they are themes.
Per. Oh, sir, proceed:
  I 'll slander you no more of wit, good sir.
Sir P. First, for your garb, it must be grave and serious,
  Very reserved, and locked; not tell a secret
  On any terms, not to your father; scarce
  A fable, but with caution: make sure choice
  Both of your company and discourse; beware
  You never speak a truth –
Per. How!
Sir P. Not to strangers,
  For those be they you must converse with most;
  Others I would not know, sir, but at distance,
  So as I still might be a saver in them:
  You shall have tricks else passed upon you hourly.
  And then, for your religion, profess none,
  But wonder at the diversity of all;
  And for your part, protest were there no other
  But simply the laws o' th' land, you could content you.
  Nic. Machiavel, and Monsieur Bodine, both
  Were of this mind. Then must you learn the use
  And handling of your silver fork at meals;

The metal of your glass; (these are main matters
With your Italian) and to know the hour
When you must eat your melons and your figs.
Per. Is that a point of state too?
Sir P. Here it is.
For your Venetian, if he see a man
Preposterous in the least, he has him straight;
He has; he strips him. I 'll acquaint you, sir,
I now have lived here, 'tis some fourteen months.
Within the first week of my landing here,
All took me for a citizen of Venice,
I knew the forms so well —
Per. And nothing else.
Sir P. I had read Contarene, took me a house,
Dealt with my Jews to furnish it with moveables —
Well, if I could but find one man, one man
To mine own heart, whom I durst trust, I would —
Per. What, what, sir?
Sir P. Make him rich; make him a fortune:
He should not think again. I would command it.
Per. As how?
Sir P. With certain projects that I have;
Which I may not discover.
Per. If I had
But one to wager with, I would lay odds now,
He tells me instantly.
Sir P. One is, and that
I care not greatly who knows, to serve the state
Of Venice with red herrings for three years,
And at a certain rate, from Rotterdam,
Where I have correspondence. There 's a letter,
Sent me from one o' the States, and to that purpose;
He cannot write his name, but that 's his mark.
Per. He is a chandler?
Sir P. No, a cheesemonger.
There are some others, too, with whom I treat
About the same negotiation;

And I will undertake it: for, 'tis thus,
I 'll do 't with ease, I have cast it all. Your hoy
Carries but three men in her, and a boy;
And she shall make me three returns a year:
So, if there come but one of three, I save,
If two, I can default. But this is now,
If my main project fail.
Per. Then you have others?
Sir P. I should be loth to draw the subtle air
Of such a place, without my thousand aims.
I 'll not dissemble, sir, where'er I come,
I love to be considerative; and 'tis true,
I have at my free hours thought upon
Some certain goods unto the state of Venice,
Which I do call my Cautions; and, sir, which
I mean, in hope of pension, to propound
To the Great Council, then unto the Forty,
So to the Ten. My means are made already –
Per. By whom?
Sir P. Sir, one that, though his place be obscure,
Yet, he can sway, and they will hear him. He's
A commandadore.
Per. What! A common sergeant?
Sir P. Sir, such as they are, put it in their mouths
What they should say, sometimes: as well as greater.
I think I have my notes to show you.
Per. Good sir.
Sir P. But you shall swear unto me, on your gentry,
Not to anticipate –
Per. I, sir?
Sir P. Nor reveal
A circumstance – My paper is not with me.
Per. Oh, but you can remember, sir.
Sir P. My first is
Concerning tinder-boxes. You must know,
No family is here without its box.
Now, sir, it being so portable a thing,

Put case, that you or I were ill-affected
Unto the state; sir, with it in our pockets,
Might not I go into the Arsenal,
Or you? come out again? and none the wiser?

Per. Except yourself, sir.

Sir P. Go to, then. I therefore
Advertise to the state, how fit it were,
That none but such as were known patriots,
Sound lovers of their country, should be suffered
To enjoy them in their houses; and even those
Sealed at some office, and at such a bigness
As might not lurk in pockets.

Per. Admirable!

Sir P. My next is, how to enquire, and be resolved,
By present demonstration, whether a ship,
Newly arrived from Syria, or from
Any suspected part of all the Levant,
Be guilty of the plague: and where they use
To lie out forty, fifty days, sometimes,
About the Lazaretto, for their trial;
I 'll save that charge and loss unto the merchant,
And in an hour clear the doubt.

Per. Indeed, sir!

Sir P. Or – I will lose my labour.

Per. 'My faith, that 's much.

Sir P. Nay, sir, conceive me. It will cost me in onions,
Some thirty livres –

Per. Which is one pound sterling.

Sir P. Beside my water-works: for this I do, sir.
First, I bring in your ship 'twixt two brick walls;
But those the state shall venture: on the one
I strain me a fair tarpaulin, and in that
I stick my onions, cut in halves: the other
Is full of loop-holes, out at which I thrust
The noses of my bellows; and those bellows
I keep, with water-works, in perpetual motion,
Which is the easiest matter of a hundred.

Now, sir, your onion, which doth naturally
Attract the infection, and your bellows blowing
The air upon him, will show, instantly,
By this changed colour, if there be contagion;
Or else remain as fair as at the first.
Now it is known, 't is nothing.

Per. You are right, sir.

Sir P. I would I had my note.

Per. Faith, so would I:
But you have done well for once, sir.

Sir P. Were I false,
Or would be made so, I could show you reasons
How I could sell this state now to the Turk,
Spite of their galleys, or their –

Per. Pray you, Sir Pol.

Sir P. I have them not about me.

Per. That I feared:
They are there, sir.

Sir P. No, this is my diary,
Wherein I note my actions of the day.

Per. Pray you, let 's see, sir. What is here? Notandum,
A rat had gnawn my spur-leathers; notwithstanding,
I put on new, and did go forth; but first
I threw three beans over the threshold. Item,
I went and bought two toothpicks, whereof one
I burst immediately, in a discourse
With a Dutch merchant, 'bout *ragion del stato*.
From him I went and paid a *moccinigo*
For piecing my silk stockings: by the way
I cheapened sprats; and at St Mark's I urined.
'Faith, these are politic notes!

Sir P. Sir, I do slip
No action of my life, thus but I quote it.

Per. Belive me, it is wise!

Sir P. Nay, sir, read forth.

ACT IV SCENE 2

LADY POLITICK WOULD-BE, NANO, WAITING-WOMEN,
SIR POLITICK WOULD-BE, PEREGRINE

Lady P. Where should this loose knight be, trow? sure,
he 's housed.

Nan. Why, then he 's fast.

Lady P. Ay, he plays both with me.
I pray you stay. This heat will do more harm
To my complexion, than his heart is worth,
(I do not care to hinder, but to take him)
How it comes off!

1st Wom. My master 's yonder.

Lady P. Where?

2nd Wom. With a young gentleman.

Lady P. That same 's the party;
In man's apparel! 'Pray you, sir, jog my knight:
I will be tender to his reputation,
However he demerit.

Sir P. My lady!

Per. Where?

Sir P. 'Tis she indeed, sir; you shall know her. She is,
Were she not mine, a lady of that merit,
For fashion and behaviour; and for beauty
I durst compare –

Per. It seems you are not jealous,
That dare commend her.

Sir P. Nay, and for discourse –

Per. Being your wife, she cannot miss that.

Sir P. Madam,
Here is a gentleman, pray you, use him fairly;
He seems a youth, but he is –

Lady P. None?

Sir P. Yes, one
Has put his face as soon into the world –

Lady P. You mean, as early? but today?

Sir P. How 's this!

Lady P. Why, in this habit, sir, you apprehend me: –
  Well, Master Would-be, this doth not become you;
  I had thought the odour, sir, of your good name
  Had been more precious to you; that you would
    not
  Have done this dire massacre on your honour;
  One of your gravity and rank besides!
  But knights, I see, care little for the oath
  They make to ladies; chiefly their own ladies.

Sir P. Now, by my spurs, the symbol of my knight-
    hood. –

Per. Lord, how his brain is humbled for an oath!

Sir P. I reach you not.

Lady P. Right, sir, your policy
  May bear it through thus. Sir, a word with you.
  I would be loth to contest publicly
  With any gentlewoman, or to seem
  Froward or violent, as the courtier says;
  It comes too near rusticity in a lady,
  Which I would shun by all means; and however
  I may deserve from Master Would-be, yet
  To have one fair gentlewoman thus be made
  The unkind instrument to wrong another,
  And one she knows not, ay, and to persevere;
  In my poor judgement, is not warranted
  From being a solecism in our sex,
  If not in manners.

Per. How is this!

Sir P. Sweet madam,
  Come nearer to your aim.

Lady P. Marry and will, sir,
  Since you provoke me with your impudence,
  And laughter of your light land-siren here,
  Your Sporus, your hermaphrodite –

Per. What's here?
  Poetic fury, and historic storms!

Sir P. The gentleman, believe it, is of worth,
　And of our nation.

Lady P. Ay, your Whitefriars nation.
　Come, I blush for you, Master Would-be, I;
　And am ashamed you should have no more forehead,
　Than thus to be the patron, or St George,
　To a lewd harlot, a base fricatrice,
　A female devil, in a male outside.

Sir P. Nay,
　And you be such an one, I must bid adieu
　To your delights. The case appears too liquid.

Lady P. Ay, you may carry it clear with your state-face!
　But for your carnival concupiscence,
　Who here is fled for liberty of conscience,
　From furious persecution of the marshal,
　Her will I disc'ple.

Per. This is fine, i' faith!
　And do you use this often? Is this part
　Of your wit's exercise, 'gainst you have occasion?
　Madam –

Lady P. Go to, sir.

Per. Do you hear me, lady!
　Why, if your knight have set you to beg shirts,
　Or to invite me home, you might have done it
　A nearer way, by far.

Lady P. This cannot work you
　Out of my snare.

Per. Why, am I in it, then?
　Indeed your husband told me you were fair.
　And so you are; only your nose inclines
　That side that 's next the sun, to the queen-apple.

Lady P. This cannot be endured by any patience.

ACT IV, SCENE 3

MOSCA, LADY POLITICK WOULD-BE, PEREGRINE

Mos. What is the matter, madam?

Lady P. If the Senate
  Right not my quest in this, I will protest them
  To all the world, no aristocracy.

Mos. What is the injury, lady?

Lady P. Why, the callet
  You told me of, here I have ta'en disguised.

Mos. Who? this? what means your ladyship? the creature
  I mentioned to you is apprehended now,
  Before the Senate; you shall see her –

Lady P. Where?

Mos. I 'll bring you to her. This young gentleman,
  I saw him land this morning at the port.

Lady P. Is 't possible! how has my judgement wandered?
  Sir, I must, blushing, say to you, I have erred;
  And plead your pardon.

Per. What, more changes yet?

Lady P. I hope you have not the malice to remember
  A gentlewoman's passion. If you stay
  In Venice here, please you to use me, sir –

Mos. Will you go, madam?

Lady P. 'Pray you, sir, use me; in faith,
  The more you see me, the more I shall conceive
  You have forgot our quarrel.

Per. This is rare!
  Sir Politick Would-be? no; Sir Politick Bawd,
  To bring me thus acquainted with his wife!
  Well, wise Sir Pol, since you have practised thus
  Upon my freshman-ship, I 'll try your salt-head,
  What proof it is against a counter-plot.

VOLTORE, CORBACCIO, CORVINO, MOSCA

Volt. Well, now you know the carriage of the business,
   Your constancy is all that is required
   Unto the safety of it.
Mos. Is the lie
   Safely conveyed amongst us? is that sure?
   Knows every man his burden?
Corv. Yes.
Mos. Then shrink not.
Corv. But knows the advocate the truth?
Mos. Oh, sir,
   By no means. I devised a formal tale,
   That salved your reputation. But be valiant, sir.
Corv. I fear no one but him, that this his pleading
   Should make him stand for a co-heir –
Mos. Co-halter!
   Hang him; we will but use his tongue, his noise,
   As we do croakers here.
Corv. Ay, what shall he do?
Mos. When we have done, you mean?
Corv. Yes.
Mos. Why, we 'll think:
   Sell him for mummia; he's half dust already.
   Do you not smile – [*to Voltore*] – to see this buffalo,
   How he doth sport it with his head? – I should,
   If all were well and past. Sir [*to Corbaccio*], only you
   Are he that shall enjoy the crop of all,
   And these not know for whom they toil.
Corb. Ay, peace,
Mos. But you shall eat it. Much! [*to Corvino, then to
    Voltore again*] Worshipful sir,
   Mercury sit upon your thundering tongue,
   Or the French Hercules, and make your language
   As conquering as his club, to beat along,

As with a tempest, flat, our adversaries;
  But, much more, yours, sir.
Volt. Here they come, have done.
Mos. I have another witness, if you need, sir,
  I can produce.
Volt. Who is it?
Mos. Sir, I have her.

—

ACT IV, SCENE 5
4 Avocatori, Bonario, Celia,
Voltore, Corbaccio, Corvino, Mosca,
Notario, Commandadori

1st Avoc. The like of this the senate never heard of.
2nd Avoc. 'Twill come most strange to them when we
  report it.
4th Avoc. The gentlewoman has been ever held
  Of unreproved name.
3rd Avoc. So the young man.
4th Avoc. The more unnatural part that of his
  father.
2nd Avoc. More of the husband.
1st Avoc. I not know to give
  His act a name, it is so monstrous!
4th Avoc. But the impostor, he's a thing created
  To exceed example!
1st Avoc. And all after times!
2nd Avoc. I never heard a true voluptuary
  Described, but him.
3rd Avoc. Appear yet those were cited?
Not. All but the old magnifico, Volpone.
1st Avoc. Why is not he here?
Mos. Please your fatherhoods,
  Here is his advocate: himself 's so weak,
  So feeble –
4th Avoc. What are you?

Bon. His parasite,
   His knave, his pandar: I beseech the court,
   He may be forced to come, that your grave eyes
   May bear strong witness of his strange impostures.
Volt. Upon my faith and credit with your virtues,
   He is not able to endure the air.
2nd Avoc. Bring him, however.
3rd Avoc. We will see him.
4th Avoc. Fetch him.
Volt. Your fatherhoods' fit pleasures be obeyed,
   But sure, the sight will rather move your pities,
   Than indignation; may it please the court,
   In the meantime, he may be heard in me:
   I know this place most void of prejudice,
   And therefore crave it, since we have no reason
   To fear our truth should hurt our cause.
3rd Avoc. Speak free.
Volt. Then know, most honoured fathers, I must now
   Discover to your strangely abused ears,
   The most prodigious and most frontless piece
   Of solid impudence and treachery,
   That ever vicious nature yet brought forth
   To shame the state of Venice. This lewd woman,
   That wants no artificial looks or tears
   To help the vizor she has now put on,
   Hath long been known a close adulteress
   To that lascivious youth there: not suspected,
   I say, but known and taken in the act
   With him; and by this man, the easy husband,
   Pardoned; whose timeless bounty makes him now
   Stand here the most unhappy, innocent person,
   That ever man's own goodness made accused.
   For these not knowing how to owe a gift
   Of that dear grace, but with their shame; being placed
   So above all powers of their gratitude,
   Began to hate the benefit; and, in place
   Of thanks, devise to extirp the memory

Of such an act. Wherein I pray your fatherhoods
To observe the malice, yea, the rage of creatures
Discovered in their evils; and what heart
Such take, even from their crimes. But that anon
Will more appear. This gentleman, the father,
Hearing of this foul fact, with many others,
Which daily struck at his too tender ears,
And grieved in nothing more than that he could not
Preserve himself a parent (his son's ills
Growing to that strange flood), at last decreed
To disinherit him.

1st Avoc. These be strange turns!

2nd Avoc. The young man's fame was ever fair and
    honest.

Volt. So much more full of danger is his vice,
  That can beguile so, under shade of virtue.
  But, as I said, my honoured sires, his father
  Having this settled purpose, by what means
  To him betrayed, we know not, and this day
  Appointed for the deed; that parricide,
  I cannot style him better, by confederacy
  Preparing this his paramour to be there,
  Entered Volpone's house (who was the man,
  Your fatherhoods must understand designed
  For the inheritance) there sought his father:
  But with what purpose sought he him, my lords?
  I tremble to pronounce it, that a son
  Unto a father, and to such a father,
  Should have so foul, felonious intent!
  It was to murder him. When, being prevented
  By his more happy absence, what then did he?
  Not check his wicked thoughts; no, now new deeds;
  (Mischief doth never end where it begins)
  An act of horror, fathers! he dragged forth
  The aged gentleman that had there lain bed-rid
  Three years and more, out of his innocent couch,
  Naked upon the floor, there left him; wounded

His servant in the face: and, with this strumpet
The stale to his forged practice, who was glad
To be so active (I shall here desire
Your fatherhoods to note but my collections,
As most remarkable), thought at once to stop
His father's ends; discredit his free choice
In the old gentleman; redeem themselves,
By laying infamy upon this man,
To whom, with blushing, they should owe their lives.

1st Avoc. What proofs have you of this?

Bon. Most honoured fathers,
I humbly crave there be no credit given
To this man's mercenary tongue.

2nd Avoc. Forbear.

Bon. His soul moves in his fee.

3rd Avoc. Oh, sir.

Bon. This fellow,
For six sols more, would plead against his maker.

1st Avoc. You do forget yourself.

Volt. Nay, nay, grave fathers,
Let him have scope: can any man imagine
That he will spare his accuser, that would not
Have spared his parent?

1st Avoc. Well, produce your proofs.

Cel. I would I could forget I were a creature.

Volt. Signior Corbaccio.

4th Avoc. What is he?

Volt. The father.

2nd Avoc. Has he had an oath?

Not. Yes.

Corb. What must I do now?

Not. Your testimony's craved.

Corb. Speak to the knave?
I 'll have my mouth first stopped with earth; my
    heart
Abhors his knowledge: I disclaim in him.

1st Avoc. But for what cause?

Corb. The mere portent of nature!
   He is an utter stranger to my loins.
Bon. Have they made you to this?
Corb. I will not hear thee,
   Monster of men, swine, goat, wolf, parricide!
   Speak not, thou viper.
Bon. Sir, I will sit down,
   And rather wish my innocence should suffer,
   Than I resist the authority of a father.
Volt. Signor Corvino!
2nd Avoc. This is strange.
1st Avoc. Who's this?
Not. The husband.
4th Avoc. Is he sworn?
Not. He is.
3rd Avoc. Speak then.
Corv. This woman, please your fatherhoods, is a strumpet
   Of most hot exercise, more than a partridge,
   Upon record –
1st Avoc. No more.
Corv. Neighs like a jennet.
Not. Preserve the honour of the court.
Corv. I shall,
   And modesty of your most reverend ears.
   And yet I hope that I may say, these eyes
   Have seen her glued into that piece of cedar,
   That fine well-timbered gallant; and that here
   The letters may be read thorough the horn,
   That make the story perfect.
Mos. Excellent! sir.
Corv. There is no shame in this now, is there?
Mos. None.
Corv. Or if I said I hoped that she were onward
   To her damnation, if there be a hell
   Greater than a foul woman; a good catholic
   May make the doubt.
3rd Avoc. His grief hath made him frantic.

1st Avoc. Remove him hence.

2nd Avoc. Look to the woman. 　　　　　　　　*[She swoons.*

Corv. Rare!

　Prettily feigned, again!

4th Avoc. Stand from about her.

1st Avoc. Give her the air.

3rd Avoc. What can you say?

Mos. My wound,

　May it please your wisdoms, speaks for me, received

　In aid of my good patron, when he missed

　His sought-for father, when that well-taught dame

　Had her cue given her to cry out a rape!

Bon. Oh, most laid impudence! Fathers –

3rd Avoc. Sir, be silent;

　You had your hearing free, so must they theirs.

2nd Avoc. I do begin to doubt the imposture here.

4th Avoc. This woman has too many moods.

Volt. Grave fathers,

　She is a creature of a most profest

　And prostituted lewdness.

Corv. Most impetuous,

　Unsatisfied, grave fathers!

Volt. May her feignings

　Not take your wisdoms; but this day she baited

　A stranger, a grave knight, with her loose eyes

　And most lascivious kisses. This man saw them

　Together on the water, in a gondola.

Mos. Here is the lady herself that saw them too,

　Without; who then had in the open streets

　Pursued them, but for saving her knight's honour.

1st Avoc. Produce that lady.

2nd Avoc. Let her come.

4th Avoc. These things,

　They strike with wonder.

3rd Avoc. I am turn'd a stone.

ACT IV, SCENE 6

MOSCA, LADY WOULD-BE, AVOCATORI, etc.

Mos. Be resolute, madam.

Lady P. Ay, this same is she.
  Out, thou chameleon harlot! Now thine eyes
  Vie tears with the hyena. Dar'st thou look
  Upon my wronged face? I cry your pardons;
  I fear I have forgettingly transgrest
  Against the dignity of the court –

2nd Avoc. No, madam.

Lady P. And been exorbitant –

2nd Avoc. You have not, lady.

4th Avoc. These proofs are strong.

Lady P. Surely, I had no purpose
  To scandalize your honours or my sex's.

3rd Avoc. We do believe it.

Lady P. Surely, you may believe it.

2nd Avoc. Madam, we do.

Lady P. Indeed you may; my breeding
  Is not so coarse –

4th Avoc. We know it.

Lady P. To offend
  With pertinacy –

3rd Avoc. Lady –

Lady P. Such a presence:
  No surely.

1st Avoc. We well think it.

Lady P. You may think it.

1st Avoc. Let her o'ercome. What witnesses have you
  To make good your report?

Bon. Our consciences.

Cel. And Heaven, that never fails the innocent.

4th Avoc. These are no testimonies.

Bon. Not in your courts,
  Where multitude and clamour overcomes.

1st Avoc. Nay, then, you do wax insolent.
                Volpone is brought in, as impotent.
Volt. Here, here,
   The testimony comes, that will convince,
   And put to utter dumbness their bold tongues.
   See here, grave fathers, here's the ravisher,
   Insulter of men's wives, the great impostor,
   The grand voluptuary! Do you not think
   These limbs should affect venery? or these eyes
   Covet a concubine? Pray you mark these hands;
   Are they not fit to stroke a lady's breasts?
   Perhaps he doth dissemble!
Bon. So he does.
Volt. Would you have him tortured?
Bon. I would have him proved.
Volt. Best try him then with goads or burning
     irons;
   Put him to the strappado; I have heard
   The rack hath cured the gout, 'faith, give it
     him,
   And help him of a malady, be courteous.
   I'll undertake, before these honoured fathers,
   He shall have yet as many left diseases
   As she has known adulterers, or thou strumpets.
   Oh, my most equal hearers, if these deeds,
   Acts of this bold and most exorbitant strain,
   May pass with sufferance, what one citizen
   But owes the forfeit of his life, yea, fame,
   To him that dares traduce him? Which of you
   Are safe, my honour'd fathers? I would ask,
   With leave of your grave fatherhoods, if their
     plot
   Have any face or colour like to truth?
   Or if unto the dullest nostril here
   It smell not rank and most abhorred slander?
   I crave your care of this good gentleman,
   Whose life is much endangered by their fable;

And as for them, I will conclude with this,
That vicious persons, when they're hot and fleshed
In impious acts, their constancy abounds;
Damn'd deeds are done with greatest confidence.

1st Avoc. Take them to custody, and sever them.

2nd Avoc. 'Tis pity two such prodigies should live.

1st Avoc. Let the old gentleman be returned with care.
I'm sorry our credulity hath wronged him.

4th Avoc. These are two creatures!

3rd Avoc. I've an earthquake in me.

2nd Avoc. Their shame even in their cradles fled their
faces.

4th Avoc. You have done a worthy service to the state, sir,
In their discovery.

1st Avoc. You shall hear, ere night,
What punishment the court decrees upon them.

Volt. We thank your fatherhoods. – How like you it?

Mos. Rare.
I'd have your tongue, sir, tipt with gold for this;
I'd have you be the heir to the whole city;
The earth I'd have want men ere you want living;
They're bound to erect your statue in St Mark's,
Signior Corvino, I would have you go
And show yourself that you have conquer'd.

Corv. Yes.

Mos. It was much better that you should profess
Yourself a cuckold thus, than that the other
Should have been proved.

Corv. Nay, I considered that:
Now it is her fault.

Mos. Then it had been yours.

Corv. True: I do doubt this advocate still.

Mos. I' faith
You need not, I dare ease you of that care.

Corv. I trust thee, Mosca.

Mos. As your own soul, sir.

Corb. Mosca!

Mos. Now for your business, sir.

Corb. How! have you business?

Mos. Yes, yours, sir.

Corb. Oh, none else?

Mos. None else, not I.

Corb. Be careful, then.

Mos. Rest you with both your eyes, sir.

Corb. Dispatch it.

Mos. Instantly.

Corb. And look that all,
　　Whatever, be put in, jewels, plate, moneys,
　　Household stuff, bedding, curtains.

Mos. Curtain-rings, sir:
　　Only the advocate's fee must be deducted.

Corb. I'll pay him now; you'll be too prodigal.

Mos. Sir, I must tender it.

Corb. Two *cecchines* is well.

Mos. No, six, sir.

Corb. 'Tis too much.

Mos. He talked a great while;
　　You must consider that, sir.

Corb. Well, there's three –

Mos. I'll give it him.

Corb. Do so, and there's for thee.

Mos. Bountiful bones! What horrid strange offence
　　Did he commit 'gainst nature, in his youth,
　　Worthy this age? You see, sir, how I work
　　Unto your ends: take you no notice?

Volt. No,
　　I'll leave you.

Mos. All is yours, the devil and all:
　　Good advocate! Madam, I'll bring you home.

Lady P. No, I'll go see your patron.

Mos. That you shall not:
　　I'll tell you why. My purpose is to urge
　　My patron to reform his will; and for
　　The zeal you have shown today, whereas before

You were but third or fourth, you shall be now
Put in the first; which would appear as begged
If you were present. Therefore –
Lady P. You shall sway me.

ACT V, SCENE 1
VOLPONE

Volp. Well, I am here, and all this brunt is past.
  I ne'er was in dislike with my disguise
  Till this fled moment: here 'twas good in private;
  But in your public, *cave,* whilst I breathe.
  'Fore God, my left leg 'gan to have the cramp,
  And I apprehended straight some power had struck
    me
  With a dead palsy: well, I must be merry,
  And shake it off. A many of these fears
  Would put me into some villainous disease,
  Should they come thick upon me; I'll prevent 'em.
  Give me a bowl of lusty wine, to fright
  This humour from my heart. [*He drinks.*] – hum, hum,
    hum!
  'Tis almost gone already; I shall conquer.
  Any device, now, of rare ingenious knavery
  That would possess me with a violent laughter,
  Would make me up again. – So, so, so! [*Drinks again.*]
  This heat is life; 't is blood by this time: – Mosca!

———

ACT V, SCENE 2
MOSCA, VOLPONE, NANO, CASTRONE

Mos. How now, sir? does the day look clear again?
  Are we recover'd, and wrought out of error,
  Into our way, to see our path before us?
  Is our trade free once more?
Volp. Exquisite Mosca!
Mos. Was it not carried learnedly?
Volp. And stoutly:
  Good wits are greatest in extremities.
Mos. It were a folly beyond thought, to trust

Any grand act unto a cowardly spirit:
You are not taken with it enough, methinks.
Volp. Oh, more than if I had enjoyed the wench:
The pleasure of all womankind's not like it.
Mos. Why, now you speak, sir. We must here be fix'd;
Here we must rest; this is our masterpiece;
We cannot think to go beyond this.
Volp. True,
Thou hast play'd thy prize, my precious Mosca.
Mos. Nay, sir,
To gull the court –
Volp. And quite divert the torrent
Upon the innocent.
Mos. Yes, and to make
So rare a music out of discords –
Volp. Right.
That yet to me's the strangest, how thou hast
borne it!
That these, being so divided 'mongst themselves,
Should not scent somewhat, or in me or thee,
Or doubt their own side.
Mos. True, they will not see 't.
Too much light blinds them, I think. Each of them
Is so possessed and stuffed with his own hopes,
That any thing unto the contrary,
Never so true, or never so apparent,
Never so palpable, they will resist it –
Volp. Like a temptation of the devil.
Mos. Right, sir.
Merchants may talk of trade, and your great signiors
Of land that yields well; but if Italy
Have any glebe more fruitful than these fellows,
I am deceiv'd. Did not your advocate rare?
Volp. Oh – 'My most honour'd fathers, my grave
fathers,
Under correction of your fatherhoods,
What face of truth is here? If these strange deeds

May pass, most honour'd fathers' – I had much ado
To forebear laughing.

Mos. It seem'd to me, you sweat, sir.

Volp. In troth, I did a little.

Mos. But confess, sir,
Were you not daunted?

Volp. In good faith, I was
A little in a mist: but not dejected:
Never, but still myself.

Mos. I think it, sir.
Now, so truth help me, I must needs say this, sir,
And out of conscience for your advocate,
He has taken pains, in faith, sir, and deserv'd,
In my poor judgement, I speak it under favour,
Not to contrary you, sir, very richly –
Well – to be cozen'd.

Volp. Troth, and I think so too,
By that I heard him, in the latter end.

Mos. Oh, but before, sir: had you heard him first
Draw it to certain heads, then aggravate,
Then use his vehement figures – I look'd still
When he would shift a shirt: and, doing this
Out of pure love, no hope of gain –

Volp. 'Tis right.
I cannot answer him, Mosca, as I would,
Not yet; but for thy sake, at thy entreaty,
I will begin, even now, to vex them all,
This very instant.

Mos. Good, sir.

Volp. Call the dwarf
And eunuch forth.

Mos. Castrone, Nano!

Nano. Here.

Volp. Shall we have a jig now?

Mos. What you please, sir.

Volp. Go,
Straight give out about the streets, you two,

   That I am dead; do it with constancy,
   Sadly, do you hear? Impute it to the grief
   Of this late slander.

Mos. What do you mean, sir?

Volp. Oh,
   I shall have instantly my vulture, crow,
   Raven, come flying hither, on the news,
   To peck for carrion, my she-wolf and all,
   Greedy and full of expectation –

Mos. And then to have it ravished from their mouths!

Volp. 'Tis true. I will have thee put on a gown,
   And take upon thee, as thou wert mine heir:
   Show them a will: open that chest, and reach
   Forth one of those that has the blanks. I'll straight
   Put in thy name.

Mos. It will be rare, sir.

Volp. Ay,
   When they e'en gape, and find themselves deluded –

Mos. Yes.

Volp. And then use them scurvily!
   Dispatch, get on thy gown.

Mos. But what, sir, if they ask
   After the body?

Volp. Say, it was corrupted.

Mos. I'll say it stank, sir; and was fain to have it
   Coffined up instantly, and sent away.

Volp. Anything, what thou wilt. Hold, here's my will.
   Get thee a cap, a count-book, pen and ink,
   Papers afore thee; sit as thou wert taking
   An inventory of parcels: I'll get up
   Behind the curtain, on a stool, and hearken;
   Sometime peep over, see how they do look,
   With what degrees their blood doth leave their
     faces!
   O, 'twill afford me a rare meal of laughter!

Mos. Your advocate will turn stark dull upon it.

Volp. It will take off his oratory's edge.

Mos. But your clarissimo, old round-back, he
    Will crump you like a hog-louse, with the touch.
Volp. And what Corvino?
Mos. Oh, sir, look for him,
    Tomorrow morning, with a rope and dagger,
    To visit all the streets; for he must run mad.
    My lady too, that came into the court
    To bear false witness for your worship –
Volp. Yes,
    And kiss'd me 'fore the fathers, when my face
    Flowed all with oils.
Mos. And sweat, sir. Why, your gold
    Is such another med'cine, it dries up
    All those offensive savours: it transforms
    The most deformed, and restores them lovely,
    As 'twere the strange poetical girdle. Jove
    Could not invent t' himself a shroud more subtle
    To pass Acrisius' guards. It is the thing
    Makes all the world her grace, her youth, her beauty.
Volp. I think she loves me.
Mos. Who? the lady, sir?
    She's jealous of you.
Volp. Dost thou say so?
Mos. Hark,
    There's some already.
Volp. Look.
Mos. It is the vulture;
    He has the quickest scent.
Volp. I'll to my place,
    Thou to thy posture.
Mos. I am set.
Volp. But, Mosca,
    Play the artificer now, torture them rarely.

ACT V, SCENE 3

Voltore, Mosca, Corbaccio, Corvino, Lady Politick, Volpone

Volt. How now, my Mosca?

Mos. Turkey carpets, nine –

Volt. Taking an inventory? that is well.

Mos. Two suits of bedding, tissue –

Volt. Where's the will?
  Let me read that the while.

Corb. So, set me down,
  And get you home.

Volt. Is he come now, to trouble us?

Mos. Of cloth of gold, two more –

Corb. Is it done, Mosca?

Mos. Of several velvets, eight –

Volt. I like his care.

Corb. Dost thou not hear?

Corv. Ha! is the hour come, Mosca?

Volp. [*Peeps from behind a traverse.*] Ay, now they muster.

Corv. What does the advocate here,
  Or this Corbaccio?

Corb. What do these here?

Lady P. Mosca!
  Is his thread spun?

Mos. Eight chests of linen –

Volp. Oh,
  My fine Dame Would-be, too!

Corv. Mosca, the will,
  That I may show it these, and rid them hence.

Mos. Six chests of diaper, four of damask –
  There.

Corb. Is that the will?

Mos. Down-beds and bolsters –

Volp. Rare!
  Be busy still. Now they begin to flutter:

They never think of me. Look, see, see, see!
How their swift eyes run over the long deed
Unto the name, and to the legacies,
What is bequeathed them there –

Mos. Ten suits of hangings –

Volp. Ay, in their garters, Mosca. Now their hopes
Are at the gasp.

Volt. Mosca the heir!

Corb. What's that?

Volp. My advocate is dumb; look to my merchant,
He has heard of some strange storm, a ship is lost,
He faints; my lady will swoon. Old glazen-eyes,
He hath not reached his despair yet.

Corb. All these
Are out of hope; I am, sure, the man.

Corv. But, Mosca –

Mos. Two cabinets.

Corv. Is this in earnest?

Mos. One
Of ebony –

Corv. Or do you but delude me?

Mos. The other, mother of pearl – I am very busy.
Good faith, it is a fortune thrown upon me –
Item, one salt of agate – not my seeking.

Lady P. Do you hear, sir?

Mos. A perfumed box – 'pray you forbear,
You see I'm troubled – made of an onyx –

Lady P. How!

Mos. Tomorrow or next day, I shall be at leisure
To talk with you all.

Corv. Is this my large hope's issue?

Lady P. Sir, I must have a fairer answer.

Mos. Madam!
Marry, and shall: 'pray you, fairly quit my house.
Nay, raise no tempest with your looks; but hark you,
Remember what your ladyship offer'd me
To put you in an heir; go to, think on it:

And what you said e'en your best madams did
For maintenance; and why not you? Enough.
Go home, and use the poor Sir Pol, your knight, well,
For fear I tell some riddles; go, be melancholy.

Volp. Oh, my fine devil!

Corv. Mosca, pray you a word.

Mos. Lord! will you not take your despatch hence yet?
Methinks, of all, you should have been the example.
Why should you stay here? with what thought, what
    promise?
Hear you, do you not know, I know you an ass,
And that you would most fain have been a wittol,
If fortune would have let you? that you are
A declared cuckold, on good terms? This pearl,
You'll say, was yours? right: this diamond?
I'll not deny't, but thank you. Much here else?
It may be so. Why, think that these good works
May help to hide your bad: I'll not betray you,
Although you be but extraordinary,
And have it only in title, it sufficeth:
Go home, be melancholic too, or mad.

Volp. Rare, Mosca! how his villainy becomes him!

Volt. Certain he doth delude all these for me.

Corb. Mosca the heir!

Volp. O, his four eyes have found it.

Corb. I am cozen'd, cheated, by a parasite slave;
Harlot, thou hast gull'd me.

Mos. Yes, sir. Stop your mouth,
Or I shall draw the only tooth is left.
Are not you he, that filthy covetous wretch,
With the three legs, that here, in hope of prey,
Have, any time this three years, snuff'd about,
With your most grovelling nose; and would have
    hired
Me to the poisoning of my patron, sir?
Are not you he that have today in court
Profess'd the disinheriting of your son?

Perjured yourself? Go home, and die, and stink;
If you but croak a syllable, all comes out:
Away, and call your porters, go, go, stink.
Volp. Excellent varlet!
Volt. Now, my faithful Mosca,
  I find thy constancy –
Mos. Sir!
Volt. Sincere.
Mos. A table
  Of porphyry – I marvel you'll be thus troublesome.
Volt. Nay, leave off now, they are gone.
Mos. Why, who are you?
  What! Who did send for you? Oh, cry you mercy,
  Reverend sir! Good faith, I am grieved for you,
  That any chance of mine should thus defeat
  Your (I must needs say) most deserving travails:
  But I protest, sir, it was cast upon me,
  And I could almost wish to be without it,
  But that the will o' the dead must be observed.
  Marry, my joy is that you need it not;
  You have a gift, sir, (thank your education),
  Will never let you want, while there are men,
  And malice, to breed causes. Would I had
  But half the like, for all my fortune, sir!
  If I have any suits, as I do hope,
  Things being so easy and direct, I shall not,
  I will make bold with your obstreperous aid,
  Conceive me, for your fee, sir. In the meantime,
  You that have so much law, I know have the conscience
  Not to be covetous of what is mine.
  Good sir, I thank you for my plate; 'twill help
  To set up a young man. Good faith, you look
  As you were costive; best go home and purge, sir.
Volp. Bid him eat lettuce well. My witty mischief,
  Let me embrace thee. Oh, that I could now
  Transform thee to a Venus – Mosca, go,
  Straight take my habit of clarissimo,

And walk the streets; be seen, torment them more:
We must pursue, as well as plot. Who would
Have lost this feast?
Mos. I doubt it will lose them.
Volp. Oh, my recovery shall recover all.
That I could now but think on some disguise
To meet them in, and ask them questions:
How I would vex them still at every turn!
Mos. Sir, I can fit you.
Volp. Can'st thou?
Mos. Yes, I know
One o' the commandadori, sir, so like you;
Him will I straight make drunk, and bring you his
habit.
Volp. A rare disguise, and answering thy brain!
Oh, I will be a sharp disease unto them.
Mos. Sir, you must look for curses –
Volp. Till they burst;
The Fox fares ever best when he is curst.

———

ACT V, SCENE 4

PEREGRINE, 3 MERCATORI, WOMAN, SIR POLITICK
WOULD-BE

Per. Am I enough disguised?
1st Mer. I warrant you.
Per. All my ambition is to fright him only.
2nd Mer. If you could ship him away, 'twere excellent.
3rd Mer. To Zant, or to Aleppo?
Per. Yes, and have his
Adventures put i' the Book of Voyages,
And his gull'd story registered for truth.
Well, gentlemen, when I am in a while,
And that you think us warm in our discourse,
Know your approaches.
1st Mer. Trust it to our care.

Per. Save you, fair lady! Is Sir Pol within?

Wom. I do not know, sir.

Per. Pray you, say unto him,
   Here is a merchant upon earnest business
   Desires to speak with him.

Wom. I will see, sir.

Per. Pray you.
   I see the family is all female here.

Wom. He says, sir, he has weighty affairs of state,
   That now require him whole; some other time
   You may possess him.

Per. Pray you say again,
   If those require him whole, these will exact him,
   Whereof I bring him tidings. What might be
   His grave affair of state now? how to make
   Bolognian sausages here in Venice, sparing
   One o' the ingredients?

Wom. Sir, he says he knows
   By your word *tidings*, that you are no statesman,
   And therefore wills you stay.

Per. Sweet, pray you return him,
   I have not read so many proclamations,
   And studied them for words, as he has done –
   But – here he deigns to come.

Sir P. Sir, I must crave
   Your courteous pardon. There hath chanced today,
   Unkind disaster 'twixt my lady and me;
   And I was penning my apology,
   To give her satisfaction, as you came now.

Per. Sir, I am grieved, I bring you worse disaster:
   The gentleman you met at the port today,
   That told you, he was newly arrived –

Sir P. Ay, was
   A fugitive punk?

Per. No, sir, a spy set on you;
   And he has made relation to the Senate,
   That you professed to him to have a plot

To sell the state of Venice to the Turk.

Sir P. O me!

Per. For which, warrants are signed by this time,
To apprehend you, and to search your study
For papers –

Sir P. Alas, sir, I have none, but notes
Drawn out of play-books –

Per. All the better, sir.

Sir P. And some essays. What shall I do?

Per. Sir, best
Convey yourself into a sugar-chest;
Or, if you could lie round, a frail were rare,
And I could send you aboard.

Sir P. Sir, I but talked so,
For discourse sake merely.   *[They knock without.*

Per. Hark! they are there.

Sir P. I am a wretch, a wretch!

Per. What will you do, sir?
Have you ne'er a currant-butt to leap into?
They'll put you to the rack; you must be sudden.

Sir P. Sir, I have an engine –

3rd Mer. Sir Politick Would-be?

2nd Mer. Where is he?

Sir P. That I have thought upon before time.

Per. What is it?

Sir P. I shall ne'er endure the torture.
Marry, it is, sir, of a tortoise-shell,
Fitted for these extremities: pray you, sir, help me.
Here I've a place, sir, to put back my legs,
Please you to lay it on, sir, with this cap
And my black gloves. I'll lie, sir, like a tortoise,
'Till they are gone.

Per. And call you this an engine?

Sir P. Mine own device – good sir, bid my wife's women
To burn my papers.   *[They rush in.*

1st Mer. Where is he hid?

3rd Mer. We must

And will, sure, find him.

2nd Mer. Which is his study?

1st Mer. What
   Are you, sir?

Per. I am a merchant, that came here
   To look upon this tortoise.

3rd Mer. How?

1st Mer. St Mark!
   What beast is this?

Per. It is a fish.

2nd Mer. Come out here!

Per. Nay, you may strike him, sir, and tread upon
      him;
   He'll bear a cart.

1st Mer. What, to run over him?

Per. Yes.

3rd Mer. Let's jump upon him.

2nd Mer. Can he not go?

Per. He creeps, sir.

1st Mer. Let 's see him creep.

Per. No, good sir, you will hurt him.

2nd Mer. Heart, I will see him creep, or prick his guts.

3rd Mer. Come out here!

Per. Pray you, sir, creep a little.

1st Mer. Forth.

2nd Mer. Yet farther.

Per. Good sir, creep.

2nd Mer. We'll see his legs.

                    [*They pull off the shell and discover him.*

3rd Mer. God's so, he has garters!

1st Mer. Ay, and gloves!

2nd Mer. Is this
   Your fearful tortoise?

Per. Now, Sir Pol, we are even;
   For your next project I shall be prepared:
   I am sorry for the funeral of your notes, sir.

1st Mer. 'Twere a rare motion to be seen in Fleet-street.

2nd Mer. Ay, in the term.

1st Mer. Or Smithfield, in the fair.

3rd Mer. Methinks 'tis but a melancholic sight.

Per. Farewell, most politic tortoise!

Sir P. Where's my lady?
   Knows she of this?

Wom. I know not, sir.

Sir P. Inquire –
   Oh, I shall be the fable of all feasts,
   The freight of the gazetti; ship-boy's tale;
   And, which is worst, even talk for ordinaries.

Wom. My lady's come most melancholic home,
   And says, sir, she will straight to sea for physic.

Sir P. And I to shun this place and clime forever,
   Creeping with house on back, and think it well
   To shrink my poor head in my politic shell.

———

ACT V, SCENE 5

VOLPONE, MOSCA, *the first in the habit of a Commandadore, the other a Clarissimo*

Volp. Am I then like him?

Mos. Oh, sir, you are he:
   No man can sever you.

Volp. Good.

Mos. But what am I?

Volp. 'Fore heaven, a brave clarissimo; thou becom'st
      it!
   Pity thou wert not born one.

Mos. If I hold
   My made one, 'twill be well.

Volp. I 'll go and see
   What news first at the court.

Mos. Do so. My Fox
   Is out of his hole, and ere he shall re-enter,
   I 'll make him languish in his borrowed case,

Except he come to composition with me.
Androgyno, Castrone, Nano!

All. Here.

Mos. Go, recreate yourselves abroad; go sport.
So, now I have the keys, and am possest.
Since he will needs be dead afore his time,
I 'll bury him, or gain by him. I am his heir;
And so will keep me, till he share at least.
To cozen him of all, were but a cheat
Well placed; no man would construe it a sin:
Let his sport pay for 't. This is called the Fox-trap.

ACT V, SCENE 6

CORBACCIO, CORVINO, VOLPONE

Corb. They say, the court is set.

Corv. We must maintain
Our first tale good, for both our reputations.

Corb. Why, mine's no tale: no son would there have killed
me.

Corv. That's true, I had forgot: mine is, I am sure.
But for your will, sir.

Corb. Ay, I 'll come upon him
For that hereafter, now his patron's dead.

Volp. Signior Corvino! and Corbaccio! Sir,
Much joy unto you.

Corv. Of what?

Volp. The sudden good
Dropped down upon you —

Corb. Where?

Volp. And none knows how,
From old Volpone, sir.

Corb. Out, arrant knave!

Volp. Let not your too much wealth, sir, make you furious.

Corb. Away, thou varlet!

Volp. Why, sir?

Corb. Dost thou mock me?

Volp. You mock the world, sir; did you not change
    wills?

Corb. Out, harlot!

Volp. O! belike you are the man,
  Signior Corvino? 'faith, you carry it well;
  You grow not mad withal; I love your spirit.
  You are not over-leavened with your fortune.
  You should have some would swell now, like a wine-
    vat,
  With such an autumn – Did he give you all, sir?

Corv. Avoid, you rascal!

Volp. Troth, your wife has shown
  Herself a very woman; but you are well,
  You need not care, you have a good estate,
  To bear it out, sir, better by this chance:
  Except Corbaccio have a share?

Corb. Hence, varlet.

Volp. You will not be a'known, sir; why, 't is wise.
  Thus do all gamesters, at all games dissemble:
  No man shall seem to win. Here comes my vulture,
  Heaving his beak up in the air, and snuffing.

ACT V, SCENE 7
VOLTORE, VOLPONE

Volt. Outstripped thus by a parasite! a slave,
  Would run on errands, and make legs for crumbs!
  Well, what I 'll do –

Volp. The court stays for your worship.
  I e'en rejoice, sir, at your worship's happiness,
  And that it fell into so learned hands,
  That understand the fingering –

Volt. What do you mean?

Volp. I mean to be a suitor to your worship,
  For the small tenement, out of reparations,

That at the end of your long row of houses,
By the Piscaria: it was, in Volpone's time,
Your predecessor, ere he grew diseased,
A handsome, pretty, customed bawdy-house
As any was in Venice, none dispraised;
But fell with him: his body and that house
Decayed together.

Volt. Come, sir, leave your prating.

Volp. Why, if your worship give me but your hand,
That I may have the refusal, I have done.
'Tis a mere toy to you, sir; candle rents;
As your learned worship knows —

Volt. What do I know?

Volp. Marry, no end of your wealth, sir: God decrease it!

Volt. Mistaking knave! what, mock'st thou my misfortune?

Volp. His blessing on your heart, sir, would 't were more.
Now to my first again, at the next corner.

———

ACT V, SCENE 8

CORBACCIO, CORVINO, MOSCA (*passant*), VOLPONE

Corb. See, in our habit! see the impudent varlet!

Corv. That I could shoot mine eyes at him like gun stones!

Volp. But is this true, sir, of the parasite?

Corb. Again, to afflict us! monster!

Volp. In good faith, sir,
I'm heartily grieved, a beard of your grave length
Should be so over-reached. I never brooked
That parasite's hair; methought his nose should cozen:
There still was somewhat in his look, did promise
The bane of a Clarissimo.

Corb. Knave —

Volp. Methinks
Yet you, that are so traded in the world,

A witty merchant, the fine bird, Corvino,
That have such moral emblems on your name,
Should not have sung your shame, and dropt your
    cheese,
To let the Fox laugh at your emptiness.
Corv. Sirrah, you think the privilege of the place,
And your red saucy cap, that seems to me
Nailed to your jolt-head with those two *cecchines*,
Can warrant your abuses; come you hither:
You shall perceive, sir, I dare beat you. Approach.
Volp. No haste, sir, I do know your valour well,
Since you durst publish what you are, sir.
Corv. Tarry,
I'd speak with you.
Volp. Sir, sir, another time –
Corv. Nay, now.
Volp. Oh, God, sir! I were a wise man,
Would stand the fury of a distracted cuckold.
                  [*Mosca walks by them.*
Corb. What, come again!
Volp. Upon 'em, Mosca; save me.
Corb. The air 's infected where he breathes.
Corv. Let 's fly him.
Volp. Excellent basilisk! turn upon the vulture.

———

ACT V, SCENE 9
VOLTORE, MOSCA, VOLPONE

Volt. Well, flesh-fly, it is summer with you now;
Your winter will come on.
Mos. Good advocate,
Prithee not rail, nor threaten out of place thus;
Thou 'lt make a solecism, as madam says.
Get you a biggin more, your brain breaks loose.
Volt. Well, sir.

Volp. Would you have me beat the insolent slave?
  Throw dirt upon his first good clothes?
Volt. This same
  Is doubtless some familiar!
Volp. Sir, the court,
  In troth, stays for you. I am mad, a mule
  That never read Justinian, should get up,
  And ride an advocate. Had you no quirk
  To avoid gullage, sir, by such a creature?
  I hope you do but jest; he has not done it;
  'Tis but confederacy, to blind the rest.
  You are the heir?
Volt. A strange, officious,
  Troublesome knave! thou dost torment me.
Volp. I know –
  It cannot be, sir, that you should be cozened;
  'Tis not within the wit of man to do it;
  You are so wise, so prudent; and 'tis fit
  That wealth and wisdom still should go together.

———

ACT V, SCENE 10

4 AVOCATORI, NOTARIO, COMMANDADORI, BONARIO, CELIA, CORBACCIO, CORVINO, VOLTORE, VOLPONE

1st Avoc. Are all the parties here?
Not. All but the advocate.
2nd Avoc. And here he comes.
1st Avoc. Then bring them forth to sentence.
Volt. O my most honoured fathers, let your mercy
  Once win upon your justice, to forgive –
  I am distracted –
Volp. What will he do now?
Volt. O,
  I know not which to address myself to first;
  Whether your fatherhoods, or these innocents –

Corv. Will he betray himself?

Volt. Whom equally
  I have abused, out of most covetous ends –

Corv. The man is mad!

Corb. What 's that?

Corv. He is possessed.

Volt. For which, now struck in conscience, here I prostrate
  Myself at your offended feet, for pardon.

1st, 2nd Avoc. Arise.

Cel. O heaven, how just thou art!

Volp. I am caught
  In mine own noose –

Corv. Be constant, sir: nought now
  Can help, but impudence.

1st Avoc. Speak forward.

Com. Silence!

Volt. It is not passion in me, reverend fathers,
  But only conscience, conscience, my good sires,
  That makes me now tell truth. That parasite,
  That knave, hath been the instrument of all.

1st Avoc. Where is that knave? fetch him.

Volp. I go.

Corv. Grave fathers,
  This man's distracted; he confessed it now:
  For, hoping to be old Volpone's heir,
  Who now is dead –

3rd Avoc. How!

2nd Avoc. Is Volpone dead?

Corv. Dead since, grave fathers.

Bon. O sure vengeance!

1st Avoc. Stay,
  Then he was no deceiver?

Volt. Oh, no, none:
  The parasite, grave fathers.

Corv. He does speak
  Out of mere envy, 'cause the servant's made
  The thing he gaped for: please your fatherhoods,

This is the truth, though I 'll not justify
The other, but he may be some-deal faulty.
Volt. Ay, to your hopes, as well as mine, Corvino:
But I 'll use modesty. Pleaseth your wisdoms,
To view these certain notes, and but confer them;
As I hope favour, they shall speak clear truth.
Corv. The devil has entered him!
Bon. Or bides in you.
4th Avoc. We have done ill, by a public officer
To send for him, if he be heir.
2nd Avoc. For whom?
4th Avoc. Him that they call the parasite.
3rd Avoc. 'Tis true.
He is a man of great estate, now left.
4th Avoc. Go you, and learn his name, and say, the Court
Entreats his presence here, but to the clearing
Of some few doubts.
2nd Avoc. This same 's a labyrinth!
1st Avoc. Stand you unto your first report?
Corv. My state,
My life, my fame –
Bon. Where is it?
Corv. Are at the stake.
1st Avoc. Is yours so too?
Corb. The advocate 's a knave,
And has a forked tongue –
2nd Avoc. Speak to the point.
Corb. So is the parasite too.
1st Avoc. This is confusion.
Volt. I do beseech your fatherhoods, read but those.
Corv. And credit nothing the false spirit hath writ:
It cannot be, but he 's possessed, grave fathers.

ACT V, SCENE 11

VOLPONE, NANO, ANDROGYNO, CASTRONE

Volp. To make a snare for mine own neck! and run
  My head into it, wilfully! with laughter!
  When I had newly 'scaped, was free, and clear,
  Out of mere wantonness! Oh, the dull devil
  Was in this brain of mine, when I devised it,
  And Mosca gave it second; he must now
  Help to sear up this vein, or we bleed dead. —
  How now! who let you loose? whither go you now?
  What, to buy gingerbread, or to drown kitlings?
Nan. Sir, Master Mosca called us out of doors,
  And bid us all go play, and took the keys.
And. Yes.
Volp. Did Master Mosca take the keys? why so!
  I 'm farther in. These are my fine conceits!
  I must be merry, with a mischief to me!
  What a vile wretch was I, that could not bear
  My fortune soberly? I must ha' my crotchets,
  And my conundrums! Well, go you, and seek him:
  His meaning may be truer than my fear.
  Bid him he straight come to me to the court;
  Thither will I, and, if 't be possible,
  Unscrew my advocate, upon new hopes:
  When I provoked him, then I lost myself.

ACT V, SCENE 12

AVOCATORI, etc.

1st Avoc. These things can ne'er be reconciled. He, here,
  Professeth, that the gentleman was wronged;
  And that the gentlewoman was brought thither,
  Forced by her husband: and there left.
Volt. Most true.

Cel. How ready is Heaven to those that pray!

1st Avoc. But that
    Volpone would have ravished her, he holds
    Utterly false, knowing his impotence.

Corv. Grave fathers, he 's possessed; again, I say,
    Possessed: nay, if there be possession,
    And obsession, he has both.

3rd Avoc. Here comes our officer.

Volp. The parasite will straight be here, grave fathers.

4th Avoc. You might invent some other name, sir varlet.

3rd Avoc. Did not the notary meet him?

Volp. Not that I know.

4th Avoc. His coming will clear all.

2nd Avoc. Yet, it is misty.

Volt. May 't please your fatherhoods –

Volp. [*whispers Voltore*] Sir, the parasite
    Will'd me to tell you, that his master lives;
    That you are still the man; your hopes the same;
    And this was only a jest –

Volt. How?

Volp. Sir, to try
    If you were firm, and how you stood affected.

Volt. Art sure he lives?

Volp. Do I live, sir?

Volt. Oh me!
    I was too violent.

Volp. Sir, you may redeem it.
    They said, you were possessed; fall down, and seem so:
    I 'll help to make it good. God bless the man!
    Stop your wind hard, and swell – See, see, see, see!
    He vomits crooked pins! His eyes are set,
    Like a dead hare's hung in a poulter's shop!
    His mouth 's running away! Do you see, signior?
    Now it is in his belly.

Corv. Ay, the devil!

Volp. Now in his throat.

Corv. Ay, I perceive it plain.

Volp. 'Twill out, 'twill out! Stand clear. See where it flies,
   In shape of a blue toad, with a bat's wings!
   Do you not see it, sir?

Corb. What? I think I do.

Corv. 'Tis too manifest.

Volp. Look! he comes to himself!

Volt. Where am I?

Volp. Take good heart, the worst is past, sir.
   You are dispossessed.

1st Avoc. What accident is this?

2nd Avoc. Sudden, and full of wonder!

3rd Avoc. If he were
   Possessed, as it appears, all this is nothing.

Corv. He has been often subject to these fits.

1st Avoc. Show him that writing: — Do you know
   it, sir?

Volp. Deny it, sir, forswear it; know not.

Volt. Yes, I do know it well, it is my hand;
   But all that it contains is false.

Bon. O practice!

2nd Avoc. What maze is this!

1st Avoc. Is he not guilty, then,
   Whom you there name the parasite?

Volt. Grave fathers,
   No more than his good patron, old Volpone.

4th Avoc. Why, he is dead.

Volt. Oh, no, my honoured fathers.
   He lives —

1st Avoc. How! lives?

Volt. Lives.

2nd Avoc. This is subtler yet!

3rd Avoc. You said he was dead.

Volt. Never.

3rd Avoc. You said so.

Corv. I heard so.

4th Avoc. Here comes the gentleman; make him way.

3rd Avoc. A stool.

4th Avoc. A proper man; and, were Volpone dead,
　　A fit match for my daughter.
3rd Avoc. Give him away.
Volp. Mosca. I was almost lost; the advocate
　　Had betrayed all; but now it is recovered;
　　All's on the hinge again – say, I am living.
Mos. What busy knave is this! Most reverend fathers,
　　I sooner had attended your grave pleasures,
　　But that my order for the funeral
　　Of my dear patron did require me –
Volp. Mosca!
Mos. Whom I intend to bury like a gentleman.
Volp. Ay, quick, and cozen me of all.
2nd Avoc. Still stranger!
　　More intricate!
1st Avoc. And come about again!
4th Avoc. It is a match, my daughter is bestow'd.
Mos. Will you give me half?
Volp. First, I 'll be hanged.
Mos. I know
　　Your voice is good, cry not so loud.
1st Avoc. Demand
　　The advocate. Sir, did you not affirm
　　Volpone was alive?
Volp. Yes, and he is;
　　This gentleman told me so. – thou shalt have half.
Mos. Whose drunkard is this same? Speak, some that
　　　　know him.
　　I never saw his face. – I cannot now
　　Afford it you so cheap.
Volp. No?
1st Avoc. What say you?
Volt. The officer told me.
Volp. I did, grave fathers,
　　And will maintain he lives with mine own life,
　　And that this creature told me. I was born
　　With all good stars my enemies.

Mos. Most grave fathers,
 If such an insolence as this must pass
 Upon me, I am silent: 'twas not this
 For which you sent, I hope.

2nd Avoc. Take him away.

Volp. Mosca!

3rd Avoc. Let him be whipped.

Volp. Wilt thou betray me?
 Cozen me?

3rd Avoc. And taught to bear himself
 Toward a person of his rank.

4th Avoc. Away.

Mos. I humbly thank your fatherhoods.

Volp. Soft, soft. Whipped?
 And lose all that I have? If I confess,
 It cannot be much more.

4th Avoc. Sir, are you married?

Volp. They'll be allied anon; I must be resolute;
 The fox shall here uncase.   [*He puts off his disguise.*

Mos. Patron!

Volp. Nay, now
 My ruins shall not come alone: your match
 I 'll hinder sure: my substance shall not glue you,
 Nor screw you into a family.

Mos. Why, patron!

Volp. I am Volpone, and this is my knave;
 This his own knave; this avarice's fool;
 This a chimera of wittol, fool, and knave:
 And, reverend fathers, since we all can hope
 Nought but a sentence, let 's not now despair it.
 You hear me brief.

Corv. May it please your fatherhoods –

Com. Silence.

1st Avoc. The knot is now undone by miracle.

2nd Avoc. Nothing can be more clear.

3rd Avoc. Or can more prove
 These innocent.

1st Avoc. Give them their liberty.

Bon. Heaven could not long let such gross crimes be hid.

2nd Avoc. If this be held the highway to get riches,
　　May I be poor!

3rd Avoc. This is not gain, but torment.

1st Avoc. These possess wealth, as sick men possess fevers,
　　Which trulier may be said to possess them.

2nd Avoc. Disrobe that parasite.

Corv., Mos. Most honoured fathers! –

1st Avoc. Can you plead aught to stay the course of justice?
　　If you can, speak.

Corv., Volt. We beg favour.

Cel. And mercy.

1st Avoc. You hurt your innocence, suing for the guilty.
　　Stand forth; and first the parasite. You appear
　　T' have been the chiefest minister, if not plotter
　　In all these lewd impostures; and now, lastly,
　　Have with your impudence abused the court
　　And habit of a gentleman of Venice,
　　Being a fellow of no birth or blood:
　　For which our sentence is, first, thou be whipped;
　　Then live perpetual prisoner in our galleys.

Volp. I thank you for him.

Mos. Bane to thy wolfish nature!

1st Avoc. Deliver him to the Saffi. Thou, Volpone,
　　By blood and rank a gentleman, canst not fall
　　Under like censure; but our judgement on thee
　　Is, that thy substance all be straight confiscate
　　To the hospital of the Incurabili:
　　And, since the most was gotten by imposture,
　　By feigning lame, gout, palsy, and such diseases,
　　Thou art to lie in prison, cramped with irons,
　　Till thou be'st sick and lame indeed. Remove him.

Volp. This is called mortifying of a Fox.

1st Avoc. Thou, Voltore, to take away the scandal
　　Thou hast given all worthy men of thy profession,
　　Art banished from their fellowship, and our state.

Corbaccio! bring him near. We here possess
Thy son of all thy state, and confine thee
To the monastery of San Spirito;
Where, since thou knewest not how to live well here,
Thou shalt be learned to die well.

Corb. Ah! what said he?

Com. You shall know anon, sir.

1st Avoc. Thou, Corvino, shalt
Be straight embarked from thine own house, and rowed
Round about Venice, through the grand canale,
Wearing a cap, with fair long ass's ears,
Instead of horns; and so to mount, a paper
Pinned on thy breast, to the Berlina –

Corv. Yes,
And have mine eyes beat out with stinking fish,
Bruised fruit, and rotten eggs – 'Tis well. I am glad
I shall not see my shame yet.

1st Avoc. And to expiate
Thy wrongs done to thy wife, thou art to send her
Home to her father, with her dowry trebled:
And these are all your judgements.

All. Honoured fathers.

1st Avoc. Which may not be revoked. Now you begin,
When crimes are done and past, and to be punished,
To think what your crimes are: away with them.
Let all that see these vices thus rewarded,
Take heart and love to study 'em! Mischiefs feed
Like beasts, till they be fat, and then they bleed.

VOLPONE

The seasoning of a play is the applause.
Now, though the Fox be punished by the laws,
He yet doth hope there is no suffering due,
For any fact which he hath done 'gainst you;
If there be, censure him; here he doubtful stands:
If not, fare jovially, and clap your hands.

THE

WAY OF THE WORLD

—

By WILLIAM CONGREVE

DRAMATIS PERSONAE

MEN

FAINALL, *in love with Mrs Marwood*

MIRABELL, *in love with Mrs Millamant*

WITWOUD
PETULANT } *followers of Mrs Millamant*

SIR WILFULL WITWOUD, *half-brother to Witwoud, and nephew to Lady Wishfort*

WAITWELL, *servant to Mirabell*

WOMEN

LADY WISHFORT, *enemy to Mirabell, for having falsely pretended to love her*

MRS MILLAMANT, *a fine lady, niece to Lady Wishfort, and loves Mirabell*

MRS MARWOOD, *friend to Mr Fainall, and likes Mirabell*

MRS FAINALL, *daughter to Lady Wishfort, and wife to Fainall, formerly friend to Mirabell*

FOIBLE, *woman to Lady Wishfort*

MINCING, *woman to Mrs Millamant*

DANCERS, FOOTMEN, *and* ATTENDANTS

SCENE – LONDON

The Time equal to that of the Presentation

THE WAY OF THE WORLD

PROLOGUE

OF those few fools, who with ill stars are curst,
Sure scribbling fools, call'd poets, fare the worst:
For they're a sort of fools which fortune makes,
And after she has made 'em fools, forsakes.
With Nature's oafs 'tis quite a diff'rent case,
For fortune favours all her idiot-race.
In her own nest the cuckoo-eggs we find,
O'er which she broods to hatch the changeling-kind.
No portion for her own she has to spare,
So much she dotes on her adopted care.

Poets are bubbles, by the town drawn in,
Suffer'd at first some trifling stakes to win:
But what unequal hazards do they run!
Each time they write they venture all they've won:
The squire that's butter'd still, is sure to be undone.
This author, heretofore, has found your favour,
But pleads no merit from his past behaviour;
To build on that might prove a vain presumption,
Should grants to poets made, admit resumption:
And in Parnassus he must lose his seat,
If that be found a forfeited estate.

He owns, with toil, he wrought the following scenes,
But if they're naught ne'er spare him for his pains:
Damn him the more; have no commiseration
For dullness on mature deliberation.
He swears he'll not resent one hiss'd-off scene
Nor, like those peevish wits, his play maintain,
Who, to assert their sense, your taste arraign.
Some plot we think he has, and some new thought;
Some humour too, no farce; but that's a fault.
Satire, he thinks, you ought not to expect;

For so reform'd a town, who dares correct?
To please, this time, has been his sole pretence,
He'll not instruct, lest it should give offence.
Should he by chance a knave or fool expose,
That hurts none here, sure here are none of those.
In short, our play shall (with your leave to show it)
Give you one instance of a passive poet
Who to your judgements yields all resignation;
So save or damn, after your own discretion.

———

ACT I, SCENE 1

A Chocolate-House
MIRABELL *and* FAINALL [*rising from cards*]
BETTY *waiting*

Mira. You are a fortunate man, Mr Fainall.

Fain. Have we done?

Mira. What you please. I'll play on to entertain you.

Fain. No, I'll give you your revenge another time, when
you are not so indifferent; you are thinking of something else now, and play too negligently; the coldness
of a losing gamester lessens the pleasure of the winner.
I'd no more play with a man that slighted his ill
fortune, than I'd make love to a woman who under-
valued the loss of her reputation.

Mira. You have a taste extremely delicate, and are for
refining on your pleasures.

Fain. Prithee, why so reserved? Something has put you
out of humour.

Mira. Not at all: I happen to be grave today; and you
are gay; that's all.

Fain. Confess, Millamant and you quarrelled last night,
after I left you; my fair cousin has some humours that
would tempt the patience of a Stoic. What, some coxcomb came in, and was well received by her, while
you were by.

Mira. Witwoud and Petulant; and what was worse, her
   aunt, your wife's mother, my evil genius; or to sum up
   all in her own name, my old Lady Wishfort came in. –

Fain. O there it is then – She has a lasting passion for you,
   and with reason – What, then my wife was there?

Mira. Yes, and Mrs Marwood and three or four more,
   whom I never saw before; seeing me, they all put on
   their grave faces, whispered one another; then com-
   plained aloud of the vapours, and after fell into a profound silence.

Fain. They had a mind to be rid of you.

Mira. For which good reason I resolved not to stir. At
   last the good old lady broke through her painful
   taciturnity, with an invective against long visits. I
   would not have understood her, but Millamant joining
   in the argument, I rose and with a constrained smile
   told her, I thought nothing was so easy as to know
   when a visit began to be troublesome; she reddened
   and I withdrew, without expecting her reply.

Fain. You were to blame to resent what she spoke only
   in compliance with her aunt.

Mira. She is more mistress of herself, than to be under the
   necessity of such a resignation.

Fain. What, though half her fortune depends upon her
   marrying with my lady's approbation?

Mira. I was then in such a humour, that I should have
   been better pleased if she had been less discreet.

Fain. Now I remember, I wonder not they were weary
   of you; last night was one of their Cabal-nights; they
   have 'em three times a week, and meet by turns, at
   one another's apartments, where they come together
   like the coroner's inquest, to sit upon the murdered
   reputations of the week. You and I are excluded; and
   it was once proposed that all the male sex should be
   excepted; but somebody moved that to avoid scandal
   there might be one man of the community; upon
   which Witwoud and Petulant were enrolled members.

Mira. And who may have been the foundress of this sect?
My Lady Wishfort, I warrant, who publishes her
detestation of mankind; and full of the vigour of
fifty-five, declares for a friend and ratafia; and let
posterity shift for itself, she'll breed no more.

Fain. The discovery of your sham addresses to her, to
conceal your love to her niece, has provoked this
separation: had you dissembled better, things might
have continued in the state of nature.

Mira. I did as much as man could, with any reasonable
conscience; I proceeded to the very last act of flattery
with her, and was guilty of a song in her commendation. Nay, I got a friend to put her into a lampoon,
and compliment her with the imputation of an affair
with a young fellow, which I carried so far, that I told
her the malicious town took notice that she was grown
fat of a sudden; and when she lay in of a dropsy, persuaded her she was reported to be in labour. The
devil's in't, if an old woman is to be flattered further,
unless a man should endeavour downright personally
to debauch her; and that my virtue forbade me. But
for the discovery of this amour, I am indebted to your
friend, or your wife's friend, Mrs Marwood.

Fain. What should provoke her to be your enemy, unless
she has made you advances, which you have slighted?
Women do not easily forgive omissions of that nature.

Mira. She was always civil to me, till of late; I confess
I am not one of those coxcombs who are apt to inter-
pret a woman's good manners to her prejudice; and
think that she who does not refuse 'em everything, can
refuse 'em nothing.

Fain. You are a gallant man, Mirabell; and though you
may have cruelty enough, not to satisfy a lady's longing, you have too much generosity, not to be tender
of her honour. Yet you speak with an indifference
which seems to be affected, and confesses you are conscious of a negligence.

Mira. You pursue the argument with a distrust that seems to be unaffected, and confesses you are conscious of a concern for which the lady is more indebted to you, than is your wife.

Fain. Fie, fie, friend, if you grow censorious I must leave you; – I'll look upon the gamesters in the next room.

Mira. Who are they?

Fain. Petulant and Witwoud. – Bring me some chocolate.

Mira. Betty, what says your clock?

Bet. Turned of the last canonical hour, Sir.

Mira. How pertinently the jade answers me! Ha? almost one o'clock! [*Looking on his watch.*] O, y'are come –

——

ACT I, SCENE 2

MIRABELL *and* FOOTMAN

Mira. Well; is the grand affair over? You have been something tedious.

Serv. Sir, there's such coupling at Pancras, that they stand behind one another, as 'twere in a country dance. Ours was the last couple to lead up; and no hopes appearing of dispatch, besides, the parson growing hoarse, we were afraid his lungs would have failed before it came to our turn; so we drove round to Duke's Place; and there they were riveted in a trice.

Mira. So, so you are sure they are married?

Serv. Married and bedded, Sir: I am witness.

Mira. Have you the certificate?

Serv. Here it is, Sir.

Mira. Has the Tailor brought Waitwell's clothes home, and the new liveries?

Serv. Yes, Sir.

Mira. That's well. Do you go home again, d'ye hear, and adjourn the consummation till farther order; bid Waitwell shake his ears, and Dame Partlet rustle up her feathers, and meet me at one o'clock by Rosamond's Pond; that I may see her before she returns to her lady: and as you tender your ears be secret.

ACT I, SCENE 3
MIRABELL, FAINALL, BETTY

Fain. Joy of your success, Mirabell; you look pleased.

Mira. Ay; I have been engaged in a matter of some sort of mirth, which is not yet ripe for discovery. I am glad this is not a Cabal-night. I wonder, Fainall, that you who are married, and of consequence should be discreet, will suffer your wife to be of such a party.

Fain. Faith, I am not jealous. Besides, most who are engaged are women and relations; and for the men, they are of a kind too contemptible to give scandal.

Mira. I am of another opinion. The greater the coxcomb, always the more scandal: for a woman who is not a fool, can have but one reason for associating with a man who is one.

Fain. Are you jealous as often as you see Witwoud entertained by Millamant?

Mira. Of her understanding I am, if not of her person.

Fain. You do her wrong; for to give her her due, she has wit.

Mira. She has beauty enough to make any man think so; and complaisance enough not to contradict him who shall tell her so.

Fain. For a passionate lover, methinks you are a man somewhat too discerning in the failings of your mistress.

Mira. And for a discerning man, somewhat too passionate a lover; for I like her with all her faults; nay, like her for her faults. Her follies are so natural, or so artful, that they become her; and those affectations which in another woman would be odious, serve but to make

her more agreeable. I'll tell thee, Fainall, she once
used me with that insolence, that in revenge I took
her to pieces, sifted her, and separated her failings;
I studied 'em, and got 'em by rote. The catalogue was
so large, that I was not without hopes, one day or
other to hate her heartily: to which end I so used myself to think of 'em, that at length, contrary to my
design and expectation, they gave me every hour less
and less disturbance; till in a few days it became
habitual to me, to remember 'em without being dis-
pleased. They are now grown as familiar to me as my
own frailties: and in all probability in a little time
longer I shall like 'em as well.

Fain. Marry her, marry her; be half as well acquainted
with her charms, as you are with her defects, and my
life on 't, you are your own man again.

Mira. Say you so?

Fain. Ay, ay, I have experience: I have a wife, and so
forth.

———

ACT I, SCENE 4

[*To them*] MESSENGER

Mess. Is one Squire Witwoud here?

Bet. Yes; what's your business?

Mess. I have a letter for him, from his brother Sir
Wilfull, which I am charged to deliver into his own
hands.

Bet. He's in the next room, friend – that way.

———

ACT I, SCENE 5

MIRABELL, FAINALL, BETTY

Mira What, is the chief of that noble family in town,
Sir Wilfull Witwoud?

Fain. He is expected to-day. Do you know him?

Mira. I have seen him, he promises to be an extra-ordinary person; I think you have the honour to be related to him.

Fain. Yes; he is half-brother to this Witwoud by a former wife, who was sister to my Lady Wishfort, my wife's mother. If you marry Millamant, you must call cousins too.

Mira. I had rather be his relation than his acquaintance.

Fain. He comes to town in order to equip himself for travel.

Mira. For travel! Why, the man that I mean is above forty.

Fain. No matter for that; 'tis for the honour of England, that all Europe should know that we have blockheads of all ages.

Mira. I wonder there is not an Act of Parliament to save the credit of the nation, and prohibit the exportation of fools.

Fain. By no means, 'tis better as 'tis; 'tis better to trade with a little loss, than to be quite eaten up with being overstocked.

Mira. Pray, are the follies of this knight-errant, and those of the squire his brother, anything related?

Fain. Not at all; Witwoud grows by the knight, like a medlar grafted on a crab. One will melt in your mouth, and t'other set your teeth on edge; one is all pulp, and the other all core.

Mira. So one will be rotten before he be ripe, and the other will be rotten without ever being ripe at all.

Fain. Sir Wilfull is an odd mixture of bashfulness and obstinacy. — But when he's drunk, he's as loving as the monster in 'The Tempest'; and much after the same manner. To give t'other his due, he has some-thing of good nature, and does not always want wit.

Mira. Not always; but as often as his memory fails him, and his commonplace of comparisons. He is a fool with a good memory, and some few scraps of other folks' wit. He is one whose conversation can never be approved, yet it is now and then to be endured. He has indeed one good quality, he is not exceptious; for he so passionately affects the reputation of understanding raillery, that he will construe an affront into a jest, and call downright rudeness and ill language, satire and fire.

Fain. If you have a mind to finish his picture, you have an opportunity to do it at full length. Behold the original.

ACT I, SCENE 6

[*To them*] WITWOUD

Wit. Afford me your compassion, my dears; pity me, Fainall, Mirabell, pity me.

Mira. I do from my soul.

Fain. Why, what's the matter?

Wit. No letters for me, Betty?

Bet. Did not a messenger bring you one but now, sir?

Wit. Ay, but no other?

Bet. No, sir.

Wit. That's hard, that's very hard; – A messenger, a mule, a beast of burden, he has brought me a letter from the fool my brother, as heavy as a panegyric in a funeral sermon, or a copy of commendatory verses from one poet to another. And what's worse, 'tis as sure a forerunner of the author, as an epistle dedicatory.

Mira. A fool, and your brother, Witwoud!

Wit. Ay, ay, my half-brother. My half-brother he is, no nearer upon honour.

Mira. Then 'tis possible he may be but half a fool.

Wit. Good, good, Mirabell, *le Drole!* Good, good, hang him, don't let's talk of him; – Fainall, how does your lady? Gad. I say anything in the world to get this fellow out of my head. I beg pardon that I should ask a man of pleasure and the town a question at once so foreign and domestic. But I talk like an old maid at a marriage, I don't know what I say: but she's the best woman in the world.

Fain. 'Tis well you don't know what you say, or else your commendation would go near to make me either vain or jealous.

Wit. No man in town lives well with a wife but Fainall. Your judgement, Mirabell?

Mira. You had better step and ask his wife; if you would be credibly informed.

Wit. Mirabell.

Mira. Ay.

Wit. My dear, I ask ten thousand pardons; – Gad, I have forgot what I was going to say to you.

Mira. I thank you heartily, heartily.

Wit. No, but prithee excuse me, – my memory is such a memory.

Mira. Have a care of such apologies, Witwoud; – for I never knew a fool but he affected to complain, either of the spleen or his memory.

Fain. What have you done with Petulant?

Wit. He's reckoning his money – my money it was – I have no luck to-day.

Fain. You may allow him to win of you at play; – for you are sure to be too hard for him at repartee: since you monopolize the wit that is between you, the fortune must be his of course.

Mira. I don't find that Petulant confesses the superiority of wit to be your talent, Witwoud.

Wit. Come, come, you are malicious now, and would breed debates – Petulant's my friend, and a very honest fellow, and a very pretty fellow, and has a smattering – faith and troth a pretty deal of an odd sort of a small wit: nay, I'll do him justice. I'm his friend, I won't wrong him. – And if he had any judgement in the world – he would not be altogether contemptible. Come, come, don't detract from the merits of my friend.

Fain. You don't take your friend to be over-nicely bred.

Wit. No, no, hang him, the rogue has no manners at all, that I must own – no more breeding than a bumbailey, that I grant you, – 'tis pity; the fellow has fire and life.

Mira. What, courage?

Wit. Hum, faith I don't know as to that, – I can't say as to that. – Yes, faith, in a controversy he'll contradict anybody.

Mira. Though 'twere a man whom he feared, or a woman whom he loved.

Wit. Well, well, he does not always think before he speaks; – we have all our failings; you are too hard upon him, you are, faith. Let me excuse him, – I can defend most of his faults, except one or two; one he has, that's the truth on't, if he were my brother, I could not acquit him – that indeed I could wish were otherwise.

Mira. Ay marry, what's that, Witwoud?

Wit. O pardon me – expose the infirmities of my friend. – No, my dear, excuse me there.

Fain. What, I warrant he's unsincere, or 'tis some such trifle.

Wit. No, no, what if he be? 'Tis no matter for that, his wit will excuse that: a wit should no more be sincere, than a woman constant; one argues a decay of parts, as t'other of beauty.

Mira. Maybe you think him too positive?

Wit. No, no, his being positive is an incentive to argument, and keeps up conversation.

Fain. Too illiterate.

Wit. That! that's his happiness. – His want of learning gives him the more opportunities to show his natural parts.

Mira. He wants words.

Wit. Ay; but I like him for that now; for his want of words gives me the pleasure very often to explain his meaning.

Fain. He's impudent.

Wit. No, that's not it.

Mira. Vain.

Wit. No.

Mira. What, he speaks unseasonable truths sometimes, because he has not wit enough to invent an evasion.

Wit. Truths! Ha, ha, ha! No, no, since you will have it, – I mean, he never speaks truth at all, – that's all. He will lie like a chambermaid, or a woman of quality's porter. Now that is a fault.

——

ACT I, SCENE 7
[*To them*] COACHMAN

Coach. Is Master Petulant here, mistress?

Bet. Yes.

Coach. Three gentlewomen in a coach would speak with him.

Fain. O brave Petulant, three!

Bet. I'll tell him.

Coach. You must bring two dishes of chocolate and a glass of cinnamon-water.

——

ACT I, SCENE 8
MIRABELL, FAINALL, WITWOUD

Wit. That should be for two fasting strumpets, and a bawd troubled with wind. Now you may know what the three are.

Mira. You are free with your friend's acquaintance.

Wit. Ay, ay, friendship without freedom is as dull as love

without enjoyment, or wine without toasting; but to
tell you a secret, these are trulls whom he allows
coach-hire, and something more by the week, to call
on him once a day at public places.

Mira. How!

Wit. You shall see he won't go to 'em because there's no
more company here to take notice of him. – Why,
this is nothing to what he used to do; – before he
found out this way, I have known him call for himself –

Fain. Call for himself? What dost thou mean?

Wit. Mean, why he would slip you out of this chocolate-
house, just when you had been talking to him – as
soon as your back was turned – whip he was gone; –
then trip to his lodging, clap on a hood and scarf,
and a mask, slap into a hackney-coach, and drive
hither to the door again in a trice; where he would
send in for himself, that I mean, call for himself, wait
for himself, nay and what's more, not finding himself,
sometimes leave a letter for himself.

Mira. I confess this is something extraordinary – I believe
he waits for himself now, he is so long a-coming; O,
I ask his pardon.

———

ACT I, SCENE 9

PETULANT, MIRABELL, FAINALL, WITWOUD, BETTY

Bet. Sir, the coach stays.

Pet. Well, well; I come – 'Sbud, a man had as good be a
professed midwife, as a professed whoremaster, at this
rate; to be knocked up and raised at all hours, and in
all places. Pox on 'em, I won't come – D'ye hear, tell
'em I won't come. – Let 'em snivel and cry their
hearts out.

Fain. You are very cruel, Petulant.

Pet. All's one, let it pass – I have a humour to be
cruel.

Mira. I hope they are not persons of condition that you use at this rate.

Pet. Condition, condition's a dried fig, if I am not in humour – By this hand, if they were your – a – a – your what-dee-call-'ems themselves, they must wait or rub off, if I want appetite.

Mira. What-dee-call-'ems! What are they, Witwoud?

Wit. Empresses, my dear. – By your what-dee-call-'ems he means sultana queens.

Pet. Ay, Roxolanas.

Mira. Cry you mercy.

Fain. Witwoud says they are –

Pet. What does he say th' are?

Wit. I; fine ladies I say.

Pet. Pass on, Witwoud – Harkee, by this light his relations – two co-heiresses his cousins, and an old aunt, who loves caterwauling better than a conventicle.

Wit. Ha, ha, ha; I had a mind to see how the rogue would come off. – Ha, ha, ha; Gad, I can't be angry with him; if he had said they were my mother and my sisters.

Mira. No!

Wit. No; the rogue's wit and readiness of invention charm me, dear Petulant.

Bet. They are gone, Sir, in great anger.

Pet. Enough, let 'em trundle. Anger helps complexion, saves paint.

Fain. This continence is all dissembled; this is in order to have something to brag of the next time he makes court to Millamant, and swear he has abandoned the whole sex for her sake.

Mira. Have you not left off your impudent pretensions there yet? I shall cut your throat, sometime or other, Petulant, about that business.

Pet. Ay, ay, let that pass. – There are other throats to be cut. –

Mira. Meaning mine, Sir?

Pet. Not I – I mean nobody – I know nothing. – But there are uncles and nephews in the world. – And they may be rivals. – What then? All's one for that –

Mira. How! Harkee Petulant, come hither. – Explain, or I shall call your interpreter.

Pet. Explain; I know nothing. – Why, you have an uncle, have you not, lately come to town, and lodges by my Lady Wishfort's?

Mira. True.

Pet. Why that's enough. – You and he are not friends; and if he should marry and have a child, you may be disinherited, ha?

Mira. Where hast thou stumbled upon all this truth?

Pet. All's one for that; why then say I know something.

Mira. Come, thou art an honest fellow, Petulant, and shalt make love to my mistress, thou shalt, faith. What hast thou heard of my uncle?

Pet. I, nothing I. If throats are to be cut, let swords clash; snug's the word, I shrug and am silent.

Mira. O raillery, raillery. Come, I know thou art in the women's secrets. – What, you're a Cabalist, I know you stayed at Millamant's last night, after I went. Was there any mention made of my uncle, or me? Tell me; if thou hadst but good nature equal to thy wit, Petulant, Tony Witwoud, who is now thy competitor in fame, would show as dim by thee as a dead whiting's eye by a pearl of orient; he would no more be seen by thee, than Mercury is by the sun: come, I'm sure thou wo't tell me.

Pet. If I do, will you grant me commonsense then, for the future?

Mira. Faith, I'll do what I can for thee, and I'll pray that heaven may grant it thee in the meantime.

Pet. Well, harkee.

Fain. Petulant and you both will find Mirabell as warm a rival as a lover.

Wit. Pshaw, pshaw, that she laughs at Petulant is plain.

And for my part. – But that it is almost a fashion to admire her, I should – harkee – to tell you a secret, but let it go no further – between friends, I shall never break my heart for her.

Fain. How!

Wit. She's handsome; but she's a sort of an uncertain woman.

Fain. I thought you had died for her.

Wit. Umh – No –

Fain. She has wit.

Wit. 'Tis what she will hardly allow anybody else. – Now, demme, I should hate that, if she were as handsome as Cleopatra. Mirabell is not so sure of her as he thinks for.

Fain. Why do you think so?

Wit. We stayed pretty late there last night; and heard something of an uncle to Mirabell, who is lately come to town – and is between him and the best part of his estate; Mirabell and he are at some distance, as my Lady Wishfort has been told; and you know she hates Mirabell, worse than a Quaker hates a parrot, or than a fishmonger hates a hard frost. Whether this uncle has seen Mrs Millamant or not, I cannot say; but there were items of such a treaty being in embryo; and if it should come to life, poor Mirabell would be in some sort unfortunately fobbed i'faith.

Fain. 'Tis impossible Millamant should hearken to it.

Wit. Faith, my dear, I can't tell; she's a woman and a kind of a humourist.

Mira. And this is the sum of what you could collect last night.

Pet. The quintessence. Maybe Witwoud knows more, he stayed longer – besides they never mind him; they say anything before him.

Mira. I thought you had been the greatest favourite.

Pet. Ay, *tête à tête*; but not in public, because I make remarks.

Mira. You do?

Pet. Ay, ay, pox. I'm malicious, man. Now he's soft, you know, they are not in awe of him. – The fellow's well-bred, he's what you call a – what-d'ye-call-'em. A fine gentleman, but he's silly withal.

Mira. I thank you, I know as much as my curiosity requires. Fainall, are you for the Mall?

Fain. Ay, I'll take a turn before dinner.

Wit. Ay, we'll all walk in the park, the ladies talked of being there.

Mira. I thought you were obliged to watch for your brother Sir Wilfull's arrival.

Wit. No, no, he's come to his aunt's, my Lady Wishfort; pox on him, I shall be troubled with him too; what shall I do with the fool?

Pet. Beg him for his estate; that I may beg you afterwards; and so have but one trouble with you both.

Wit. O rare Petulant; thou art as quick as fire in a frosty morning; thou shalt to the Mall with us; and we'll be very severe.

Pet. Enough, I'm in a humour to be severe.

Mira. Are you? Pray then walk by yourselves, – let not us be accessory to your putting the ladies out of countenance, with your senseless ribaldry; which you roar out aloud as often as they pass by you; and when you have made a handsome woman blush, then you think you have been severe.

Pet. What, what? Then let 'em either show their innocence by not understanding what they hear, or else show their discretion by not hearing what they would not be thought to understand.

Mira. But hast not thou then sense enough to know that thou oughtest to be most ashamed thyself, when thou hast put another out of countenance?

Pet. Not I, by this hand – I always take blushing either for a sign of guilt, or ill-breeding.

Mira. I confess you ought to think so. You are in the

right, that you may plead the error of your judgement in defence of your practice.

> *Where modesty's ill manners, 'tis but fit*
> *That impudence and malice pass for wit.*

End of the First Act

ACT II, SCENE 1

St James's Park

MRS FAINALL *and* MRS MARWOOD

Mrs Fain. Ay, ay, dear Marwood, if we will be happy, we must find the means in ourselves, and among ourselves. Men are ever in extremes; either doting or averse. While they are lovers, if they have fire and sense, their jealousies are insupportable: and when they cease to love (we ought to think at least), they loathe; they look upon us with horror and distaste; they meet us like the ghosts of what we were, and as from such, fly from us.

Mrs Mar. True, 'tis an unhappy circumstance of life, that love should ever die before us; and that the man so often should out-live the lover. But say what you will, 'tis better to be left, than never to have been loved. To pass our youth in dull indifference, to refuse the sweets of life because they once must leave us, is as preposterous as to wish to have been born old, because we one day must be old. For my part, my youth may wear and waste, but it shall never rust in my possession.

Mrs Fain. Then it seems you dissemble an aversion to mankind, only in compliance to my mother's humour.

Mrs Mar. Certainly. To be free; I have no taste of those insipid dry discourses, with which our sex of force must entertain themselves, apart from men. We may affect endearments to each other, profess eternal friendships, and seem to dote like lovers; but 'tis not in our natures long to persevere. Love will resume his empire in our breasts, and every heart, or soon or late, receive and readmit him as its lawful tyrant.

Mrs Fain. Bless me, how have I been deceived! Why, you profess a libertine.

Mrs Mar. You see my friendship by my freedom. Come, be as sincere, acknowledge that your sentiments agree with mine.

Mrs Fain. Never.

Mrs Mar. You hate mankind?

Mrs Fain. Heartily, inveterately.

Mrs Mar. Your husband?

Mrs Fain. Most transcendently; ay, though I say it, meritoriously.

Mrs Mar. Give me your hand upon it.

Mrs Fain. There.

Mrs Mar. I join with you; what I have said has been to try you.

Mrs Fain. Is it possible? Dost thou hate those vipers, men?

Mrs Mar. I have done hating 'em, and am now come to despise 'em; the next thing I have to do, is eternally to forget 'em.

Mrs Fain. There spoke the spirit of an Amazon, a Penthesilea.

Mrs Mar. And yet I am thinking sometimes to carry my aversion further.

Mrs Fain. How?

Mrs Mar. Faith, by marrying; if I could but find one that loved me very well, and would be thoroughly sensible of ill-usage, I think I should do myself the violence of undergoing the ceremony.

Mrs Fain. You would not make him a cuckold?

Mrs Mar. No; but I'd make him believe I did, and that's as bad.

Mrs Fain. Why had not you as good do it?

Mrs Mar. O if he should ever discover it, he would then know the worst, and be out of his pain; but I would have him ever to continue upon the rack of fear and jealousy.

Mrs Fain. Ingenious mischief! Would thou wert married to Mirabell.

Mrs Mar. Would I were.

Mrs Fain. You change colour.

Mrs Mar. Because I hate him.

Mrs Fain. So do I; but I can hear him named. But what reason have you to hate him in particular?

Mrs Mar. I never loved him; he is, and always was, insufferably proud.

Mrs Fain. By the reason you give for your aversion, one would think it dissembled; for you have laid a fault to his charge, of which his enemies must acquit him.

Mrs Mar. O then it seems you are one of his favourable enemies. Methinks you look a little pale, and now you flush again.

Mrs Fain. Do I? I think I am a little sick o' the sudden.

Mrs Mar. What ails you?

Mrs Fain. My husband. Don't you see him? He turned short upon me unawares, and has almost overcome me.

———

ACT II, SCENE 2

[*To them*] FAINALL *and* MIRABELL

Mrs Mar. Ha, ha, ha; he comes opportunely for you.

Mrs Fain. For you, for he has brought Mirabell with him.

Fain. My dear.

Mrs Fain. My soul.

Fain. You don't look well today, child.

Mrs Fain. D'ye think so?

Mira. He is the only man that does, madam.

Mrs Fain. The only man that would tell me so, at least; and the only man from whom I could hear it without mortification.

Fain. O my dear, I am satisfied of your tenderness; I know you cannot resent anything from me; especially what is an effect of my concern.

Mrs Fain. Mr Mirabell, my mother interrupted you in

a pleasant relation last night: I would fain hear it out.

Mira. The persons concerned in that affair have yet a tolerable reputation. – I am afraid Mr Fainall will be censorious.

Mrs Fain. He has a humour more prevailing than his curiosity, and will willingly dispense with the hearing of one scandalous story, to avoid giving an occasion to make another by being seen to walk with his wife. This way, Mr Mirabell, and I dare promise you will oblige us both.

ACT II, SCENE 3
FAINALL, MRS MARWOOD

Fain. Excellent creature! Well, sure if I should live to be rid of my wife, I should be a miserable man.

Mrs Mar. Ay!

Fain. For having only that one hope, the accomplishment of it of consequence must put an end to all my hopes; and what a wretch is he who must survive his hopes! Nothing remains when that day comes, but to sit down and weep like Alexander, when he wanted other worlds to conquer.

Mrs Mar. Will you not follow 'em?

Fain. Faith, I think not.

Mrs Mar. Pray let us; I have a reason.

Fain. You are not jealous?

Mrs Mar. Of whom?

Fain. Of Mirabell.

Mrs Mar. If I am, is it inconsistent with my love to you that I am tender of your honour?

Fain. You would intimate then, as if there were a fellow-feeling between my wife and him.

Mrs Mar. I think she does not hate him to that degree she would be thought.

Fain. But he, I fear, is too insensible.

Mrs Mar. It may be you are deceived.

Fain. It may be so. I do not now begin to apprehend it.

Mrs Mar. What?

Fain. That I have been deceived, madam, and you are false.

Mrs Mar. That I am false! What mean you?

Fain. To let you know I see through all your little arts. — Come, you both love him; and both have equally dissembled your aversion. Your mutual jealousies of one another have made you clash till you have both struck fire. I have seen the warm confession reddening on your cheeks, and sparkling from your eyes.

Mrs Mar. You do me wrong.

Fain. I do not. — 'Twas for my ease to oversee and wilfully neglect the gross advances made him by my wife; that by permitting her to be engaged, I might continue unsuspected in my pleasures; and take you oftener to my arms in full security. But could you think, because the nodding husband would not wake, that e'er the watchful lover slept?

Mrs Mar. And wherewithal can you reproach me?

Fain. With infidelity, with loving another, with love of Mirabell.

Mrs Mar. 'Tis false. I challenge you to show an instance that can confirm your groundless accusation. I hate him.

Fain. And wherefore do you hate him? He is insensible, and your resentment follows his neglect. An instance! The injuries you have done him are a proof: your interposing in his love. What cause had you to make discoveries of his pretended passion? To undeceive the credulous aunt, and be the officious obstacle of his match with Millamant?

Mrs Mar. My obligations to my lady urged me: I had professed a friendship to her; and could not see her easy nature so abused by that dissembler.

Fain. What, was it conscience then? Professed a friendship! O the pious friendships of the female sex!

Mrs Mar. More tender, more sincere, and more enduring,
than all the vain and empty vows of men, whether
professing love to us, or mutual faith to one another.

Fain. Ha, ha, ha; you are my wife's friend too.

Mrs Mar. Shame and ingratitude! Do you reproach me?
You, you upbraid me! Have I been false to her,
through strict fidelity to you, and sacrificed my friendship to keep my love inviolate? And have you the
baseness to charge me with the guilt, unmindful of
the merit! To you it should be meritorious, that I
have been vicious: and do you reflect that guilt upon
me, which should lie buried in your bosom?

Fain. You misinterpret my reproof. I meant but to
remind you of the slight account you once could make
of strictest ties, when set in competition with your love
to me.

Mrs Mar. 'Tis false, you urged it with deliberate malice.
– 'Twas spoke in scorn, and I never will forgive it.

Fain. Your guilt, not your resentment, begets your rage.
If yet you loved, you could forgive a jealousy: but
you are stung to find you are discovered.

Mrs Mar. It shall be all discovered. You too shall be
discovered; be sure you shall. I can but be exposed. –
If I do it myself I shall prevent your baseness.

Fain. Why, what will you do?

Mrs Mar. Disclose it to your wife; own what has passed
between us.

Fain. Frenzy!

Mrs Mar. By all my wrongs I'll do 't – I'll publish to the
world the injuries you have done me, both in my
fame and fortune: with both I trusted you, you bankrupt in honour, as indigent of wealth.

Fain. Your fame I have preserved. Your fortune has been
bestowed as the prodigality of your love would have
it, in pleasures which we both have shared. Yet, had

not you been false, I had ere this repaid it. – 'Tis true –
had you permitted Mirabell with Millamant to have
stolen their marriage, my lady had been incensed
beyond all means of reconcilement: Millamant had
forfeited the moiety of her fortune; which then would
have descended to my wife; – and wherefore did I
marry, but to make lawful prize of a rich widow's
wealth, and squander it on love and you?

Mrs Mar. Deceit and frivolous pretence.

Fain. Death, am I not married? What's pretence? Am
I not imprisoned, fettered? Have I not a wife? Nay,
a wife that was a widow, a young widow, a handsome
widow; and would be again a widow, but that I have
a heart of proof, and something of a constitution to
bustle through the ways of wedlock and this world.
Will you yet be reconciled to truth and me?

Mrs Mar. Impossible. Truth and you are inconsistent –
I hate you, and shall for ever.

Fain. For loving you?

Mrs Mar. I loathe the name of love after such usage;
and next to the guilt with which you would asperse
me, I scorn you most. Farewell.

Fain. Nay, we must not part thus.

Mrs Mar. Let me go.

Fain. Come, I'm sorry.

Mrs Mar. I care not – let me go – break my hands,
do – I'd leave 'em to get loose.

Fain. I would not hurt you for the world. Have I no
other hold to keep you here?

Mrs Mar. Well, I have deserved it all.

Fain. You know I love you.

Mrs Mar. Poor dissembling! – O that – well, it is not
yet –

Fain. What? What is it not? What is it not yet? It is not
yet too late –

Mrs Mar. No, it is not yet too late – I have that comfort.

Fain. It is, to love another.

Mrs Mar. But not to loathe, detest, abhor mankind, myself, and the whole treacherous world.

Fain. Nay, this is extravagance. – Come, I ask your pardon – no tears – I was to blame, I could not love you and be easy in my doubts. – Pray forbear – I believe you; I'm convinced I've done you wrong; and any way, every way will make amends; – I'll hate my wife yet more, damn her, I'll part with her, rob her of all she's worth, and we'll retire somewhere, any-where, to another world, I'll marry thee. – Be pacified – 'Sdeath, they come, hide your face, your tears. – You have a mask, wear it a moment. This way, this way, be persuaded.

———

ACT II, SCENE 4
Mirabell *and* Mrs Fainall

Mrs Fain. They are here yet.

Mira. They are turning into the other walk.

Mrs Fain. While I only hated my husband, I could bear to see him; but since I have despised him, he's too offensive.

Mira. O you should hate with prudence.

Mrs Fain. Yes, for I have loved with indiscretion.

Mira. You should have just so much disgust for your husband, as may be sufficient to make you relish your lover.

Mrs Fain. You have been the cause that I have loved without bounds, and would you set limits to that aversion, of which you have been the occasion? Why did you make me marry this man?

Mira. Why do we daily commit disagreeable and danger-ous actions? To save that idol reputation. If the familiarities of our loves had produced that conse-quence of which you were apprehensive, where could you have fixed a father's name with credit, but on a

husband? I knew Fainall to be a man lavish of his
morals, an interested and professing friend, a false and
a designing lover; yet one whose wit and outward fair
behaviour have gained a reputation with the town,
enough to make that woman stand excused, who has
suffered herself to be won by his addresses. A better
man ought not to have been sacrificed to the occasion;
a worse had not answered to the purpose. When you
are weary of him, you know your remedy.

Mrs Fain. I ought to stand in some degree of credit with
you, Mirabell.

Mira. In justice to you, I have made you privy to my
whole design, and put it in your power to ruin or
advance my fortune.

Mrs Fain. Whom have you instructed to represent your
pretended uncle?

Mira. Waitwell, my servant.

Mrs Fain. He is an humble servant to Foible, my
mother's woman, and may win her to your interest.

Mira. Care is taken for that. – She is won and worn by
this time. They were married this morning.

Mrs Fain. Who?

Mira. Waitwell and Foible. I would not tempt my
servant to betray me by trusting him too far. If your
mother, in hopes to ruin me, should consent to marry
my pretended uncle, he might, like Mosca in 'The
Fox', stand upon terms; so I made him sure beforehand.

Mrs Fain. So, if my poor mother is caught in a contract,
you will discover the imposture betimes; and release
her by producing a certificate of her gallant's former
marriage.

Mira. Yes, upon condition that she consent to my
marriage with her niece, and surrender the moiety of
her fortune in her possession.

Mrs Fain. She talked last night of endeavouring at a
match between Millamant and your uncle.

Mira. That was by Foible's direction, and my instruction, that she might seem to carry it more privately.

Mrs Fain. Well, I have an opinion of your success; for I believe my lady will do anything to get a husband; and when she has this, which you have provided for her, I suppose she will submit to anything to get rid of him.

Mira. Yes, I think the good lady would marry anything that resembled a man, though 'twere no more than what a butler could pinch out of a napkin.

Mrs Fain. Female frailty! We must all come to it, if we live to be old, and feel the craving of a false appetite when the true is decayed.

Mira. An old woman's appetite is depraved like that of a girl. – 'Tis the green-sickness of a second childhood; and like the faint offer of a latter spring, serves but to usher in the fall, and withers in an affected bloom.

Mrs Fain. Here's your mistress.

ACT II, SCENE 5

[*To them*] Mrs MILLAMANT, WITWOUD, MINCING

Mira. Here she comes i'faith full sail, with her fan spread and streamers out, and a shoal of fools for tenders. – Ha, no, I cry her mercy.

Mrs Fain. I see but one poor empty sculler; and he tows her woman after him.

Mira. You seem to be unattended, madam, – you used to have the *Beau-monde* throng after you; and a flock of gay fine perukes hovering round you.

Wit. Like moths about a candle. – I had like to have lost my comparison for want of breath.

Milla. O I have denied myself airs to-day. I have walked as fast through the crowd –

Wit. As a favourite just disgraced; and with as few followers.

Milla. Dear Mr Witwoud, truce with your similitudes: for I am as sick of 'em –

Wit. As a physician of a good air. – I cannot help it, madam, though 'tis against myself.

Milla. Yet again! Mincing, stand between me and his wit.

Wit. Do, Mrs Mincing, like a screen before a great fire. I confess I do blaze today, I am too bright.

Mrs Fain. But dear Millamant, why were you so long?

Milla. Long! Lord, have I not made violent haste? I have asked every living thing I met for you: I have enquired after you, as after a new fashion.

Wit. Madam, truce with your similitudes. – No, you met her husband, and did not ask him for her.

Mira. By your leave, Witwoud, that were like enquiring after an old fashion, to ask a husband for his wife.

Wit. Hum, a hit, a hit, a palpable hit, I confess it.

Mrs Fain. You were dressed before I came abroad.

Milla. Ay, that's true. – O but then I had – Mincing, what had I? Why was I so long?

Minc. O mem, your laship staid to peruse a packet of letters.

Milla. O ay, letters – I had letters – I am persecuted with letters – I hate letters – nobody knows how to write letters; and yet one has 'em, one does not know why. – They serve one to pin up one's hair.

Wit. Is that the way? Pray, madam, do you pin up your hair with all your letters; I find I must keep copies.

Milla. Only with those in verse, Mr Witwoud. I never pin up my hair with prose. I think I tried once, Mincing.

Minc. O mem, I shall never forget it.

Milla. Ay, poor Mincing, tift and tift all the morning.

Minc. 'Till I had the cramp in my fingers, I'll vow, mem. And all to no purpose. But when your laship pins it up with poetry, it sits so pleasant the next day as anything, and is so pure and so crips.

Wit. Indeed, so crips?

Minc. You're such a critic, Mr Witwoud.

Milla. Mirabell, did you take exceptions last night? O ay, and went away. – Now I think on't I'm angry. – No, now I think on't I'm pleased. – For I believe I gave you some pain.

Mira. Does that please you?

Milla. Infinitely; I love to give pain.

Mira. You would affect a cruelty which is not in your nature; your true vanity is in the power of pleasing.

Milla. O I ask your pardon for that – one's cruelty is one's power, and when one parts with one's cruelty, one parts with one's power; and when one has parted with that, I fancy one's old and ugly.

Mira. Ay, ay, suffer your cruelty to ruin the object of your power, to destroy your lover – and then how vain, how lost a thing you'll be? Nay, 'tis true: you are no longer handsome when you've lost your lover; your beauty dies upon the instant: for beauty is the lover's gift; 'tis he bestows your charms – your glass is all a cheat. The ugly and the old, whom the looking-glass mortifies, yet after commendation can be flattered by it, and discover beauties in it: for that reflects our praises, rather than your face.

Milla. O the vanity of these men! Fainall, d'ye hear him? If they did not commend us, we were not handsome! Now you must know they could not commend one, if one was not handsome. Beauty the lover's gift – Lord, what is a lover, that it can give? Why, one makes lovers as fast as one pleases, and they live as long as one pleases, and they die as soon as one pleases: and then if one pleases one makes more.

Wit. Very pretty. Why you make no more of making of lovers, madam, than of making so many card-matches.

Milla. One no more owes one's beauty to a lover, than

one's wit to an echo: they can but reflect what we look and say; vain empty things if we are silent or unseen, and want a being.

Mira. Yet, to those two vain empty things, you owe two of the greatest pleasures of your life.

Milla. How so?

Mira. To your lover you owe the pleasure of hearing yourselves praised; and to an echo the pleasure of hearing yourselves talk.

Wit. But I know a lady that loves talking so incessantly, she won't give an echo fair play; she has that ever-lasting rotation of tongue, that an echo must wait till she dies, before it can catch her last words.

Milla. O fiction; Fainall, let us leave these men.

Mira. Draw off Witwoud.   [*Aside to Mrs Fainall.*

Mrs Fain. Immediately; I have a word or two for Mr Witwoud.

———

ACT II, SCENE 6

Mrs Millamant, Mirabell, Mincing

Mira. I would beg a little private audience too. – You had the tyranny to deny me last night; though you knew I came to impart a secret to you that concerned my love.

Milla. You saw I was engaged.

Mira. Unkind. You had the leisure to entertain a herd of fools; things who visit you from their excessive idle-ness; bestowing on your easiness that time, which is the encumbrance of their lives. How can you find delight in such society? It is impossible they should admire you, they are not capable: or if they were, it should be to you as a mortification; for sure to please a fool is some degree of folly.

Milla. I please myself. – Besides, sometimes to converse with fools is for my health.

Mira. Your health! Is there a worse disease than the conversation of fools?

Milla. Yes, the vapours; fools are physic for it, next to *assafoetida.*

Mira. You are not in a course of fools?

Milla. Mirabell, if you persist in this offensive freedom – you'll displease me. – I think I must resolve after all, not to have you. – We shan't agree.

Mira. Not in our physic it may be.

Milla. And yet our distemper in all likelihood will be the same; for we shall be sick of one another. I shan't endure to be reprimanded, nor instructed; 'tis so dull to act always by advice, and so tedious to be told of one's faults – I can't bear it. Well, I won't have you Mirabell – I'm resolved – I think – you may go. – Ha, ha, ha. What would you give, that you could help loving me?

Mira. I would give something that you did not know I could not help it.

Milla. Come, don't look grave then. Well, what do you say to me?

Mira. I say that a man may as soon make a friend by his wit, or a fortune by his honesty, as win a woman with plain-dealing and sincerity.

Milla. Sententious Mirabell! Prithee don't look with that violent and inflexible wise face, like Solomon at the dividing of the child in an old tapestry hanging.

Mira. You are merry, madam, but I would persuade you for a moment to be serious.

Milla. What, with that face? No, if you keep your countenance, 'tis impossible I should hold mine. Well, after all, there is something very moving in a lovesick face. Ha, ha, ha. – Well I won't laugh, don't be peevish. – Heigho! Now I'll be melancholy, as melancholy as a watchlight. Well Mirabell, if ever you will win me woo me now. – Nay, if you are so tedious, fare you well; – I see they are walking away.

Mira. Can you not find in the variety of your disposition
  one moment –

Milla. To hear you tell me Foible's married, and your
  plot like to speed – No.

Mira. But how came you to know it –

Milla. Without the help of the devil, you can't imagine;
  unless she should tell me herself. Which of the two
  it may have been, I will leave you to consider; and
  when you have done thinking of that, think of me.

ACT II, SCENE 7

MIRABELL *alone*

Mira. I have something more – gone. – Think of you!
  To think of a whirlwind, tho' 'twere in a whirlwind,
  were a case of more steady contemplation; a very
  tranquillity of mind and mansion. A fellow that lives
  in a windmill has not a more whimsical dwelling
  than the heart of a man that is lodged in a woman.
  There is no point of the compass to which they cannot
  turn, and by which they are not turned; and by one
  as well as another; for motion not method is their
  occupation. To know this, and yet continue to be in
  love, is to be made wise from the dictates of reason,
  and yet persevere to play the fool by the force of
  instinct. – O here come my pair of turtles. – What,
  billing so sweetly! Is not Valentine's Day over with
  you yet?

ACT II, SCENE 8

[*To him*] WAITWELL, FOIBLE

Mira. Sirrah, Waitwell, why sure you think you were
  married for your own recreation, and not for my
  conveniency.

Wait. Your pardon, Sir. With submission, we have indeed been solacing in lawful delights; but still with an eye to business, Sir. I have instructed her as well as I could. If she can take your directions as readily as my instructions, Sir, your affairs are in a prosperous way.

Mira. Give you joy, Mrs Foible.

Foib. O-las, Sir, I'm so ashamed – I'm afraid my lady has been in a thousand inquietudes for me. But I protest, Sir, I made as much haste as I could.

Wait. That she did indeed, Sir. It was my fault that she did not make more.

Mira. That I believe.

Foib. But I told my lady as you instructed me, Sir, that I had a prospect of seeing Sir Rowland your uncle; and that I would put her ladyship's picture in my pocket to show him; which I'll be sure to say has made him so enamoured of her beauty, that he burns with impatience to lie at her ladyship's feet and worship the original.

Mira. Excellent Foible! Matrimony has made you eloquent in love.

Wait. I think she has profited, Sir. I think so.

Foib. You have seen Madam Millamant, Sir?

Mira. Yes.

Foib. I told her, Sir, because I did not know that you might find an opportunity; she had so much company last night.

Mira. Your diligence will merit more. – In the meantime –   [*Gives money.*

Foib. O dear Sir, your humble servant.

Wait. Spouse.

Mira. Stand off Sir, not a penny. – Go on and prosper, Foible – the lease shall be made good and the farm stocked, if we succeed.

Foib. I don't question your generosity, Sir: and you need not doubt of success. If you have no more commands,

Sir, I'll be gone; I'm sure my lady is at her toilet, and can't dress till I come. – O dear, I'm sure that [*Looking out*] was Mrs Marwood that went by in a mask; if she has seen me with you I'm sure she'll tell my lady. I'll make haste home and prevent her. Your servant Sir. B'w'y Waitwell.

———

ACT II, SCENE 9
MIRABELL, WAITWELL

Wait. Sir Rowland if you please. The jade's so pert upon her preferment she forgets herself.

Mira. Come sir, will you endeavour to forget yourself – and transform into Sir Rowland.

Wait. Why Sir; it will be impossible I should remember myself – married, knighted and attended all in one day! 'Tis enough to make any man forget himself. The difficulty will be how to recover my acquaintance and familiarity with my former self; and fall from my transformation to a reformation into Waitwell. Nay, I shan't be quite the same Waitwell neither – for now I remember me, I'm married, and can't be my own man again.

> *Ay there's my grief; that's the sad change of life;*
> *To lose my title, and yet keep my wife.*

End of the Second Act

———

ACT III, SCENE 1

A Room in Lady Wishfort's House

LADY WISHFORT *at her toilet,* PEG *waiting*

Lady. Merciful, no news of Foible yet?

Peg. No, madam.

Lady. I have no more patience. – If I have not fretted myself till I am pale again, there's no veracity in me. Fetch me the red – the red, do you hear, sweetheart? An arrant ash colour, as I'm a person. Look you how this wench stirs! Why dost thou not fetch me a little red? Didst thou not hear me, Mopus?

Peg. The red ratafia does your ladyship mean, or the cherry-brandy?

Lady. Ratafia, fool. No, fool. Not the ratafia, fool – grant me patience! I mean the Spanish paper, idiot, complexion, darling. Paint, paint, paint, dost thou understand that, changeling, dangling thy hands like bobbins before thee? Why doest thou not stir, puppet? thou wooden thing upon wires.

Peg. Lord, Madam, your ladyship is so impatient – I cannot come at the paint, madam, Mrs Foible has locked it up, and carried the key with her.

Lady. A pox take you both – fetch me the cherry-brandy then.

———

ACT III, SCENE 2

LADY WISHFORT

Lady. I'm as pale and as faint, I look like Mrs Qualmsick the curate's wife, that's always breeding. – Wench, come, come, wench, what art thou doing, sipping? tasting? Save thee, dost thou not know the bottle?

———

ACT III, SCENE 3

LADY WISHFORT, PEG *with a bottle and china cup*

Peg. Madam, I was looking for a cup.

Lady. A cup, save thee, and what a cup hast thou brought! Dost thou take me for a fairy, to drink out of an acorn? Why didst thou not bring thy thimble? Hast thou ne'er a brass thimble clinking in thy pocket with a bit of nutmeg? I warrant thee. Come, fill, fill. – So – again. See who that is – [*One knocks.*] Set down the bottle first. Here, here, under the table – what, wouldst thou go with the bottle in thy hand like a tapster? As I'm a person, this wench has lived in an inn upon the road, before she came to me, like Maritornes the Asturian in 'Don Quixote'. No Foible yet?

Peg. No, madam, Mrs Marwood.

Lady. O Marwood, let her come in. Come in good Marwood.

—

ACT III, SCENE 4

[*To them*] MRS MARWOOD

Mrs Mar. I'm surprised to find your ladyship in *dishabillé* at this time of day.

Lady. Foible's a lost thing; has been abroad since morning, and never heard of since.

Mrs Mar. I saw her but now, as I came masked through the park, in conference with Mirabell.

Lady. With Mirabell! You call my blood into my face, with mentioning that traitor. She durst not have the confidence. I sent her to negotiate an affair, in which if I'm detected I'm undone. If that wheedling villain has wrought upon Foible to detect me, I'm ruined.

Oh my dear friend, I'm a wretch of wretches if I'm detected.

Mrs Mar. O madam, you cannot suspect Mrs Foible's integrity.

Lady. O, he carries poison in his tongue that would corrupt integrity itself. If she has given him an opportunity, she has as good as put her integrity into his hands. Ah dear Marwood, what's integrity to an opportunity? – Hark! I hear her. – Dear friend, retire into my closet, that I may examine her with more freedom. – You'll pardon me, dear friend, I can make bold with you – there are books over the chimney – Quarles and Prynne, and the 'Short View of the Stage', with Bunyan's works to entertain you. – Go, you thing, and send her in.   [*To* Peg.

ACT III, SCENE 5
LADY WISHFORT, FOIBLE

Lady. O Foible, where hast thou been? What hast thou been doing?

Foib. Madam, I have seen the party.

Lady. But what hast thou done?

Foib. Nay, 'tis your ladyship has done, and are to do; I have only promised. But a man so enamoured – so transported! Well, if worshipping of pictures be a sin – poor Sir Rowland, I say.

Lady. The miniature has been counted like. – But hast thou not betrayed me, Foible? Hast thou not detected me to that faithless Mirabell? – What hadst thou to do with him in the park? Answer me, has he got nothing out of thee?

Foib. So, the devil has been beforehand with me, what shall I say? Alas, madam, could I help it, if I met that confident thing? Was I in fault? If you had heard how he used me, and all upon your ladyship's account,

I'm sure you would not suspect my fidelity. Nay, if
that had been the worst I could have borne: but he
had a fling at your ladyship too; and then I could
not hold: but i'faith I gave him his own.

Lady. Me? What did the filthy fellow say?

Foib. O madam; 'tis a shame to say what he said –
With his taunts and his fleers, tossing up his nose.
Humh (says he) what, you are a-hatching some plot
(says he) you are so early abroad, or catering (says he)
ferreting for some disbanded officer, I warrant – half
pay is but thin subsistence (says he) – well, what
pension does your lady propose? Let me see (says he)
what she must come down pretty deep now, she's
superannuated (says he) and –

Lady. Ods my life, I'll have him, I'll have him murdered.
I'll have him poisoned. Where does he eat? I'll marry
a drawer to have him poisoned in his wine. I'll send
for Robin from Lockets – immediately.

Foib. Poison him? Poisoning's too good for him. Starve
him, madam, starve him; marry Sir Rowland, and
get him disinherited. O you would bless yourself, to
hear what he said.

Lady. A villain, superannuated!

Foib. Humh (says he) I hear you are laying designs
against me too (says he) and Mrs Millamant is to
marry my uncle; (he does not suspect a word of your
ladyship) but (says he) I'll fit you for that, I warrant
you (says he) I'll hamper you for that (says he) you
and your old frippery too (says he) I'll handle you –

Lady. Audacious villain! handle me, would he durst. –
Frippery? old frippery! Was there ever such a foul-
mouthed fellow? I'll be married tomorrow, I'll be
contracted tonight.

Foib. The sooner the better, madam.

Lady. Will Sir Rowland be here, sayest thou? When,
Foible?

Foib. Incontinently, madam. No new sheriff's wife expects

the return of her husband after knighthood, with
that impatience in which Sir Rowland burns for the
dear hour of kissing your ladyship's hand after dinner.

Lady. Frippery! superannuated frippery! I'll frippery the
villain; I'll reduce him to frippery and rags: a tatter-
demallion – I hope to see him hung with tatters, like
a Long-Lane penthouse, or a gibbet-thief. A slander-
mouthed railer: I warrant the spendthrift prodigal's
in debt as much as the million lottery, or the whole
court upon a birthday. I'll spoil his credit with his
tailor. Yes, he shall have my niece with her fortune,
he shall.

Foib. He! I hope to see him lodge in Ludgate first, and
angle into Blackfriars for brass farthings, with an old
mitten.

Lady. Ay dear Foible; thank thee for that, dear Foible.
He has put me out of all patience. I shall never
recompose my features, to receive Sir Rowland with
any economy of face. This wretch has fretted me that
I am absolutely decayed. Look, Foible.

Foib. Your ladyship has frowned a little too rashly,
indeed madam. There are some cracks discernible in
the white varnish.

Lady. Let me see the glass – cracks, sayest thou? Why
I am arrantly flayed – I look like an old peeled wall.
Thou must repair me, Foible, before Sir Rowland
comes; or I shall never keep up to my picture.

Foib. I warrant you, madam; a little art once made
your picture like you; and now a little of the same art
must make you like your picture. Your picture must
sit for you, madam.

Lady. But art thou sure Sir Rowland will not fail to
come? Or will a' not fail when he does come? Will he
be importunate, Foible, and push? For if he should
not be importunate – I shall never break decorums –
I shall die with confusion, if I am forced to advance. –
Oh no, I can never advance – I shall swoon if he

should expect advances. No, I hope Sir Rowland is better bred, than to put a lady to the necessity of breaking her forms. I won't be too coy neither. – I won't give him despair – but a little disdain is not amiss; a little scorn is alluring.

Foib. A little scorn becomes your ladyship.

Lady. Yes, but tenderness becomes me best – A sort of dyingness. – You see that picture has a sort of a – ha Foible? A swimmingness in the eyes. – Yes, I'll look so. – My niece affects it; but she wants features. Is Sir Rowland handsome? Let my toilet be removed – I'll dress above. I'll receive Sir Rowland here. Is he handsome? Don't answer me. I won't know: I'll be surprised. I'll be taken by surprise.

Foib. By storm, madam. Sir Rowland's a brisk man.

Lady. Is he! O then he'll importune, if he's a brisk man. I shall save decorums if Sir Rowland importunes. I have a mortal terror at the apprehension of offending against decorums. O I'm glad he's a brisk man. Let my things be removed, good Foible.

———

ACT III, SCENE 6
MRS FAINALL, FOIBLE

Mrs Fain. O Foible, I have been in a fright, lest I should come too late. That devil, Marwood, saw you in the park with Mirabell, and I'm afraid will discover it to my lady.

Foib. Discover what, madam?

Mrs Fain. Nay, nay, put not on that strange face. I am privy to the whole design, and know Waitwell, to whom thou wert this morning married, is to personate Mirabell's uncle, and as such, winning my lady, to involve her in those difficulties from which Mirabell only must release her, by his making his conditions to have my cousin and her fortune left to her own disposal.

Foib. O dear madam, I beg your pardon. It was not my confidence in your ladyship that was deficient; but I thought the former good correspondence between your ladyship and Mr Mirabell might have hindered his communicating this secret.

Mrs Fain. Dear Foible, forget that.

Foib. O dear madam, Mr Mirabell is such a sweet winning gentleman – but your ladyship is the pattern of generosity. – Sweet lady, to be so good! Mr Mirabell cannot choose but to be grateful. I find your ladyship has his heart still. Now, madam, I can safely tell your ladyship our success. Mrs Marwood had told my lady; but I warrant I managed myself. I turned it all for the better. I told my lady that Mr Mirabell railed at her. I laid horrid things to his charge, I'll vow; and my lady is so incensed that she'll be contracted to Sir Rowland tonight, she says; – I warrant I worked her up, that he may have her for asking for, as they say of a Welsh maidenhead.

Mrs Fain. O rare Foible!

Foib. Madam, I beg your ladyship to acquaint Mr Mirabell of his success. I would be seen as little as possible to speak to him – besides, I believe Madam Marwood watches me. – She has a month's mind; but I know Mr Mirabell can't abide her. – [*Calls.*] John – remove my lady's toilet. Madam, your servant. My lady is so impatient, I fear she'll come for me, if I stay.

Mrs Fain. I'll go with you up the back stairs, lest I should meet her.

———

ACT III, SCENE 7
Mrs Marwood *alone*

Mrs Mar. Indeed, Mrs Engine, is it thus with you? Are you become a go-between of this importance? Yes, I shall watch you. Why this wench is the *passe-partout*, a very master-key to everybody's strong box. My friend Fainall, have you carried it so swimmingly? I thought there was something in it; but it seems it's over with you. Your loathing is not from a want of appetite then, but from a surfeit. Else you could never be so cool to fall from a principal to be an assistant; to procure for him! A pattern of generosity, that I confess. Well, Mr Fainall, you have met with your match. – O Man, Man! Woman, Woman! The devil's an ass: if I were a painter, I would draw him like an idiot, a driveller with a bib and bells. Man should have his head and horns, and woman the rest of him. Poor simple fiend! Madam Marwood has a month's mind, but he can't abide her. – 'Twere better for him you had not been his confessor in that affair; without you could have kept his counsel closer. I shall not prove another pattern of generosity – he has not obliged me to that with those excesses of himself; and now I'll have none of him. Here comes the good lady, panting ripe; with a heart full of hope, and a head full of care, like any chymist upon the day of projection.

ACT III, SCENE 8

[*To her*] LADY WISHFORT

Lady. O dear Marwood, what shall I say for this rude forgetfulness – But my dear friend is all goodness.

Mrs Mar. No apologies, dear madam. I have been very well entertained.

Lady. As I'm a person I am in a very chaos to think I should so forget myself – But I have such an olio of affairs really I know not what to do. – [*Calls*] – Foible – I expect my nephew Sir Wilfull every moment too: – why Foible – he means to travel for improvement.

Mrs Mar. Methinks Sir Wilfull should rather think of

marrying than travelling at his years. I hear he is turned of forty.

Lady. O he's in less danger of being spoiled by his travels – I am against my nephew's marrying too young. It will be time enough when he comes back, and has acquired discretion to choose for himself.

Mrs Mar. Methinks Mrs Millamant and he would make a very fit match. He may travel afterwards. 'Tis a thing very usual with young gentlemen.

Lady. I promise you I have thought on't – and since 'tis your judgement, I'll think on't again. I assure you I will; I value your judgement extremely. On my word I'll propose it.

———

ACT III, SCENE 9
[*To them*] FOIBLE

Lady. Come, come Foible – I had forgot my nephew will be here before dinner – I must make haste.

Foib. Mr Witwoud and Mr Petulant are come to dine with your ladyship.

Lady. O dear, I can't appear till I am dressed. Dear Marwood, shall I be free with you again, and beg you to entertain 'em. I'll make all imaginable haste. Dear friend excuse me.

———

ACT III, SCENE 10
MRS MARWOOD, MRS MILLAMANT, MINCING

Milla. Sure never anything was so unbred as that odious man. – Marwood, your servant.

Mrs Mar. You have a colour, what's the matter?

Milla. That horrid fellow Petulant has provoked me into a flame – I have broke my fan – Mincing, lend me yours. – Is not all the powder out of my hair?

Mrs Mar. No. What has he done?

Milla. Nay, he has done nothing; he has only talked. —
Nay, he has said nothing neither; but he has contra-
dicted everything that has been said. For my part, I
thought Witwoud and he would have quarrelled.

Minc. I vow mem, I thought once they would have fitt.

Milla. Well, 'tis a lamentable thing I swear, that one
has not the liberty of choosing one's acquaintance as
one does one's clothes.

Mrs Mar. If we had that liberty, we should be as weary
of one set of acquaintance, though never so good, as
we are of one suit, though never so fine. A fool and a
doily stuff would now and then find days of grace,
and be worn for variety.

Milla. I could consent to wear 'em, if they would wear
alike; but fools never wear out. — They are such
drap-de-berry things! Without one could give 'em to
one's chamber-maid after a day or two.

Mrs Mar. 'Twere better so indeed. Or what think you
of the play-house? A fine gay glossy fool should be
given there, like a new masking habit, after the
masquerade is over, and we have done with the disguise. For a fool's visit is always a disguise; and never
admitted by a woman of wit, but to blind her affair
with a lover of sense. If you would but appear bare-
faced now, and own Mirabell; you might as easily put
off Petulant and Witwoud, as your hood and scarf.
And indeed 'tis time, for the town has found it: the
secret is grown too big for the pretence: 'tis like Mrs
Primly's great belly; she may lace it down before, but
it burnishes on her hips. Indeed, Millamant, you can
no more conceal it, than my Lady Strammel can her
face, that goodly face, which in defiance of her Rhen-
ish-wine tea, will not be comprehended in a mask.

Milla. I'll take my death, Marwood, you are more
censorious than a decayed beauty, or a discarded
toast; Mincing, tell the men they may come up. My

aunt is not dressing here; their folly is less provoking than your malice.

———

ACT III, SCENE II
Mrs Millamant, Marwood

Milla. The town has found it. What has it found? That Mirabell loves me is no more a secret, than it is a secret that you discovered it to my aunt, or than the reason why you discovered it is a secret.

Mrs Mar. You are nettled.

Milla. You're mistaken. Ridiculous!

Mrs Mar. Indeed, my dear, you'll tear another fan, if you don't mitigate those violent airs.

Milla. O silly! Ha, ha, ha. I could laugh immoderately. Poor Mirabell! His constancy to me has quite destroyed his complaisance for all the world beside. I swear, I never enjoined it him, to be so coy. – If I had the vanity to think he would obey me; I would command him to show more gallantry. – 'Tis hardly well bred to be so particular on one hand, and so insensible on the other. But I despair to prevail, and so let him follow his own way. Ha, ha, ha. Pardon me, dear creature, I must laugh, ha, ha, ha; though I grant you 'tis a little barbarous, ha, ha, ha.

Mrs Mar. What pity 'tis, so much fine raillery, and delivered with so significant gesture, should be so unhappily directed to miscarry.

Milla. Ha? Dear creature, I ask your pardon – I swear I did not mind you.

Mrs Mar. Mr Mirabell and you both may think it a thing impossible, when I shall tell him by telling you –

Milla. O dear, what? for it is the same thing, if I hear it – ha, ha, ha.

Mrs Mar. That I detest him, hate him, madam.

Milla. O madam, why so do I. – And yet the creature

loves me, ha, ha, ha. How can one forbear laughing
to think of it – I am a sybil if I am not amazed to
think what he can see in me. I'll take my death, I
think you are handsomer – and within a year or two
as young. – If you could but stay for me, I should
overtake you – but that cannot be. – Well, that
thought makes me melancholic. – Now I'll be sad.

Mrs Mar. Your merry note may be changed sooner than
you think.

Milla. D'ye say so? Then I'm resolved I'll have a song
to keep up my spirits.

ACT III, SCENE 12

[*To them*] MINCING

Minc. The gentlemen stay but to comb, madam; and
will wait on you.

Milla. Desire Mrs – that is in the next room to sing the
song I would have learnt yesterday. You shall hear it,
madam. – Not that there's any great matter in it –
but 'tis agreeable to my humour.

SONG

I

Love's but the frailty of the mind,
When 'tis not with ambition join'd;
A sickly flame, which if not fed expires;
And feeding, wastes in self-consuming fires.

II

'Tis not to wound a wanton boy
Or am'rous youth, that gives the joy;
But 'tis the glory to have pierc'd a swain,
For whom inferior beauties sigh'd in vain.

III

Then I alone the conquest prize,
When I insult a rival's eyes:
If there's delight in love, 'tis when I see
That heart which others bleed for, bleed for me.

ACT III, SCENE 13

[*To them*] PETULANT, WITWOUD

Milla. Is your animosity composed, gentlemen?

Wit. Raillery, raillery, madam, we have no animosity –
We hit off a little wit now and then, but no animosity –
The falling out of wits is like the falling out of lovers –
we agree in the main, like treble and bass. Ha,
Petulant!

Pet. Ay, in the main – but when I have a humour to
contradict –

Wit. Ay, when he has a humour to contradict, then I
contradict too. What, I know my cue. Then we contradict one another like two battledores; for contradictions beget one another like Jews.

Pet. If he says black's black – if I have a humour to say
'tis blue – let that pass – all's one for that. If I have a
humour to prove it, it must be granted.

Wit. Not positively must – but it may – it may.

Pet. Yes, it positively must, upon proof positive.

Wit. Ay, upon proof positive it must; but upon proof
presumptive it only may. That's a logical distinction
now, madam.

Mrs Mar. I perceive your debates are of importance,
and very learnedly handled.

Pet. Importance is one thing, and learning's another;
but a debate's a debate, that I assert.

Wit. Petulant's an enemy to learning; he relies altogether
on his parts.

Pet. No, I'm no enemy to learning; it hurts not me.

Mrs Mar. That's a sign indeed it's no enemy to you.

Pet. No, no, it's no enemy to anybody, but them that
have it.

Milla. Well, an illiterate man's my aversion. I wonder at
the impudence of any illiterate man, to offer to make
love.

Wit. That I confess I wonder at too.

Milla. Ah! to marry an ignorant! that can hardly read or write.

Pet. Why should a man be any further from being married though he can't read, than he is from being hanged. The ordinary's paid for setting the Psalm, and the parish-priest for reading the ceremony. And for the rest which is to follow in both cases, a man may do it without book. – So all's one for that.

Milla. D'ye hear the creature? Lord, here's company, I'll be gone.

———

ACT III, SCENE 14

Sir Wilfull Witwoud *in a riding dress,*
Mrs Marwood, Petulant, Witwoud, Footman

Wit. In the name of Bartlemew and his Fair, what have we here?

Mrs Mar. 'Tis your brother, I fancy. Don't you know him?

Wit. Not I. – Yes, I think it is he – I've almost forgot him; I have not seen him since the Revolution.

Foot. Sir, my lady's dressing. Here's company; if you please to walk in, in the mean-time.

Sir Wil. Dressing! What, it's but morning here I warrant with you in London; we should count it towards afternoon in our parts, down in Shropshire. – Why then belike my aunt han't dined yet – ha, friend? ...

Foot. Your aunt, Sir?

Sir Wil. My aunt, Sir, yes, my aunt, Sir, and your lady, Sir, your lady is my aunt, Sir – Why, what do'st thou not know me, friend? Why then, send somebody hither that does. How long hast thou lived with thy lady, fellow, ha?

Foot. A week, Sir; longer than anybody in the house, except my lady's woman.

Sir Wil. Why then belike thou do'st not know thy lady,
   if thou see'st her, ha friend?
Foot. Why truly, Sir, I cannot safely swear to her face
   in a morning, before she is dress'd. 'Tis like I may
   give a shrewd guess at her by this time.
Sir Wil. Well, prithee try what thou canst do; if thou
   canst not guess, enquire her out, do'st hear, fellow?
   And tell her, her nephew, Sir Wilfull Witwoud, is in
   the house.
Foot. I shall, Sir.
Sir Wil. Hold ye, hear me, friend; a word with you in
   your ear, prithee who are these gallants?
Foot. Really, Sir, I can't tell; here come so many here,
   'tis hard to know 'em all.

———

ACT III, SCENE 15

Sir Wilfull Witwoud, Petulant, Witwoud, Mrs Marwood

Sir Wil. Oons, this fellow knows less than a starling; I
   don't think a'knows his own name.
Mrs Mar. Mr Witwoud, your brother is not behind hand
   in forgetfulness — I fancy he has forgot you too.
Wit. I hope so — the Devil take him that remembers first,
   I say.
Sir Wil. Save you, gentlemen and lady.
Mrs Mar. For shame, Mr Witwoud; why don't you speak
   to him? — And you, Sir.
Wit. Petulant speak.
Pet. And you, Sir.
Sir Wil. No offence, I hope.   [*Salutes Marwood.*
Mrs Mar. No sure, Sir.
Wit. This is a vile dog, I see that already. No offence!
   Ha, ha, ha, to him; to him, Petulant, smoke him.
Pet. It seems as if you had come a journey, Sir; hem,
   hem.   [*Surveying him round.*

Sir Wil. Very likely, Sir, that it may seem so.

Pet. No offence, I hope, Sir.

Wit. Smoke the boots, the boots; Petulant, the boots; Ha, ha, ha.

Sir Wil. May be not, Sir; thereafter as 'tis meant, Sir.

Pet. Sir, I presume upon the information of your boots.

Sir Wil. Why, 'tis like you may, Sir: if you are not satisfied with the information of my boots, Sir, if you will step to the stable, you may enquire further of my horse, Sir.

Pet. Your horse, Sir! Your horse is an ass, Sir!

Sir Wil. Do you speak by way of offence, Sir?

Mrs Mar. The gentleman's merry, that's all, Sir – S'life, we shall have a quarrel betwixt a horse and an ass, before they find one another out. You must not take anything amiss from your friends, Sir. You are among your friends, here, though it may be you don't know it. – If I am not mistaken, you are Sir Wilfull Witwoud.

Sir Wil. Right lady; I am Sir Wilfull Witwoud, so I write myself; no offence to anybody, I hope; and nephew to the Lady Wishfort of this mansion.

Mrs Mar. Don't you know this gentleman, Sir?

Sir Wil. Hum! what, sure 'tis not. – Yea by'r Lady, but 'tis – 'Sheart I know not whether 'tis or no – Yea but 'tis, by the Wrekin. Brother Antony! What Tony, i'faith! What, do'st thou not know me? By'r lady nor I thee, thou art so becravated, and so beperriwigged – 'Sheart why do'st not speak? Art thou o'erjoy'd?

Wit. Odso brother, is it you? Your servant, brother.

Sir Wil. Your servant! Why yours, Sir. Your servant again – 'Sheart, and your friend and servant to that – And a – (*puff*) and a flap-dragon for your service, Sir: And a hare's foot, and a hare's scut for your service, Sir; an you be so cold and so courtly!

Wit. No offence, I hope, brother.

Sir Wil. 'Sheart, Sir, but there is, and much offence. – A pox, is this your Inns o' Court breeding, not to *know* your friends and your relations, your elders, and your betters?

Wit. Why, brother Wilfull of Salop, you may be as short as a Shrewsbury cake, if you please. But I tell you 'tis not modish to know relations in town. You think you're in the country, where great lubberly brothers slabber and kiss one another when they meet, like a call of Serjeants. – 'Tis not the fashion here; 'tis not indeed, dear brother.

Sir Wil. The fashion's a fool; and you're a fop, dear brother. 'Sheart, I've suspected this. – By'r lady I conjectured you were a fop, since you began to change the style of your letters, and write in a scrap of paper, gilt round the edges, no bigger than a subpoena. I might expect this when you left off Honoured Brother; and hoping you are in good health, and so forth – to begin with a Rat me, Knight, I'm so sick of a last night's debauch. – Od's heart, and then tell a familiar tale of a cock and a bull, and a whore and a bottle, and so conclude. – You could write news before you were out of your time, when you lived with honest Pumple-Nose the attorney of Furnival's Inn. – You could entreat to be remembered then to your friends round the Wrekin. We could have Gazettes then, and Dawks's Letter, and the Weekly Bill, 'till of late days.

Pet. 'Slife, Witwoud, were you ever an attorney's clerk? Of the family of the Furnivals. Ha, ha, ha!

Wit. Ay, ay, but that was but for a while. Not long, not long; pshaw, I was not in my own power then. An orphan, and this fellow was my guardian; ay, ay, I was glad to consent to that man to come to London. He had the disposal of me then. If I had not agreed to that, I might have been bound prentice to a felt-maker in Shrewsbury; this fellow would have bound me to a maker of felts.

Sir Wil. 'Sheart, and better than to be bound to a maker

of fops; where, I suppose, you have served your time; and now you may set up for yourself.

Mrs Mar. You intend to travel, Sir, as I'm inform'd.

Sir Wil. Belike I may, madam. I may chance to sail upon the salt seas, if my mind hold.

Pet. And the wind serve.

Sir Wil. Serve or not serve, I shan't ask licence of you, sir; nor the weather-cock your companion. I direct my discourse to the lady, sir; 'tis like my aunt may have told you, madam. – Yes, I have settled my concerns, I may say now, and am minded to see foreign parts. If an' how that the peace holds, whereby that is taxes abate.

Mrs Mar. I thought you had designed for France at all adventures.

Sir Wil. I can't tell that; 'tis like I may, and 'tis like I may not. I am somewhat dainty in making a resolution, – because when I make it I keep it. I don't stand shill I, shall I, then; if I say't, I'll do't. But I have thoughts to tarry a small matter in town, to learn somewhat of your lingo first, before I cross the seas. I'd gladly have a spice of your French as they say, whereby to hold discourse in foreign countries.

Mrs Mar. Here's an academy in town for that use.

Sir Wil. There is? 'Tis like there may.

Mrs Mar. No doubt you will return very much improved.

Wit. Yes, refined like a Dutch skipper from a whale-fishing.

———

ACT III, SCENE 16

[*To them*] LADY WISHFORT *and* FAINALL

Lady. Nephew, you are welcome.

Sir Wil. Aunt, your servant.

Fain. Sir Wilfull, your most faithful servant.

Sir Wil. Cousin Fainall, give me your hand.

Lady. Cousin Witwoud, your servant; Mr Petulant, your
servant – nephew, you are welcome again. Will you
drink anything after your journey, nephew, before you
eat? Dinner's almost ready.

Sir Wil. I'm very well I thank you, aunt. – However, I
thank you for your courteous offer. 'Sheart I was
afraid you would have been in the fashion too, and
have remembered to have forgot your relations. Here's
your cousin Tony, belike, I mayn't call him brother
for fear of offence.

Lady. O he's a rallier, nephew – my cousin's a wit: and
your great wits always rally their best friends to choose.
When you have been abroad, nephew, you'll understand raillery better.

[*Fainall and Mrs Marwood talk apart.*

Sir Wil. Why then let him hold his tongue in the meantime; and rail when that day comes.

———

ACT III, SCENE 17
[*To them*] MINCING

Minc. Mem, I come to acquaint your laship that dinner
is impatient.

Sir Wil. Impatient? Why then belike it won't stay till I
pull off my boots. Sweetheart, can you help me to a
pair of slippers? – My man's with his horses, I warrant.

Lady. Fie, fie, nephew, you would not pull off your boots
here – go down into the hall – dinner shall stay for
you. – My nephew's a little unbred, you'll pardon him,
madam. – Gentlemen will you walk? Marwood?

Mrs Mar. I'll follow you, madam, – before Sir Wilfull
is ready.

———

MRS. MARWOOD, FAINALL

Fain. Why then Foible's a bawd, an errant, rank, match-
making bawd. And I it seems am a husband, a rank-
husband; and my wife a very errant, rank-wife, – all
in the Way of the World. 'Sdeath to be a cuckold by
anticipation, a cuckold in embryo? Sure I was born
with budding antlers like a young satyr, or a citizen's
child. 'Sdeath to be out-witted, to be out-jilted – out-
matrimonied, – if I had kept my speed like a stag,
'twere somewhat, – but to crawl after, with my horns
like a snail, and be out-stripped by my wife – 'tis
scurvy wedlock.

Mrs Mar. Then shake it off, you have often wished for
an opportunity to part; – and now you have it. But
first prevent their plot, – the half of Millamant's
fortune is too considerable to be parted with, to a foe,
to Mirabell.

Fain. Damn him, that had been mine – had you not
made that fond discovery, – that had been forfeited,
had they been married. My wife had added lustre to
my horns, by that increase of fortune, I could have
worn 'em tipped with gold, though my forehead had
been furnished like a deputy-lieutenant's hall.

Mrs Mar. They may prove a cap of maintenance to you
still, if you can away with your wife. And she's no
worse than when you had her – I dare swear she had
given up her game, before she was married.

Fain. Hum! That may be –

Mrs Mar. You married her to keep you; and if you can
contrive to have her keep you better than you expected; why should you not keep her longer than you
intended?

Fain. The means, the means.

Mrs Mar. Discover to my lady your wife's conduct;

threaten to part with her. – My lady loves her, and
will come to any composition to save her reputation.
Take the opportunity of breaking it, just upon the
discovery of this imposture. My lady will be enraged
beyond bounds, and sacrifice niece, and fortune, and
all at that conjuncture. And let me alone to keep her
warm; if she should flag in her part, I will not fail to
prompt her.

Fain. Faith, this has an appearance.

Mrs Mar. I'm sorry I hinted to my lady to endeavour a
match between Millamant and Sir Wilfull, that may
be an obstacle.

Fain. O for that matter leave me to manage him; I'll
disable him for that, he will drink like a Dane: after
dinner, I'll set his hand in.

Mrs Mar. Well, how do you stand affected towards your
lady?

Fain. Why faith, I'm thinking of it. – Let me see – I am
married already; so that's over. – My wife has played
the jade with me – well, that's over too – I never loved
her, or if I had, why that would have been over too
by this time – jealous of her I cannot be, for I am
certain; so there's an end of jealousy. Weary of her,
I am and shall be – no, there's no end of that; no,
no, that were too much to hope. Thus far concerning
my repose. Now for my reputation. – As to my own,
I married not for it; so that's out of the question. –
And as to my part in my wife's – why she had parted
with hers before; so bringing none to me, she can take
none from me; 'tis against all rule of play, that I
should lose to one, who has not wherewithal to
stake.

Mrs Mar. Besides you forget, marriage is honourable.

Fain. Hum! Faith and that's well thought on; marriage
is honourable, as you say; and if so, wherefore should
cuckoldom be a discredit, being deriv'd from so
honourable a root?

Mrs Mar. Nay I know not; if the root be honourable, why not the branches?

Fain. So, so, why this point's clear. – Well, how do we proceed?

Mrs Mar. I will contrive a letter which shall be delivered to my lady at the time when that rascal who is to act Sir Rowland is with her. It shall come as from an unknown hand – for the less I appear to know of the truth, the better I can play the incendiary. Besides, I would not have Foible provoked if I could help it, – because you know she knows some passages. – Nay I expect all will come out – But let the mine be sprung first, and then I care not if I am discovered.

Fain. If the worst come to the worst. – I'll turn my wife to grass – I have already a deed of settlement of the best part of her estate: which I wheedled out of her; and that you shall partake at least.

Mrs Mar. I hope you are convinced that I hate Mirabell now: you'll be no more jealous?

Fain. Jealous, no, – by this kiss – let husbands be jealous; but let the lover still believe: or if he doubt, let it be only to endear his pleasure, and prepare the joy that follows, when he proves his mistress true. But let husbands' doubts convert to endless jealousy; or if they have belief, let it corrupt to superstition, and blind credulity. I am single, and will herd no more with 'em. True, I wear the badge, but I'll disown the order. And since I take my leave of 'em, I care not if I leave 'em a common motto to their common crest.

> *All husbands must, or pain, or shame, endure;*
> *The wise too jealous are, fools too secure.*

End of the Third Act.

[Scene continues]
LADY WISHFORT *and* FOIBLE

Lady. Is Sir Rowland coming sayest thou, Foible, and
   are things in order?
Foib. Yes, madam. I have put wax-lights in the sconces;
   and placed the footmen in a row in the hall, in their
   best liveries, with the coachman and postilion to fill
   up the equipage.
Lady. Have you pullvilled the coachman and postilion,
   that they may not stink of the stable, when Sir Rowland comes by?
Foib. Yes, madam.
Lady. And are the dancers and the music ready, that he
   may be entertained in all points with correspondence
   to his passion?
Foib. All is ready, madam.
Lady. And – well – and how do I look, Foible?
Foib. Most killing well, madam.
Lady. Well, and how shall I receive him? In what figure
   shall I give his heart the first impression? There is a
   great deal in the first impression. Shall I sit? – No, I
   won't sit – I'll walk – ay, I'll walk from the door upon
   his entrance; and then turn full upon him. – No, that
   will be too sudden. I'll lie – ay, I'll lie down – I'll
   receive him in my little dressing-room, there's a couch
   – yes, yes, I'll give the first impression on a couch – I
   won't lie neither, but loll and lean upon one elbow;
   with one foot a little dangling off, jogging in a thoughtful way – yes – and then as soon as he appears, start,
   ay, start and be surprised, and rise to meet him in a
   pretty disorder – yes – O, nothing is more alluring
   than a levee from a couch in some confusion. – It
   shows the foot to advantage, and furnishes with
   blushes, and re-composing airs beyond comparison.

Hark! There's a coach.

Foib. 'Tis he, madam.

Lady. O dear, has my nephew made his addresses to Millamant? I ordered him.

Foib. Sir Wilfull is set in to drinking, madam, in the parlour.

Lady. Odds my life, I'll send him to her. Call her down, Foible; bring her hither. I'll send him as I go. – When they are together, then come to me, Foible, that I may not be too long alone with Sir Rowland.

———

ACT IV, SCENE 2

Mrs Millamant, Mrs Fainall, Foible

Foib. Madam, I stayed here to tell your ladyship that Mr Mirabell has waited this half hour for an opportunity to talk with you. Though my lady's orders were to leave you and Sir Wilfull together. Shall I tell Mr Mirabell that you are at leisure?

Milla. No – what would the dear man have? I am thoughtful, and would amuse myself, – bid him come another time.

> There never yet was Woman made,
> Nor shall, but to be cursed.

[*Repeating and walking about.*

That's hard!

Mrs Fain. You are very fond of Sir John Suckling today, Millamant, and the poets.

Milla. He? Ay, and filthy verses. – So I am.

Foib. Sir Wilfull is coming, madam. Shall I send Mr Mirabell away?

Milla. Ay, if you please, Foible, send him away, – or send him hither, – just as you will, dear Foible. – I think I'll see him. – Shall I? Ay, let the wretch come.

> Thyrsis, a Youth of the Inspir'd Train.

[*Repeating.*

Dear Fainall, entertain Sir Wilfull. – Thou hast philosophy to undergo a fool, thou art married and hast patience – I would confer with my own thoughts.

Mrs Fain. I am obliged to you, that you would make me your proxy in this affair; but I have business of my own.

ACT IV, SCENE 3
[*To them*] SIR WILFULL

Mrs Fain. O Sir Wilfull; you are come at the critical instant. There's your mistress up to the ears in love and contemplation, pursue your point, now or never.

Sir Wil. Yes; my Aunt will have it so, – I would gladly have been encouraged with a bottle or two, because I'm somewhat wary at first, before I am acquainted; – But I hope, after a time, I *{ This while Milla., walks about repeating to herself.* shall break my mind – that is upon further acquaintance. – So for the present, cousin, I'll take my leave – If so be you'll be so kind to make my excuse, I'll return to my company –

Mrs Fain. O fie, Sir Wilfull! What, you must not be daunted.

Sir Wil. Daunted, no, that's not it, it is not so much for that – for if so be that I set on't, I'll do't. But only for the present, 'tis sufficient till further acquaintance, that's all – your servant.

Mrs Fain. Nay, I'll swear you shall never lose so favourable an opportunity, if I can help it. I'll leave you together, and lock the door.

ACT IV, SCENE 4

Sir Wilfull, Mrs Millamant

Sir Wil. Nay, nay, cousin, – I have forgot my gloves. –
What d'ye do? 'Sheart, a'has lock'd the door indeed,
I think. – Nay, Cousin Fainall, open the door – pshaw,
what a vixen trick is this? – Nay, now a'has seen me
too. – Cousin, I made bold to pass through as it were –
I think this door's enchanted –

Milla. [*Repeating*].

> I prithee spare me, gentle Boy,
> Press me no more for that slight Toy.

Sir Wil. Anan? Cousin, your servant.

Milla. – That Foolish Trifle of a Heart – Sir Wilfull!

Sir Wil. Yes – your servant. No offence I hope, cousin.

Milla. [*Repeating*].

> I swear it will not do its Part,
> Tho' thou dost thine, employ'st thy Power and Art.

Natural, easy Suckling!

Sir Wil. Anan? Suckling? No such suckling neither,
cousin, nor stripling: I thank heaven I'm no minor.

Milla. Ah rustic, ruder than Gothic.

Sir Wil. Well, well, I shall understand your lingo one of
these days, cousin, in the meanwhile I must answer in
plain English.

Milla. Have you any business with me, Sir Wilfull?

Sir Wil. Not at present, cousin. – Yes, I made bold to
see, to come and know if that how you were disposed
to fetch a walk this evening, if so be that I might not
be troublesome, I would have sought a walk with
you.

Milla. A walk? What then?

Sir Wil. Nay nothing – only for the walk's sake, that's
all –

Milla. I nauseate walking; 'tis a country diversion, I
loathe the country and everything that relates to it.

Sir Wil. Indeed! Hah! Look ye, look ye, you do? Nay, 'tis like you may. – Here are choice of pastimes here in town, as plays and the like, that must be confessed indeed. –

Milla. Ah *l'étourdie!* I hate the town too.

Sir Wil. Dear heart, that's much. – Hah! that you should hate 'em both! Hah! 'tis like you may; there are some can't relish the town, and others can't away with the country, – 'tis like you may be one of those, cousin.

Milla. Ha, ha, ha. Yes, 'tis like I may. – You have nothing further to say to me?

Sir Wil. Not at present, cousin. – 'Tis like when I have an opportunity to be more private, – I may break my mind in some measure – I conjecture you partly guess. – However, that's as time shall try – but spare to speak and spare to speed, as they say.

Milla. If it is of no great importance, Sir Wilfull, you will oblige me to leave me: I have just now a little business –

Sir Wil. Enough, enough, cousin: yes, yes, all a case – When you're disposed, when you're disposed. Now's as well as another time; and another time as well as now. All's one for that. – Yes, yes, if your concerns call you, there's no haste; it will keep cold as they say. – Cousin, your servant. – I think this door's locked.

Milla. You may go this way, sir.

Sir Wil. Your servant, then with your leave I'll return to my company.

Milla. Ay ay; ha, ha, ha.

Like Phoebus sung the no less am'rous boy.

Mrs Millamant, Mirabell

Mira. *Like Daphne she, as lovely and as coy.* Do you lock yourself up from me, to make my search more curious? Or is this pretty artifice contrived, to signify that here the chase must end, and my pursuit be crowned, for you can fly no further? –

Milla. Vanity! No, – I'll fly and be followed to the last moment, though I am upon the very verge of matrimony, I expect you should solicit me as much as if I were wavering at the gate of a monastery, with one foot over the threshold. I'll be solicited to the very last, nay and afterwards.

Mira. What, after the last?

Milla. O, I should think I was poor and had nothing to bestow, if I were reduced to an inglorious ease; and freed from the agreeable fatigues of solicitation.

Mira. But do not you know, that when favours are conferred upon instant and tedious solicitation, that they diminish in their value, and that both the giver loses the grace, and the receiver lessens his pleasure?

Milla. It may be in things of common application; but never sure in love. O, I hate a lover, that can dare to think he draws a moment's air, independent of the bounty of his mistress. There is not so impudent a thing in nature, as the saucy look of an assured man, confident of success. The pedantic arrogance of a very husband, has not so pragmatical an air. Ah! I'll never marry, unless I am first made sure of my will and pleasure.

Mira. Would you have 'em both before marriage? Or will you be contented with the first now, and stay for the other till after grace?

Milla. Ah, don't be impertinent – My dear liberty, shall I leave thee? My faithful solitude, my darling

contemplation, must I bid you then adieu? Ay-h adieu
– my morning thoughts, agreeable wakings, indolent
slumbers, all ye *douceurs*, ye *sommeils du matin*, adieu –
I can't do it, 'tis more than impossible. – Positively,
Mirabell, I'll lie a-bed in a morning as long as I please.

Mira. Then I'll get up in a morning as early as I
please.

Milla. Ah! Idle creature, get up when you will – And
d'ye hear, I won't be called names after I'm married;
positively I won't be call'd names.

Mira. Names!

Milla. Ay, as wife, spouse, my dear, joy, jewel, love,
sweetheart, and the rest of that nauseous cant, in
which men and their wives are so fulsomely familiar, –
I shall never bear that. – Good Mirabell don't let us
be familiar or fond, nor kiss before folks, like my Lady
Fadler and Sir Francis: nor go to Hyde Park together
the first Sunday in a new chariot, to provoke eyes and
whispers; and then never be seen there together again;
as if we were proud of one another the first week, and
ashamed of one another ever after. Let us never visit
together, nor go to a play together, but let us be very
strange and wellbred: let us be as strange as if we had
been married a great while; and as wellbred as if we
were not married at all.

Mira. Have you any more conditions to offer? Hitherto
your demands are pretty reasonable.

Milla. Trifles, – as liberty to pay and receive visits to
and from whom I please; to write and receive letters,
without interrogatories or wry faces on your part; to
wear what I please; and choose conversation with
regard only to my own taste; to have no obligation
upon me to converse with wits that I don't like,
because they are your acquaintance; or to be intimate
with fools, because they may be your relations. Come
to dinner when I please, dine in my dressing-room
when I'm out of humour, without giving a reason.

To have my closet inviolate; to be sole empress of my tea-table, which you must never presume to approach without first asking leave. And lastly wherever I am, you shall always knock at the door before you come in. These articles subscribed, if I continue to endure you a little longer, I may by degrees dwindle into a wife.

Mira. Your bill of fare is something advanced in this latter account. Well, have I liberty to offer conditions – that when you are dwindled into a wife, I may not be beyond measure enlarged into a husband.

Milla. You have free leave, propose your utmost, speak and spare not.

Mira. I thank you. *Imprimis* then, I covenant that your acquaintance be general; that you admit no sworn confidante, or intimate of your own sex; no she friend to screen her affairs under your countenance, and tempt you to make trial of a mutual secrecy. No decoy-duck to wheedle you a fop – scrambling to the play in a mask – then bring you home in a pretended fright, when you think you shall be found out – and rail at me for missing the play, and disappointing the frolic which you had to pick me up and prove my constancy.

Milla. Detestable *Imprimis*! I go to the play in a mask!

Mira. *Item,* I article that you continue to like your own face, as long as I shall: and while it passes current with me, that you endeavour not to new coin it. To which end, together with all vizards for the day, I prohibit all masks for the night, made of oiled-skins and I know not what – hog's bones, hare's gall, pig water, and the marrow of a roasted cat. In short, I forbid all commerce with the gentlewoman in what-d'ye-call-it Court. *Item,* I shut my doors against all bawds with baskets, and penny-worths of muslin, china, fans, atlases, &c. – *Item,* when you shall be breeding –

Milla. Ah! Name it not.

Mira. Which may be presumed, with a blessing on our endeavours –

Milla. Odious endeavours!

Mira. I denounce against all strait lacing, squeezing for a shape, till you mould my boy's head like a sugar-loaf; and instead of a man-child, make me father to a crooked billet. Lastly, to the dominion of the tea-table I submit. – But with proviso, that you exceed not in your province; but restrain yourself to native and simple tea-table drinks, as tea, chocolate, and coffee. As likewise to genuine and authorized tea-table talk – such as mending of fashions, spoiling reputations, railing at absent friends, and so forth – but that on no account you encroach upon the men's prerogative, and presume to drink healths, or toast fellows; for prevention of which, I banish all foreign forces, all auxiliaries to the tea-table, as orange-brandy, all aniseed, cinnamon, citron and Barbadoes-waters, together with ratafia and the most noble spirit of clary. – But for cowslip-wine, poppy-water, and all dormitives, those I allow. – These provisoes admitted, in other things I may prove a tractable and complying husband.

Milla. O horrid provisoes! filthy strong waters! I toast fellows, odious men! I hate your odious provisoes.

Mira. Then we're agreed. Shall I kiss your hand upon the contract? And here comes one to be a witness to the sealing of the deed.

ACT IV, SCENE 6
[*To them*] MRS FAINALL

Milla. Fainall, what shall I do? Shall I have him? I think I must have him.

Mrs Fain. Ay, ay, take him, take him, what should you do?

Milla. Well then – I'll take my death I'm in a horrid fright – Fainall, I shall never say it – well – I think – I'll endure you.

Mrs Fain. Fie, fie, have him, have him, and tell him so in plain terms: for I am sure you have a mind to him.

Milla. Are you? I think I have – and the horrid man looks as if he thought so too. – Well, you ridiculous thing you, I'll have you – I won't be kissed, nor I won't be thanked. – Here, kiss my hand though – so, hold your tongue now, don't say a word.

Mrs Fain. Mirabell, there's a necessity for your obedience; – you have neither time to talk nor stay. My mother is coming; and in my conscience if she should see you, would fall into fits, and may be not recover in time enough to return to Sir Rowland; who, as Foible tells me, is in a fair way to succeed. Therefore spare your ecstasies for another occasion, and slip down the back stairs, where Foible waits to consult you.

Milla. Ay, go, go. In the meantime I suppose you have said something to please me.

Mira. I am all obedience.

ACT IV, SCENE 7

Mrs Millamant, Mrs Fainall

Mrs Fain. Yonder Sir Wilfull's drunk; and so noisy that my mother has been forced to leave Sir Rowland to appease him; but he answers her only with singing and drinking. – What they may have done by this time I know not; but Petulant and he were upon quarrelling as I came by.

Milla. Well, if Mirabell should not make a good husband, I am a lost thing; – for I find I love him violently.

Mrs Fain. So it seems; for you mind not what's said to you. – If you doubt him, you had best take up with Sir Wilfull.

Milla. How can you name that superannuated lubber?
Foh!

———

ACT IV, SCENE 8

[To them] WITWOUD *from drinking*

Mrs Fain. So, is the fray made up, that you have left
'em?

Wit. Left 'em? I could stay no longer. – I have laugh'd
like ten christenings – I am tipsy with laughing. – If
I had stayed any longer I should have burst, – I must
have been let out and pieced in the sides like an
unsized camlet. – Yes, yes, the fray is composed; my
lady came in like a *Nolle prosequi*, and stopped the
proceedings.

Milla. What was the dispute?

Wit. That's the jest; there was no dispute. They could
neither of 'em speak for rage; and so fell a-sputtering
at one another like two roasting apples.

———

ACT IV, SCENE 9

[To them] PETULANT *drunk*

Wit. Now Petulant! All's over, all's well? Gad my head
begins to whim it about – Why dost thou not speak?
Thou art both as drunk and as mute as a fish.

Pet. Look you, Mrs Millamant – if you can love me, dear
nymph – say it – and that's the conclusion. – Pass on,
or pass off, – that's all.

Wit. Thou hast uttered volumes, folios, in less than
decimo sexto, my dear Lacedemonian. Sirrah, Petulant, thou art an epitomizer of words.

Pet. Witwoud – you are an annihilator of sense.

Wit. Thou art a retailer of phrases; and dost deal in
remnants of remnants, like a maker of pincushions –

thou art in truth (metaphorically speaking) a speaker of shorthand.

Pet. Thou art (without a figure) just one half of an ass, and Baldwin yonder, thy half-brother, is the rest – a Gemini of asses split would make just four of you.

Wit. Thou dost bite, my dear mustard-seed; kiss me for that?

Pet. Stand off – I'll kiss no more males, – I have kissed your twin yonder in a humour of reconciliation, till he (*hiccup*) rises upon my stomach like a radish.

Milla. Eh! filthy creature – what was the quarrel?

Pet. There was no quarrel – there might have been a quarrel.

Wit. If there had been words enow between 'em to have expressed provocation, they had gone together by the ears like a pair of castanets.

Pet. You were the quarrel.

Milla. Me!

Pet. If I have a humour to quarrel, I can make less matters conclude premises. – If you are not handsome, what then; if I have a humour to prove it? – If I shall have my reward, say so; if not, fight for your face the next time yourself – I'll go sleep.

Wit. Do, wrap thyself up like a woodlouse, and dream revenge. – And hear me, if thou canst learn to write by tomorrow morning, pen me a challenge – I'll carry it for thee.

Pet. Carry your mistress's monkey a spider, – go flea dogs, and read romances – I'll go to bed to my maid.

Mrs Fain. He's horridly drunk – how came you all in this pickle?

Wit. A plot, a plot, to get rid of the knight, – your husband's advice; but he sneaked off.

SIR WILFULL *drunk*, LADY WISHFORT,
WITWOUD, MRS MILLAMANT, MRS FAINALL

Lady. Out upon't, out upon't, at years of discretion, and comport yourself at this rantipole rate.

Sir Wil. No offence, aunt.

Lady. Offence? As I'm a person, I'm ashamed of you. – Foh! how you stink of wine! D'ye think my niece will ever endure such a Borachio! you're an absolute Borachio.

Sir Wil. Borachio!

Lady. At a time when you should commence an amour, and put your best foot foremost –

Sir Wil. 'Sheart, an you grutch me your liquor, make a bill. – Give me more drink, and take my purse.

Sings

> Prithee fill me the glass
> Till it laugh in my face,
> With ale that is potent and mellow;
> He that whines for a lass
> Is an ignorant ass,
> For a bumper has not its fellow.

But if you would have me marry my cousin, – say the word, and I'll do 't – Wilfull will do 't, that's the word – Wilfull will do 't, that's my crest – my motto I have forgot.

Lady. My nephew's a little overtaken, cousin – but 'tis with drinking your health. – O' my word you are obliged to him –

Sir Wil. In vino veritas, aunt: – If I drunk your health today, cousin, – I am a Borachio. But if you have a mind to be married, say the word, and send for the piper, Wilfull will do 't. If not, dust it away, and let's have t'other round – Tony, Odds-heart where's Tony –

Tony's an honest fellow, but he spits after a bumper, and that's a fault.

Sings

> We'll drink and we'll never ha' done boys
> Put the glass then around with the sun boys,
> Let Apollo's example invite us;
> For he's drunk ev'ry night,
> And that makes him so bright,
> That he's able next morning to light us.

The sun's a good pimple, an honest soaker, he has a cellar at your Antipodes. If I travel, aunt, I touch at your Antipodes – your Antipodes are a good rascally sort of topsy turvy fellows. – If I had a bumper I'd stand upon my head and drink a health to 'em. – A match or no match, Cousin, with the hard name – Aunt, Wilfull will do 't. If she has her maidenhead let her look to 't; if she has not, let her keep her own counsel in the meantime, and cry out at the nine months' end.

Milla. Your pardon, madam, I can stay no longer – Sir Wilfull grows very powerful. Egh! how he smells! I shall be overcome if I stay. Come, cousin.

———

ACT IV, SCENE 11

Lady Wishfort, Sir Wilfull Witwoud, Mr Witwoud, Foible

Lady. Smells! he would poison a tallow-chandler and his family. Beastly creature, I know not what to do with him. – Travel, quoth a; ay, travel, travel, get thee gone, get thee but far enough, to the Saracens, or the Tartars, or the Turks – for thou art not fit to live in a Christian commonwealth, thou beastly pagan.

Sir Wil. Turks, no; no Turks, Aunt: your Turks are infidels, and believe not in the grape. Your Mahometan, your Mussulman is a dry stinkard – no offence,

aunt. My map says that your Turk is not so honest a
man as your Christian – I cannot find by the map
that your Mufti is orthodox – whereby it is a plain
case, that orthodox is a hard word, aunt, and (*hiccup*)
Greek for claret.

Sings

To drink is a Christian diversion.
Unknown to the Turk or the Persian:
    Let Mahometan fools
    Live by heathenish rules,
And be damn'd over tea-cups and coffee.
    But let British lads sing,
    Crown a health to the King,
And a fig for your Sultan and Sophy.

Ah, Tony!   [*Foible whispers Lady W.*

Lady. Sir Rowland impatient? Good lack! what shall I
do with this beastly tumbril? – Go lie down and
sleep, you sot – or as I'm a person, I'll have you
bastinadoed with broomsticks. Call up the wenches
with broomsticks.

Sir Wil. Ahay? Wenches, where are the wenches?

Lady. Dear Cousin Witwoud, get him away, and you will
bind me to you inviolably. I have an affair of moment
that invades me with some precipitation – you will
oblige me to all futurity.

Wit. Come, Knight. – Pox on him, I don't know what to
say to him – will you go to a cock-match?

Sir Wil. With a wench, Tony? Is she a shakebag, sirrah?
Let me bite your cheek for that.

Wit. Horrible! He has a breath like a bagpipe. – Ay, ay,
come will you march, my Salopian?

Sir Wil. Lead on, little Tony – I'll follow thee my
Anthony, my Tantony. Sirrah, thou shalt be my
Tantony, and I'll be thy Pig.

    – And a Fig for your Sultan and Sophy.

Lady. This will never do. It will never make a match. –
At least before he has been abroad.

ACT IV, SCENE 12

LADY WISHFORT, WAITWELL *disguised as for*
SIR ROWLAND

Lady. Dear Sir Rowland, I am confounded with confusion at the retrospection of my own rudeness, – I
have more pardons to ask than the Pope distributes in
the Year of Jubilee. But I hope where there is likely
to be so near an alliance, – we may unbend the
severity of decorum – and dispense with a little
ceremony.

Wait. My impatience, madam, is the effect of my trans-
port; – and till I have the possession of your adorable
person, I am tantalized on the rack; and do but hang,
madam, on the tenter of expectation.

Lady. You have excess of gallantry, Sir Rowland; and
press things to a conclusion, with a most prevailing
vehemence. – But a day or two for decency of marriage. –

Wait. For decency of funeral, madam. The delay will
break my heart – or if that should fail, I shall be
poisoned. My nephew will get an inkling of my
designs, and poison me – and I would willingly starve
him before I die – I would gladly go out of the world
with that satisfaction. – That would be some comfort
to me, if I could but live so long as to be revenged on
that unnatural viper.

Lady. Is he so unnatural, say you? Truly I would contribute much both to the saving of your life, and the
accomplishment of your revenge – not that I respect
myself; though he has been a perfidious wretch to
me.

Wait. Perfidious to you!

Lady. O Sir Rowland, the hours that he has died away
at my feet, the tears that he has shed, the oaths that
he has sworn, the palpitations that he has felt, the
trances and the tremblings, the ardours and the

ecstasies, the kneelings, and the risings, the heart-
heavings and the hand-grippings, the pangs and the
pathetic regards of his protesting eyes! Oh no memory
can register.

Wait. What, my rival! Is the rebel my rival? a'dies.

Lady. No, don't kill him at once, Sir Rowland, starve
him gradually inch by inch.

Wait. I'll do 't. In three weeks he shall be barefoot; in a
month out at knees with begging an alms, – he shall
starve upward and upward, till he has nothing living
but his head, and then go out in a stink like a candle's
end upon a saveall.

Lady. Well, Sir Rowland, you have the way – you are
no novice in the labyrinth of love – you have the clue.
– But as I am a person, Sir Rowland, you must not
attribute my yielding to any sinister appetite, or in-
digestion of widowhood; nor impute my complacency
to any lethargy of continence – I hope you do not
think me prone to any iteration of nuptials. –

Wait. Far be it from me –

Lady. If you do, I protest I must recede – or think that I
have made a prostitution of decorums, but in the
vehemence of compassion, and to save the life of a
person of so much importance –

Wait. I esteem it so –

Lady. Or else you wrong my condescension –

Wait. I do not, I do not –

Lady. Indeed you do.

Wait. I do not, fair shrine of virtue.

Lady. If you think the least scruple of carnality was an
ingredient –

Wait. Dear madam, no. You are all camphire and
frankincense, all chastity and odour.

Lady. Or that –

ACT IV, SCENE 13

[*To them*] FOIBLE

Foib. Madam, the dancers are ready, and there's one
with a letter, who must deliver it into your own
hands.

Lady. Sir Rowland, will you give me leave? Think
favourably, judge candidly, and conclude you have
found a person who would suffer racks in honour's
cause, dear Sir Rowland, and will wait on you
incessantly.

——

ACT IV, SCENE 14

WAITWELL, FOIBLE

Wait. Fie, fie! – What a slavery have I undergone;
spouse, hast thou any cordial, I want spirits.

Foib. What a washy rogue art thou, to pant thus for a
quarter of an hour's lying and swearing to a fine lady?

Wait. O, she is the antidote to desire. Spouse, thou wilt
fare the worse for 't – I shall have no appetite to iteration of nuptials – this eight and forty hours. – By this
hand I'd rather be a chairman in the dog-days – than
act Sir Rowland till this time tomorrow.

——

ACT IV, SCENE 15

[*To them*] LADY *with a letter*

Lady. Call in the dancers; Sir Rowland, we'll sit, if you
please, and see the entertainment.   [*Dance.*
Now with your permission, Sir Rowland, I will peruse
my letter – I would open it in your presence, because
I would not make you uneasy. If it should make
you uneasy I would burn it – speak if it does – but

you may see, the superscription is like a woman's
hand.

Foib. By Heaven! Mrs Marwood's, I know it, – my
heart aches – get it from her –   [*To him.*

Wait. A woman's hand? No, madam, that's no woman's
hand, I see that already. That's somebody whose
throat must be cut.

Lady. Nay, Sir Rowland, since you give me a proof of
your passion by your jealousy, I promise you I'll make
a return, by a frank communication – You shall see it –
we'll open it together – look you here.

[*Reads*]. – *Madam, though unknown to you* [Look you
there, 'tis from nobody that I know] – *I have that
honour for your character, that I think myself obliged to let
you know you are abused. He who pretends to be Sir Rowland
is a cheat and a rascal* –

Oh Heavens! what's this?

Foib. Unfortunate, all's ruined.

Wait. How, how, let me see, let me see – [*reading*], *a
rascal and disguised, and suborned for that imposture,* – O
villainy! O villainy! – *by the contrivance of* –

Lady. I shall faint, I shall die, oh!

Foib. Say, 'tis your nephew's hand. – Quickly, his plot,
swear, swear it. –   [*To him.*

Wait. Here's a villain! Madam, don't you perceive it,
don't you see it?

Lady. Too well, too well. I have seen too much.

Wait. I told you at first, I knew the hand – a woman's
hand? The rascal writes a sort of a large hand; your
Roman hand – I saw there was a throat to be cut
presently. If he were my son, as he is my nephew,
I'd pistol him –

Foib. O treachery! But are you sure, Sir Rowland, it is
his writing?

Wait. Sure? Am I here? Do I live? Do I love this pearl
of India? I have twenty letters in my pocket from him,
in the same character.

Lady. How!

Foib. O what luck it is, Sir Rowland, that you were present at this juncture! This was the business that brought Mr Mirabell disguised to Madam Millamant this afternoon. I thought something was contriving, when he stole by me and would have hid his face.

Lady. How, how! – I heard the villain was in the house indeed; and now I remember, my niece went away abruptly, when Sir Wilfull was to have made his addresses.

Foib. Then, then madam, Mr Mirabell waited for her in her chamber; but I would not tell your ladyship to discompose you when you were to receive Sir Rowland.

Wait. Enough, his date is short.

Foib. No, good Sir Rowland, don't incur the law.

Wait. Law! I care not for law. I can but die, and 'tis in a good cause. – My lady shall be satisfied of my truth and innocence, though it cost me my life.

Lady. No, dear Sir Rowland, don't fight, if you should be killed I must never show my face; or hanged, – O consider my reputation, Sir Rowland. – No you shan't fight, – I'll go and examine my niece; I'll make her confess. I conjure you Sir Rowland, by all your love not to fight.

Wait. I am charmed madam, I obey. But some proof you must let me give you; – I'll go for a black box, which contains the writings of my whole estate, and deliver that into your hands.

Lady. Ay dear Sir Rowland, that will be some comfort, bring the black box.

Wait. And may I presume to bring a contract to be signed this night? May I hope so far?

Lady. Bring what you will; but come alive, pray come alive. O this is a happy discovery.

Wait. Dead or alive I'll come – and married we will be in spite of treachery; ay, and get an heir that shall defeat the last remaining glimpse of hope in my abandoned nephew. Come, my buxom widow:

E'er long you shall substantial proof receive
That I'm an arrant knight –

Foib. Or arrant knave.

End of the Fourth Act.

ACT V, SCENE 1

Scene continues

LADY WISHFORT *and* FOIBLE

Lady. Out of my house, out of my house, thou viper, thou serpent, that I have fostered; thou bosom traitress, that I raised from nothing – Begone, begone, begone, go, go, – that I took from washing of old gauze and weaving of dead hair, with a bleak blue nose, over a chafing-dish of starved embers, and dining behind a traverse rag, in a shop no bigger than a bird-cage, – go, go, starve again, do, do.

Foib. Dear madam, I'll beg pardon on my knees.

Lady. Away, out, out, go set up for yourself again – do, drive a trade, do, with your threepenny-worth of small ware, flaunting upon a packthread, under a brandy-seller's bulk, or against a dead wall by a ballad-monger. Go, hand out an old frisoneer-gorget, with a yard of yellow colberteen again; do; an old gnawed mask, two rows of pins and a child's fiddle; a glass necklace with the beads broken, and a quilted night-cap with one ear. Go, go, drive a trade. – These were your commodities, you treacherous trull, this was the merchandise you dealt in, when I took you into my house, placed you next myself, and made you gover-nante of my whole family. You have forgot this, have you, now you have feathered your nest?

Foib. No, no, dear madam. Do but hear me, have but a moment's patience – I'll confess all. Mr Mirabell seduced me; I am not the first that he has wheedled with his dissembling tongue; your ladyship's own wisdom has been deluded by him, then how should I, a poor ignorant, defend myself? O madam, if you knew but what he promised me, and how he assured me your ladyship should come to no damage – or else the wealth of the Indies should not have bribed

me to conspire against so good, so sweet, so kind a
lady as you have been to me.

Lady. No damage? What, to betray me, to marry me to
a cast serving-man; to make me a receptacle, an
hospital for a decayed pimp? No damage? O thou
frontless impudence, more than a big-bellied actress.

Foib. Pray do but hear me madam, he could not marry
your ladyship, madam. – No indeed, his marriage was
to have been void in law; for he was married to me
first, to secure your ladyship. He could not have
bedded your ladyship; for if he had consummated
with your ladyship, he must have run the risk of the
law, and been put upon his clergy. – Yes indeed, I
enquired of the law in that case before I would meddle
or make.

Lady. What, then I have been your property, have I?
I have been convenient to you, it seems, – while you
were catering for Mirabell; I have been broker for
you? What, have you made a passive bawd of me? –
This exceeds all precedent; I am brought to fine uses,
to become a botcher of second-hand marriages between Abigails and Andrews! I'll couple you. Yes,
I'll baste you together, you and your Philander, I'll
Duke's Place you, as I'm a person. Your turtle is in
custody already: you shall coo in the same cage, if
there be constable or warrant in the parish.

Foib. O that ever I was born, O that I was ever married,
– a bride, ay I shall be a Bridewell-bride. Oh!

ACT V, SCENE 2

Mrs Fainall, Foible

Mrs Fain. Poor Foible, what's the matter?

Foib. O madam, my lady's gone for a constable; I shall
be had to a justice, and put to Bridewell to beat hemp;
poor Waitwell's gone to prison already.

Mrs Fain. Have a good heart. Foible, Mirabell's gone to give security for him. This is all Marwood's and my husband's doing.

Foib. Yes, yes, I know it, madam; she was in my lady's closet, and overheard all that you said to me before dinner. She sent the letter to my lady; and that missing effect, Mr Fainall laid this plot to arrest Waitwell, when he pretended to go for the papers; and in the meantime Mrs Marwood declared all to my lady.

Mrs Fain. Was there no mention made of me in the letter? – My mother does not suspect my being in the confederacy? I fancy Marwood has not told her, though she has told my husband.

Foib. Yes, madam; but my lady did not see that part: we stifled the letter before she read so far. Has that mischievous devil told Mr Fainall of your ladyship then?

Mrs Fain. Ay, all's out, my affair with Mirabell, everything discovered. This is the last day of our living together, that's my comfort.

Foib. Indeed madam, and so 'tis a comfort if you knew all, – he has been even with your ladyship; which I could have told you long enough since, but I love to keep peace and quietness by my good will: I had rather bring friends together, than set 'em at distance. But Mrs Marwood and he are nearer related than ever their parents thought for.

Mrs Fain. Say'st thou so, Foible? Canst thou prove this?

Foib. I can take my oath of it, madam, so can Mrs Mincing; we have had many a fair word from Madam Marwood, to conceal something that passed in our chamber one evening when you were at Hyde Park; – and we were thought to have gone a-walking: but we went up unawares, – though we were sworn to secrecy too; Madam Marwood took a book and swore us upon it: but it was but a book of poems – so long as it was not a Bible-oath, we may break it with a safe conscience.

Mrs Fain. This discovery is the most opportune thing I could wish. Now Mincing?

──

ACT V, SCENE 3
[*To them*] MINCING

Minc. My lady would speak with Mrs Foible, mem. Mr Mirabell is with her; he has set your spouse at liberty, Mrs Foible, and would have you hide yourself in my lady's closet, till my old lady's anger is abated. O, my old lady is in a perilous passion, at something Mr Fainall has said; he swears, and my old lady cries. There's a fearful hurricane I vow. He says, mem, how that he'll have my lady's fortune made over to him, or he'll be divorced.

Mrs Fain. Does your lady or Mirabell know that?

Minc. Yes, mem, they have sent me to see if Sir Wilfull be sober, and to bring him to them. My lady is resolved to have him I think, rather than lose such a vast sum as six thousand pound. O, come Mrs Foible, I hear my old lady.

Mrs Fain. Foible, you must tell Mincing that she must prepare to vouch when I call her.

Foib. Yes, yes, madam.

Minc. O yes mem, I'll vouch anything for your ladyship's service, be what it will.

──

ACT V, SCENE 4
MRS FAINALL, LADY WISHFORT, MRS MARWOOD

Lady. O my dear friend, how can I enumerate the benefits that I have received from your goodness? To you I owe the timely discovery of the false vows of Mirabell; to you I owe the detection of the impostor Sir Rowland. And now you are become an intercessor with my son-in-law, to save the honour of my house, and compound for the frailties of my daughter. Well friend, you are enough to reconcile me to the bad world, or else I would retire to deserts and solitudes; and feed harmless sheep by groves and purling streams. Dear Marwood, let us leave the world, and retire by ourselves and be shepherdesses.

Mrs Mar. Let us first dispatch the affair in hand, madam. We shall have leisure to think of retirement afterwards. Here is one who is concerned in the treaty.

Lady. O daughter, daughter, is it possible thou shouldst be my child, bone of my bone, and flesh of my flesh, and as I may say, another me, and yet transgress the most minute particle of severe virtue? Is it possible you should lean aside to iniquity, who have been cast in the direct mould of virtue? I have not only been a mould but a pattern for you, and a model for you, after you were brought into the world.

Mrs Fain. I don't understand your ladyship.

Lady. Not understand? Why, have you not been naught? Have you not been sophisticated? Not understand? Here I am ruined to compound for your caprices and your cuckoldoms. I must pawn my plate and my jewels, and ruin my niece, and all little enough –

Mrs Fain. I am wronged and abused, and so are you. 'Tis a false accusation, as false as hell, as false as your friend there, ay or your friend's friend, my false husband.

Mrs Mar. My friend, Mrs Fainall? Your husband my friend, what do you mean?

Mrs Fain. I know what I mean, madam, and so do you; and so shall the world at a time convenient.

Mrs Mar. I am sorry to see you so passionate, madam. More temper would look more like innocence. But I have done. I am sorry my zeal to serve your ladyship and family, should admit of misconstruction, or make me liable to affront. You will pardon me, madam, if

I meddle no more with an affair, in which I am not
personally concerned.

Lady. O dear friend, I am so ashamed that you should
meet with such returns; – you ought to ask pardon on
your knees, ungrateful creature; she deserves more
from you, than all your life can accomplish – O don't
leave me destitute in this perplexity; – no, stick to me,
my good genius.

Mrs Fain. I tell you, madam, you're abused. – Stick to
you? Ay, like a leech, to suck your best blood – she'll
drop off when she's full. Madam, you shan't pawn a
bodkin, nor part with a brass counter, in composition
for me. I defy 'em all. Let 'em prove their aspersions:
I know my own innocence, and dare stand a trial.

ACT V, SCENE 5
LADY WISHFORT, MRS MARWOOD

Lady. Why, if she should be innocent, if she should be
wronged after all, ha? I don't know what to think,
and I promise you, her education has been unex-
ceptionable – I may say it; for I chiefly made it my
own care to initiate her very infancy in the rudiments
of virtue, and to impress upon her tender years a
young odium and aversion to the very sight of men. –
Ay friend, she would have shrieked if she had but seen
a man, till she was in her teens. As I'm a person 'tis
true – she was never suffer'd to play with a male child,
though but in coats; nay, her very babies were of the
feminine gender – O, she never looked a man in the
face but her own father, or the chaplain, and him we
made a shift to put upon her for a woman, by the help
of his long garments, and his sleek face; till she was
going in her fifteen.

Mrs Mar. 'Twas much she should be deceived so long.

Lady. I warrant you, or she would never have borne to

have been catechized by him; and have heard his long
lectures against singing and dancing, and such de-
baucheries; and going to filthy plays; and profane
music-meetings, where the lewd trebles squeak nothing
but bawdy, and the basses roar blasphemy. O, she
would have swooned at the sight or name of an
obscene play book – and can I think after all this, that
my daughter can be naught? What, a whore? And
thought it excommunication to set her foot within the
door of a playhouse. O dear friend, I can't believe it,
no, no; as she says, let him prove it, let him prove
it.

Mrs Mar. Prove it, madam? What, and have your
name prostituted in a public court; yours and your
daughter's reputation worried at the bar by a pack
of bawling lawyers? To be ushered in with an *O Yes*
of scandal; and have your case opened by an old
fumbler lecher in a coif like a man midwife, to bring
your daughter's infamy to light; to be a theme for
legal punsters, and quibblers by the statute; and become a jest, against a rule of court, where there is no
precedent for a jest in any record; not even in Domes-
day-book: to discompose the gravity of the bench, and
provoke naughty interrogatories in more naughty Law
Latin; while the good judge, tickled with the pro-
ceeding, simpers under a grey beard, and fidgets off
and on his cushion as if he had swallowed cantharides,
or sate upon cow-itch.

Lady. O, 'tis very hard!

Mrs Mar. And then to have my young revellers of the
Temple take notes, like prentices at a conventicle;
and after talk it over again in Commons, or before
drawers in an eating-house.

Lady. Worse and worse.

Mrs Mar. Nay, this is nothing; if it would end here,
'twere well. But it must after this be consigned by the
shorthand writers to the public press; and from thence

be transferred to the hands, nay into the throats and
lungs of hawkers, with voices more licentious than the
loud flounderman's: and this you must hear till you are
stunned; nay, you must hear nothing else for some
days.

Lady. O, 'tis insupportable. No, no, dear friend, make it
up, make it up; ay, ay, I'll compound. I'll give up all,
myself and my all, my niece and her all – anything,
everything for composition.

Mrs Mar. Nay, madam, I advise nothing, I only lay before you, as a friend, the inconveniences which perhaps you have overseen. Here comes Mr Fainall, if he
will be satisfied to huddle up all in silence, I shall be
glad. You must think I would rather congratulate than
condole with you.

─

ACT V, SCENE 6

Fainall, Lady Wishfort, Mrs Marwood

Lady. Ay, ay, I do not doubt it, dear Marwood: no, no,
I do not doubt it.

Fain. Well, madam; I have suffered myself to be overcome by the importunity of this lady your friend; and
am content you shall enjoy your own proper estate
during life; on condition you oblige yourself never to
marry, under such penalty as I think convenient.

Lady. Never to marry?

Fain. No more Sir Rowlands, – the next imposture may
not be so timely detected.

Mrs Mar. That condition, I dare answer, my lady will
consent to, without difficulty; she has already but too
much experienced the perfidiousness of men. Besides,
madam, when we retire to our pastoral solitude we
shall bid adieu to all other thoughts.

Lady. Ay, that's true; but in case of necessity; as of
health, or some such emergency –

Fain. O, if you are prescribed marriage, you shall be considered; I will only reserve to myself the power to choose for you. If your physic be wholesome, it matters not who is your apothecary. Next, my wife shall settle on me the remainder of her fortune, not made over already; and for her maintenance depend entirely on my discretion.

Lady. This is most inhumanly savage; exceeding the barbarity of a Muscovite husband.

Fain. I learned it from his Czarish Majesty's retinue, in a winter evening's conference over brandy and pepper, amongst other secrets of matrimony and policy, as they are at present practised in the northern hemisphere. But this must be agreed unto, and that positively. Lastly, I will be endowed, in right of my wife, with that six thousand pound, which is the moiety of Mrs Millamant's fortune in your possession; and which she has forfeited (as will appear by the last will and testament of your deceased husband, Sir Jonathan Wishfort) by her disobedience in contracting herself against your consent or knowledge; and by refusing the offered match with Sir Wilfull Witwoud, which you, like a careful aunt, had provided for her.

Lady. My nephew was *non compos*; and could not make his addresses.

Fain. I come to make demands – I'll hear no objections.

Lady. You will grant me time to consider?

Fain. Yes, while the instrument is drawing, to which you must set your hand till more sufficient deeds can be perfected: which I will take care shall be done with all possible speed. In the meanwhile I will go for the said instrument, and till my return you may balance this matter in your own discretion.

ACT V, SCENE 7

Lady Wishfort, Mrs Marwood

Lady. This insolence is beyond all precedent, all parallel; must I be subject to this merciless villain?

Mrs Mar. 'Tis severe indeed, madam, that you should smart for your daughter's wantonness.

Lady. 'Twas against my consent that she married this barbarian, but she would have him, though her year was not out. – Ah! her first husband, my son Languish, would not have carried it thus. Well, that was my choice, this is hers; she is matched now with a witness – I shall be mad, dear friend, is there no comfort for me? Must I live to be confiscated at this rebel-rate? – Here come two more of my Egyptian plagues too.

ACT V, SCENE 8

[*To them*] Mrs Millamant, Sir Wilfull

Sir Wil. Aunt, your servant.

Lady. Out caterpillar, call not me aunt; I know thee not.

Sir Wil. I confess I have been a little in disguise, as they say – 'Sheart! and I'm sorry for 't. What would you have? I hope I committed no offence, aunt – and if I did I am willing to make satisfaction; and what can a man say fairer? If I have broke anything I'll pay for 't, an it cost a pound. And so let that content for what's past, and make no more words. For what's to come, to pleasure you I'm willing to marry my cousin. So pray let's all be friends, she and I are agreed upon the matter before a witness.

Lady. How's this, dear niece? Have I any comfort? Can this be true?

Milla. I am content to be a sacrifice to your repose, madam; and to convince you that I had no hand in

the plot, as you were misinformed, I have laid my
commands on Mirabell to come in person, and be a
witness that I give my hand to this flower of knighthood; and for the contract that passed between Mirabell and me, I have obliged him to make a resignation
of it in your ladyship's presence; – he is without, and
waits your leave for admittance.

Lady. Well, I'll swear I am something revived at this
testimony of your obedience; but I cannot admit that
traitor, – I fear I cannot fortify myself to support his
appearance. He is as terrible to me as a Gorgon; if I
see him I fear I shall turn to stone, petrify instantly.

Milla. If you disoblige him he may resent your refusal,
and insist upon the contract still. Then 'tis the last time
he will be offensive to you.

Lady. Are you sure it will be the last time? – If I were
sure of that – shall I never see him again?

Milla. Sir Wilfull, you and he are to travel together, are
you not?

Sir Wil. 'Sheart the gentleman's a civil gentleman, aunt,
let him come in; why we are sworn brothers and
fellow-travellers. – We are to be Pylades and Orestes,
he and I – he is to be my interpreter in foreign parts.
He has been overseas once already; and with proviso
that I marry my cousin, will cross 'em once again, only
to bear me company. – 'Sheart, I'll call him in, – an
I set on 't once, he shall come in; and see who 'll hinder
him.   [*Goes to the door and hems.*

Mrs Mar. This is precious fooling, if it would pass; but
I'll know the bottom of it.

Lady. O dear Marwood, you are not going?

Mar. Not far, madam; I'll return immediately.

Lady Wishfort, Mrs Millamant,
Sir Wilfull, Mirabell

Sir Wil. Look up, man, I'll stand by you, 'sbud an she
  do frown, she can't kill you; – besides – harkee she dare
  not frown desperately, because her face is none of her
  own; 'sheart, and she should, her forehead would
  wrinkle like the coat of a cream cheese; but mum for
  that, fellow-traveller.

Mira. If a deep sense of the many injuries I have offered
  to so good a lady, with a sincere remorse, and a hearty
  contrition, can but obtain the least glance of compassion, I am too happy. – Ah madam, there was a
  time – but let it be forgotten – I confess I have
  deservedly forfeited the high place I once held, of
  sighing at your feet; nay, kill me not by turning from
  me in disdain – I come not to plead for favour; – nay
  not for pardon; I am a suppliant only for pity – I am
  going where I never shall behold you more –

Sir Wil. How, fellow-traveller! – you shall go by yourself
  then.

Mira. Let me be pitied first; and afterwards forgotten –
  I ask no more.

Sir Wil. By'r Lady, a very reasonable request, and will
  cost you nothing, aunt – come, come, forgive and forget, aunt, why you must, an you are a Christian.

Mira. Consider madam, in reality you could not receive
  much prejudice; it was an innocent device: though I
  confess it had a face of guiltiness, – it was at most an
  artifice which love contrived – and errors which love
  produces have ever been accounted venial. At least
  think it is punishment enough, that I have lost what in
  my heart I hold most dear, that to your cruel indignation, I have offered up this beauty, and with her my
  peace and quiet; nay, all my hopes of future comfort.

Sir Wil. An he does not move me, would I may never be o' the Quorum, – an it were not as good a deed as to drink, to give her to him again, – I would I might never take shipping – Aunt, if you don't forgive quickly I shall melt, I can tell you that. My contract went no farther than a little mouth-glue, and that's hardly dry; one doleful sigh more from my fellow-traveller and 'tis dissolved.

Lady. Well nephew, upon your account – ah, he has a false insinuating tongue. – Well sir, I will stifle my just resentment at my nephew's request. – I will endeavour what I can to forget, – but on proviso that you resign the contract with my niece immediately.

Mira. It is in writing and with papers of concern; but I have sent my servant for it, and will deliver it to you, with all acknowledgements for your transcendent goodness.

Lady. Oh, he has witchcraft in his eyes and tongue; – when I did not see him I could have bribed a villain to his assassination; but his appearance rakes the embers which have so long lain smothered in my breast. –   [*Aside.*

———

ACT V, SCENE 10

[*To them*] FAINALL, MRS MARWOOD

Fain. Your date of deliberation, madam, is expired. Here is the instrument. Are you prepared to sign?

Lady. If I were prepared, I am not empowered. My niece exerts a lawful claim, having matched herself by my direction to Sir Wilfull.

Fain. That sham is too gross to pass on me – though 'tis imposed on you, madam.

Milla. Sir, I have given my consent.

Mira. And, sir, I have resigned my pretensions.

Sir Wil. And, sir, I assert my right; and will maintain it in defiance of you, sir, and of your instrument. 'Sheart

an you talk of an instrument sir, I have an old fox by
my thigh shall hack your instrument of ram vellum to
shreds, sir. It shall not be sufficient for a Mittimus or a
tailor's measure; therefore withdraw your instrument
sir, or by 'r Lady I shall draw mine.

Lady. Hold, nephew, hold.

Milla. Good Sir Wilfull, respite your valour.

Fain. Indeed? Are you provided of your guard, with
your single beef-eater there? But I'm prepared for you;
and insist upon my first proposal. You shall submit
your own estate to my management, and absolutely
make over my wife's to my sole use; as pursuant to the
purport and tenor of this other covenant. – I suppose,
madam, your consent is not requisite in this case; nor,
Mr Mirabell, your resignation; nor, Sir Wilfull, your
right. – You may draw your fox if you please sir, and
make a bear-garden flourish somewhere else: for here
it will not avail. This, my Lady Wishfort, must be
subscribed, or your darling daughter's turned adrift,
like a leaky hulk to sink or swim, as she and the current
of this lewd town can agree.

Lady. Is there no means, no remedy, to stop my ruin?
Ungrateful wretch! dost thou not owe thy being, thy
subsistence to my daughter's fortune?

Fain. I'll answer you when I have the rest of it in my
possession.

Mira. But that you would not accept of a remedy from
my hands – I own I have not deserved you should owe
any obligation to me; or else perhaps I could advise, –

Lady. O what? what? to save me and my child from ruin,
from want, I'll forgive all that's past; nay, I'll consent
to anything to come, to be delivered from this tyranny.

Mira. Ay madam; but that is too late, my reward is
intercepted. You have disposed of her, who only could
have made me a compensation for all my services; –
but be it as it may, I am resolved I 'll serve you, you
shall not be wronged in this savage manner.

Lady. How! Dear Mr Mirabell, can you be so generous at last! But it is not possible. Harkee, I'll break my nephew's match, you shall have my niece yet, and all her fortune; if you can but save me from this imminent danger.

Mira. Will you? I take you at your word. I ask no more. I must have leave for two criminals to appear.

Lady. Ay, ay, anybody, anybody.

Mira. Foible is one, and a penitent.

———

ACT V, SCENE 11

[*To them*] MRS FAINALL, FOIBLE, MINCING

Mrs Mar. O my shame! these corrupt things are brought hither to expose me.

       [*Mira. and Lady go to Mrs Fain. and Foib.*

Fain. If it must all come out, why let 'em know it, it's but the Way of the World. That shall not urge me to relinquish or abate one tittle of my terms, no, I will insist the more.

Foib. Yes indeed, madam, I'll take my Bible-oath of it.

Minc. And so will I, mem.

Lady. O Marwood, Marwood, art thou false? my friend deceive me? Hast thou been a wicked accomplice with that profligate man?

Mrs Mar. Have you so much ingratitude and injustice, to give credit against your friend, to the aspersions of two such mercenary trulls?

Minc. Mercenary, mem? I scorn your words. 'Tis true we found you and Mr Fainall in the blue garret; by the same token, you swore us to secrecy upon Messalinas's poems. Mercenary? No, if we would have been mercenary, we should have held our tongues; you would have bribed us sufficiently.

Fain. Go, you are an insignificant thing. – Well, what are you the better for this! Is this Mr Mirabell's

expedient? I'll be put off no longer – You, thing, that
was a wife, shall smart for this. I will not leave thee
wherewithal to hide thy shame: your body shall be
naked as your reputation.

Mrs Fain. I despise you, and defy your malice. – You
have aspersed me wrongfully – I have proved your
falsehood. – Go you and your treacherous – I will not
name it, but starve together – perish.

Fain. Not while you are worth a groat, indeed my dear.
Madam, I'll be fooled no longer.

Lady. Ah Mr Mirabell, this is small comfort, the detection
of this affair.

Mira. O in good time. – Your leave for the other offender
and penitent to appear, madam.

ACT V, SCENE 12

[To them] WAITWELL *with a box of writings*

Lady. O Sir Rowland – well, rascal.

Wait. What your ladyship pleases – I have brought the
black box at last, madam.

Mira. Give it me. Madam, you remember your promise.

Lady. Ay, dear sir.

Mira. Where are the gentlemen?

Wait. At hand sir, rubbing their eyes, – just risen from
sleep.

Fain. S'death what's this to me? I'll not wait your private
concerns.

ACT V, SCENE 13

[To them] PETULANT, WITWOUD

Pet. How now? what's the matter? whose hand's out?

Wit. Hey-day! what, are you all got together, like
players at the end of the last act?

Mira. You may remember, gentlemen, I once requested
your hands as witnesses to a certain parchment.

Wit. Ay I do, my hand I remember – Petulant set his
mark.

Mira. You wrong him, his name is fairly written, as shall
appear. – You do not remember, gentlemen, anything
of what that parchment contained –? [*Undoing the box.*

Wit. No.

Pet. Not I. I writ, I read nothing.

Mira. Very well, now you shall know. – Madam your
promise.

Lady. Ay, ay, sir, upon my honour.

Mira. Mr Fainall, it is now time that you should know,
that your lady, while she was at her own disposal, and
before you had by your insinuations wheedled her out
of a pretended settlement of the greatest part of her
fortune –

Fain. Sir! pretended!

Mira. Yes, sir. I say that this lady while a widow, having,
it seems, received some cautions respecting your inconstancy and tyranny of temper, which from her own
partial opinion and fondness of you she could never
have suspected – she did, I say, by the wholesome
advice of friends and of sages learned in the laws of
this land, deliver this same as her act and deed to me
in trust, and to the uses within mentioned. You may
read if you please – [*Holding out the parchment*] though
perhaps what is written on the back may serve your
occasions.

Fain. Very likely, Sir. What's here? Damnation?
[*Reads*] A Deed of Conveyance of the whole Estate real
of Arabella Languish, Widow, in Trust to Edward
Mirabell.
Confusion!

Mira. Even so, sir, 'tis the Way of the World, sir; of the
widows of the world. I suppose this deed may bear an
elder date than what you have obtained from your lady.

Fain. Perfidious fiend! then thus I'll be revenged –

         [*Offers to run at Mrs Fain.*

Sir Wil. Hold, Sir, now you may make your bear-garden
flourish somewhere else, Sir.

Fain. Mirabell, you shall hear of this, sir, be sure you
shall. – Let me pass, oaf.

Mrs Fain. Madam, you seem to stifle your resentment:
you had better give it vent.

Mrs Mar. Yes, it shall have vent – and to your confusion,
or I'll perish in the attempt.

———

ACT V, SCENE THE LAST [14]

LADY WISHFORT, MRS MILLAMONT, MIRABELL,
MRS FAINALL, SIR WILFULL, PETULANT,
WITWOUD, FOIBLE, MINCING, WAITWELL

Lady. O daughter, daughter, 'tis plain thou hast inherited
thy mother's prudence.

Mrs Fain. Thank Mr Mirabell, a cautious friend, to
whose advice all is owing.

Lady. Well Mr Mirabell, you have kept your promise –
and I must perform mine. – First I pardon for your
sake Sir Rowland there and Foible. – The next thing
is to break the matter to my nephew – and how to do
that –

Mira. For that, madam, give yourself no trouble, – let
me have your consent – Sir Wilfull is my friend; he
has had compassion upon lovers, and generously
engaged a volunteer in this action, for our service; and
now designs to prosecute his travels.

Sir Wil. 'Sheart, aunt, I have no mind to marry. My
cousin 's a fine lady, and the gentleman loves her, and
she loves him, and they deserve one another; my resolution is to see foreign parts – I have set on 't – and
when I'm set on 't, I must do 't. And if these two gentlemen would travel too, I think they may be spared.

Pet. For my part, I say little – I think things are best off or on.

Wit. Egad I understand nothing of the matter, – I'm in a maze yet, like a dog in a dancing-school.

Lady. Well, sir, take her, and with her all the joy I can give you.

Milla. Why does not the man take me? Would you have me give myself to you over again?

Mira. Ay, and over and over again; [*Kisses her hand.* I would have you as often as possibly I can. Well, heaven grant I love you not too well, that's all my fear.

Sir Wil. 'Sheart you'll have time enough to toy after you're married; or if you will toy now, let us have a dance in the meantime; that we who are not lovers may have some other emp'oyment, besides looking on.

Mira. With all my heart, dear Sir Wilfull. What shall we do for music?

Foib. O sir, some that were provided for Sir Rowland's entertainment are yet within call.   [*A Dance.*

Lady. As I am a person I can hold out no longer; – I have wasted my spirits so today already, that I am ready to sink under the fatigue; and I cannot but have some fears upon me yet, that my son Fainall will pursue some desperate course.

Mira. Madam, disquiet not yourself on that account; to my knowledge his circumstances are such, he must of force comply. For my part I will contribute all that in me lies to a reunion: in the meantime, madam [*To Mrs Fain.*], let me before these witnesses restore to you this deed of trust; it may be a means, well managed, to make you live easily together.

> From hence let those be warn'd, who mean to wed;
> Lest mutual falsehood stain the bridal-bed:
> For each deceiver to his cost may find,
> That marriage frauds too oft are paid in kind.
>   [*Exeunt Omnes.*

EPILOGUE

AFTER our Epilogue this crowd dismisses,
I'm thinking how this play'll be pull'd to pieces.
But pray consider, ere you doom its fall,
How hard a thing t'would be, to please you all.
There are some critics so with spleen diseas'd,
They scarcely come inclining to be pleas'd:
And sure he must have more than mortal skill,
Who pleases any one against his will.
Then, all bad poets we are sure are foes,
And how their number's swell'd the town well knows:
In shoals, I've mark'd 'em judging in the pit;
Though they're on no pretence for judgement fit,
But that they have been damn'd for want of wit.
Since when, they by their own offences taught,
Set up for spies on plays, and finding fault.
Others there are, whose malice we 'd prevent;
Such, who watch plays, with scurrilous intent
To mark out who by characters are meant.
And though no perfect likeness they can trace,
Yet each pretends to know the copied face.
These, with false glosses feed their own ill-nature,
And turn to libel, what was meant a satire.
May such malicious fops this fortune find,
To think themselves alone the fools design'd:
If any are so arrogantly vain,
To think they singly can support a scene,
And furnish fool enough to entertain.
For well the learn'd and the judicious know,
That satire scorns to stoop so meanly low,
As any one abstracted fop to show.
For, as when painters form a matchless face,
They from each fair one catch some diff'rent grace;

And shining features in one portrait blend,
To which no single beauty must pretend:
So poets oft do in one piece expose
Whole *Belles Assemblées* of coquettes and beaux.

SHE STOOPS TO CONQUER

or, *The Mistakes of a Night*

By OLIVER GOLDSMITH

DRAMATIS PERSONAE

MEN

SIR CHARLES MARLOW

YOUNG MARLOW, *his son*

HARDCASTLE

HASTINGS

TONY LUMPKIN

DIGGORY

WOMEN

MRS HARDCASTLE

MISS HARDCASTLE

MISS NEVILLE

MAID

LANDLORD, SERVANTS, *etc.*

SHE STOOPS TO CONQUER
OR, THE MISTAKES OF A NIGHT

—

PROLOGUE
BY DAVID GARRICK, ESQ.

*Enter Mr Woodward, dressed in black, and holding a
handkerchief to his eyes*

EXCUSE me, sirs, I pray – I can't yet speak –
  I'm crying now – and have been all the week.
"Tis not alone this mourning suit,' good masters;
  'I've that within' – for which there are no plasters!
Pray would you know the reason why I'm crying?
  The comic muse, long sick, is now a-dying!
And if she goes, my tears will never stop;
  For as a player, I can't squeeze out one drop:
I am undone, that's all – shall lose my bread –
  I'd rather, but that's nothing – lose my head.
When the sweet maid is laid upon the bier,
  Shuter and I shall be chief mourners here.
To her a mawkish drab of spurious breed,
  Who deal in Sentimentals will succeed!
Poor Ned and I are dead to all intents;
  We can as soon speak Greek as Sentiments.
Both nervous grown, to keep our spirits up,
  We now and then take down a hearty cup.
What shall we do? – If Comedy forsake us!
  They'll turn us out, and no one else will take us,
But, why can't I be moral? – Let me try –
  My heart thus pressing – fix'd my face and eye –
With a sententious look, that nothing means
  (Faces are blocks, in sentimental scenes),
Thus I begin – 'All is not gold that glitters,
  'Pleasure seems sweet, but proves a glass of bitters.
'When ignorance enters, folly is at hand:

'Learning is better far than house and land.
'Let not your virtue trip, who trips may stumble,
  'And virtue is not virtue, if she tumble.'
I give it up – morals won't do for me;
  To make you laugh, I must play tragedy.
One hope remains – hearing the maid was ill,
  A Doctor comes this night to show his skill.
To cheer her heart, and give your muscles motion,
  He in Five Draughts prepar'd, presents a potion:
A kind of magic charm – for be assur'd,
  If you will swallow it, the maid is cur'd.
But desperate the Doctor, and her case is,
  If you reject the dose, and make wry faces!
This truth he boasts, will boast it while he lives,
  No poisonous drugs are mix'd in what he gives.
Should he succeed, you'll give him his degree;
  If not, within he will receive no fee!
The college You, must his pretensions back,
  Pronounce him Regular, or dub him Quack.

———

ACT I, SCENE 1

A Chamber in an old-fashioned house
Enter MRS HARDCASTLE *and* MR HARDCASTLE

Mrs Hard. I vow, Mr Hardcastle, you're very particular.
Is there a creature in the whole country, but ourselves,
that does not take a trip to town now and then, to rub
off the rust a little? There's the two Miss Hoggs, and
our neighbour, Mrs Grigsby, go to take a month's
polishing every winter.

Hard. Ay, and bring back vanity and affectation to last
them the whole year. I wonder why London cannot
keep its own fools at home. In my time, the follies of
the town crept slowly among us, but now they travel
faster than a stage-coach. Its fopperies come down, not
only as inside passengers, but in the very basket.

Mrs Hard. Ay, your times were fine times, indeed; you have been telling us of them for many a long year. Here we live in an old rambling mansion, that looks for all the world like an inn, but that we never see company. Our best visitors are old Mrs Oddfish, the curate's wife, and little Cripplegate, the lame dancing-master: and all our entertainment your old stories of Prince Eugene and the Duke of Marlborough. I hate such old-fashioned trumpery.

Hard. And I love it. I love everything that's old: old friends, old times, old manners, old books, old wine; and, I believe, Dorothy (*taking her hand*), you'll own I have been pretty fond of an old wife.

Mrs Hard. Lord, Mr Hardcastle, you're for ever at your Dorothys and your old wives. You may be a Darby, but I'll be no Joan, I promise you. I'm not so old as you'd make me, by more than one good year. Add twenty to twenty, and make money of that.

Hard. Let me see; twenty added to twenty makes just fifty and seven.

Mrs Hard. It's false, Mr Hardcastle: I was but twenty when Tony was born, the son of Mr Lumpkin, my first husband; and he's not come to years of discretion yet.

Hard. Nor ever will, I dare answer for him. Ay, you have taught him finely!

Mrs Hard. No matter, Tony Lumpkin has a good fortune. My son is not to live by his learning. I don't think a boy wants much learning to spend fifteen hundred a-year.

Hard. Learning, quotha! a mere composition of tricks and mischief!

Mrs Hard. Humour, my dear: nothing but humour. Come, Mr Hardcastle, you must allow the boy a little humour.

Hard. I'd sooner allow him a horse-pond! If burning the footmen's shoes, frightening the maids, and worrying the kittens be humour, he has it. It was but yesterday he fastened my wig to the back of my chair, and when I went to make a bow, I popt my bald head in Mrs Frizzle's face!

Mrs Hard. And am I to blame? The poor boy was always too sickly to do any good. A school would be his death. When he comes to be a little stronger, who knows what a year or two's Latin may do for him?

Hard. Latin for him! A cat and fiddle! No, no, the alehouse and the stable are the only schools he'll ever go to.

Mrs Hard. Well, we must not snub the poor boy now, for I believe we shan't have him long among us. Anybody that looks in his face may see he's consumptive.

Hard. Ay, if growing too fat be one of the symptoms.

Mrs Hard. He coughs sometimes.

Hard. Yes, when his liquor goes the wrong way.

Mrs Hard. I'm actually afraid of his lungs.

Hard. And truly, so am I; for he sometimes whoops like a speaking-trumpet – (*Tony halloing behind the scenes*) – O, there he goes – a very consumptive figure, truly!

Enter TONY, *crossing the stage.*

Mrs Hard. Tony, where are going, my charmer? Won't you give papa and I a little of your company, lovee?

Tony. I'm in haste, mother; I cannot stay.

Mrs Hard. You shan't venture out this raw evening, my dear; you look most shockingly.

Tony. I can't stay, I tell you. The Three Pigeons expects me down every moment. There's some fun going forward.

Hard. Ay; the alehouse, the old place: I thought so.

Mrs Hard. A low, paltry set of fellows.

Tony. Not so low, neither. There's Dick Muggins the exciseman, Jack Slang the horse doctor, Little Aminadab that grinds the music-box, and Tom Twist that spins the pewter platter.

Mrs Hard. Pray, my dear, disappoint them for one night, at least.

Tony. As for disappointing them I should not so much mind; but I can't abide to disappoint myself!

Mrs Hard. (*Detaining him.*) You shan't go.

Tony. I will, I tell you.

Mrs Hard. I say you shan't.

Tony. We'll see which is strongest, you or I.

[*Exit, hauling her out.*

HARDCASTLE *solus*

Hard. Ay, there goes a pair that only spoil each other. But is not the whole age in a combination to drive sense and discretion out of doors? There's my pretty darling Kate! the fashions of the times have almost infected her too. By living a year or two in town, she's as fond of gauze and French frippery as the best of them.

Enter MISS HARDCASTLE

Hard. Blessings on my pretty innocence! drest out as usual, my Kate. Goodness! What a quantity of superfluous silk hast thou got about thee, girl! I could never teach the fools of this age, that the indigent world could be clothed out of the trimmings of the vain.

Miss Hard. You know our agreement, sir. You allow me the morning to receive and pay visits, and to dress in my own manner; and in the evening I put on my housewife's dress to please you.

Hard. Well, remember, I insist on the terms of our agreement; and, by the by, I believe I shall have occasion to try your obedience this very evening.

Miss Hard. I protest, sir, I don't comprehend your meaning.

Hard. Then, to be plain with you, Kate, I expect the young gentleman I have chosen to be your husband from town this very day. I have his father's letter, in which he informs me his son is set out, and that he intends to follow himself shortly after.

Miss Hard. Indeed! I wish I had known something of this

before. Bless me, how shall I behave? It's a thousand to one I shan't like him; our meeting will be so formal, and so like a thing of business, that I shall find no room for friendship or esteem.

Hard. Depend upon it, child, I never will control your choice; but Mr Marlow, whom I have pitched upon, is the son of my old friend, Sir Charles Marlow, of whom you have heard me talk so often. The young gentleman has been bred a scholar, and is designed for an employment in the service of his country. I am told he's a man of an excellent understanding.

Miss Hard. Is he?

Hard. Very generous.

Miss Hard. I believe I shall like him.

Hard. Young and brave.

Miss Hard. I am sure I shall like him.

Hard. And very handsome.

Miss Hard. My dear papa, say no more (*kissing his hand*). He's mine, I'll have him.

Hard. And, to crown all, Kate, he's one of the most bashful and reserved young fellows in all the world.

Miss Hard. Eh! you have frozen me to death again. That word *reserved* has undone all the rest of his accomplishments. A reserved lover, it is said, always makes a suspicious husband.

Hard. On the contrary, modesty seldom resides in a breast that is not enriched with nobler virtues. It was the very feature in his character that first struck me.

Miss Hard. He must have more striking features to catch me, I promise you. However, if he be so young, so handsome, and so everything as you mention, I believe he'll do still. I think I'll have him.

Hard. Ay, Kate, but there is still an obstacle. It is more than an even wager, he may not have you.

Miss Hard. My dear papa, why will you mortify one so? Well, if he refuses, instead of breaking my heart at his indifference, I'll only break my glass for its flattery,

set my cap to some newer fashion, and look out for
some less difficult admirer.

Hard. Bravely resolved! In the meantime I'll go prepare
the servants for his reception; as we seldom see company, they want as much training as a company of
recruits the first day's muster.   [*Exit.*

Miss Hard. (*Alone.*) Lud, this news of papa's puts me all
in a flutter. Young, handsome; these he put last; but I
put them foremost. Sensible, good-natured; I like all
that. But then reserved, and sheepish, that's much
against him. Yet can't he be cured of his timidity, by
being taught to be proud of his wife? Yes, and can't I –
but I vow I'm disposing of the husband before I have
secured the lover.

Enter MISS NEVILLE

Miss Hard. I'm glad you're come, Neville, my dear. Tell
me, Constance, how do I look this evening? Is there
anything whimsical about me? Is it one of my well-
looking days, child? Am I in face to-day?

Miss Neville. Perfectly, my dear. Yet, now I look again –
bless me! – sure no accident has happened among the
canary birds or the goldfishes? Has your brother or the
cat been meddling? Or has the last novel been too
moving?

Miss Hard. No; nothing of all this. I have been threatened
– I can scarce get it out – I have been threatened with
a lover.

Miss Neville. And his name –

Miss Hard. Is Marlow.

Miss Neville. Indeed!

Miss Hard. The son of Sir Charles Marlow.

Miss Neville. As I live, the most intimate friend of Mr
Hastings, my admirer. They are never asunder. I
believe you must have seen him when we lived in
town.

Miss Hard. Never.

Miss Neville. He's a very singular character, I assure you. Among women of reputation he is the modestest man alive; but his acquaintance give him a very different character among creatures of another stamp: you understand me.

Miss Hard. An odd character, indeed. I shall never be able to manage him. What shall I do? Pshaw, think no more of him, but trust to occurrences for success. But how goes on your own affair, my dear? Has my mother been courting you for my brother Tony as usual?

Miss Neville. I have just come from one of our agreeable *tête-à-têtes.* She has been saying a hundred tender things, and setting off her pretty monster as the very pink of perfection.

Miss Hard. And her partiality is such, that she actually thinks him so. A fortune like yours is no small temptation. Besides, as she has the sole management of it, I'm not surprised to see her unwilling to let it go out of the family.

Miss Neville. A fortune like mine, which chiefly consists in jewels, is not such mighty temptation. But at any rate, if my dear Hastings be but constant, I make no doubt to be too hard for her at last. However, I let her suppose that I am in love with her son, and she never once dreams that my affections are fixed upon another.

Miss Hard. My good brother holds out stoutly. I could almost love him for hating you so.

Miss Neville. It is a good-natured creature at bottom, and I'm sure would wish to see me married to anybody but himself. But my aunt's bell rings for our afternoon's walk round the improvements. *Allons.* Courage is necessary, as our affairs are critical.

Miss Hard. 'Would it were bed-time and all were well.'

[*Exeunt.*

ACT I, SCENE 2

An Alehouse Room

Several shabby fellows, with punch and tobacco. Tony *at the head of the table, a little higher than the rest, a mallet in his hand*

Omnes. Hurrea! hurrea! hurrea! bravo!

First Fellow. Now, gentlemen, silence for a song. The 'squire is going to knock himself down for a song.

Omnes. Ay, a song, a song.

Tony. Then I'll sing you, gentlemen, a song I made upon this alehouse, the Three Pigeons.

Song

Let school-masters puzzle their brain
    With grammar, and nonsense, and learning;
Good liquor, I stoutly maintain,
    Gives genius a better discerning,
Let them brag of their heathenish gods,
    Their Lethes, their Styxes, and Stygians;
Their Quis, and their Quaes, and their Quods,
    They're all but a parcel of pigeons.
        Toroddle, toroddle, toroll!

When Methodist preachers come down,
    A-preaching that drinking is sinful,
I'll wager the rascals a crown,
    They always preach best with a skinful.
But when you come down with your pence,
    For a slice of their scurvy religion,
I'll leave it to all men of sense,
    But you, my good friend, are the pigeon.
        Toroddle, toroddle, toroll!

Then come, put the jorum about,
    And let us be merry and clever,
Our hearts and our liquors are stout,
    Here's the Three Jolly Pigeons for ever.
Let some cry up woodcock or hare,
    Your bustards, your ducks, and your widgeons;
But of all the birds in the air,
    Here's a health to the Three Jolly Pigeons.
        Toroddle, toroddle, toroll!

Omnes. Bravo, bravo!

First Fellow. The 'squire has got spunk in him.

Second Fellow. I loves to hear him sing, bekeays he never gives us nothing that's low.

Third Fellow. O damn anything that's low, I cannot bear it.

Fourth Fellow. The genteel thing is the genteel thing at any time: if so be that a gentleman bees in a concatenation accordingly.

Third Fellow. I like the maxum of it, Master Muggins. What, though I am obligated to dance a bear, a man may be a gentleman for all that. May this be my poison if my bear ever dances but to the very genteelest of tunes; Water Parted, or the minuet in *Ariadne*.

Second Fellow. What a pity it is the 'squire is not come to his own. It would be well for all the publicans within ten miles round of him.

Tony. Ecod, and so it would, Master Slang. I'd then show what it was to keep choice of company.

Second Fellow. Oh, he takes after his own father for that. To be sure, old 'squire Lumpkin was the finest gentleman I ever set my eyes on. For winding the straight horn, or beating a thicket for a hare, or a wench, he never had his fellow. It was a saying in the place, that he kept the best horses, dogs, and girls, in the whole county.

Tony. Ecod, and when I'm of age I'll be no bastard, I promise you. I have been thinking of Bet Bouncer and the miller's grey mare to begin with. But come, my boys, drink about and be merry, for you pay no reckoning. Well, Stingo, what's the matter?

Enter LANDLORD

Landlord. There be two gentlemen in a postchaise at the door. They have lost their way upo' the forest; and they are talking something about Mr Hardcastle.

Tony. As sure as can be, one of them must be the gentleman that's coming down to court my sister. Do they seem to be Londoners?

Landlord. I believe they may. They look woundily like
  Frenchmen.

Tony. Then desire them to step this way, and I'll set them
  right in a twinkling. [*Exit Landlord.*] Gentlemen, as
  they mayn't be good enough company for you, step
  down for a moment, and I'll be with you in the
  squeezing of a lemon.   [*Exeunt Mob.*

Tony. (*Alone.*) Father-in-law has been calling me whelp
  and hound this half-year. Now, if I pleased, I could
  be so revenged upon the old grumbletonian. But then
  I'm afraid – afraid of what? I shall soon be worth
  fifteen hundred a year, and let him frighten me out of
  that if he can!

Enter the Landlord, conducting MARLOW *and* HASTINGS

Marlow. What a tedious uncomfortable day have we had
  of it! We were told it was but forty miles across the
  country, and we have come above threescore!

Hastings. And all, Marlow, from that unaccountable
  reserve of yours that would not let us inquire more
  frequently on the way.

Marlow. I own, Hastings, I am unwilling to lay myself
  under an obligation to everyone I meet, and often
  stand the chance of an unmannerly answer.

Hastings. At present, however, we are not likely to receive any answer.

Tony. No offence, gentlemen. But I'm told you have been
  inquiring for one Mr Hardcastle in these parts. Do
  you know what part of the country you are in?

Hastings. Not in the least, sir, but should thank you for
  information.

Tony. Nor the way you came?

Hastings. No, sir; but if you can inform us –

Tony. Why, gentlemen, if you know neither the road you
  are going, nor where you are, nor the road you came,
  the first thing I have to inform you is, that – you have
  jost your way.

Marlow. We wanted no ghost to tell us that.

Tony. Pray, gentlemen, may I be so bold as to ask the place from whence you came?

Marlow. That's not necessary towards directing us where we are to go.

Tony. No offence; but question for question is all fair, you know. – Pray, gentlemen, is not this same Hardcastle a cross-grained, old-fashioned, whimsical fellow with an ugly face, a daughter, and a pretty son?

Hastings. We have not seen the gentleman; but he has the family you mention.

Tony. The daughter, a tall, trapesing, trolloping, talkative maypole – the son, a pretty, well-bred, agreeable youth, that everybody is fond of?

Marlow. Our information differs in this. The daughter is said to be well-bred, and beautiful; the son, an awkward booby, reared up and spoiled at his mother's apron-string.

Tony. He-he-hem! – Then gentlemen, all I have to tell you is, that you won't reach Mr Hardcastle's house this night, I believe.

Hastings. Unfortunate!

Tony. It's a damned long, dark, boggy, dirty, dangerous way. Stingo, tell the gentlemen the way to Mr Hardcastle's. (*Winking upon the Landlord.*) Mr Hardcastle's of Quagmire Marsh, you understand me.

Landlord. Master Hardcastle's! Lock-a-daisy, my masters, you're come a deadly deal wrong! When you came to the bottom of the hill, you should have crossed down Squash Lane.

Marlow. Cross down Squash Lane!

Landlord. Then you were to keep straight forward, until you came to four roads.

Marlow. Come to where four roads meet!

Tony. Ay, but you must be sure to take only one of them.

Marlow. O, sir, you're facetious!

Tony. Then, keeping to the right, you are to go sideways

till you come upon Crack-skull common: there you
must look sharp for the track of the wheel, and go
forward, till you come to Farmer Murrain's barn.
Coming to the farmer's barn, you are to turn to the
right, and then to the left, and then to the right about
again, till you find out the old mill.

Marlow. Zounds, man! we could as soon find out the
longitude!

Hastings. What's to be done, Marlow?

Marlow. This house promises but a poor reception;
though perhaps the landlord can accommodate us.

Landlord. Alack, master, we have but one spare bed in
the whole house.

Tony. And to my knowledge, that's taken up by three
lodgers already. (*After a pause, in which the rest seem disconcerted.*) I have hit it. Don't you think, Stingo, our
landlady could accommodate the gentlemen by the
fireside, with – three chairs and a bolster?

Hastings. I hate sleeping by the fireside.

Marlow. And I detest your three chairs and a bolster.

Tony. You do, do you? – then let me see – what if you
go on a mile farther, to the Buck's Head; the old
Buck's Head on the hill, one of the best inns in the
whole county?

Hastings. Oho! so we have escaped an adventure for this
night, however.

Landlord. (*Apart to Tony.*) Sure, you ben't sending them
to your father's as an inn, be you?

Tony. Mum, you fool, you. Let them find that out. (*To
them.*) You have only to keep on straight forward, till
you come to a large old house by the roadside. You'll
see a pair of large horns over the door. That's the sign.
Drive up the yard, and call stoutly about you.

Hastings. Sir, we are obliged to you. The servants can't
miss the way?

Tony. No, no: but I tell you, though, the landlord is rich,
and going to leave off business; so he wants to be

thought a gentleman, saving your presence, he! he! he! He'll be for giving you his company, and, ecod, if you mind him, he'll persuade you that his mother was an alderman, and his aunt a justice of peace!

Landlord. A troublesome old blade, to be sure; but 'a keeps as good wines and beds as any in the whole country.

Marlow. Well, if he supplies us with these, we shall want no further connexion. We are to turn to the right, did you say?

Tony. No, no; straight forward. I'll just step myself, and show you a piece of the way. (*To the Landlord.*) Mum.

Landlord. Ah, bless your heart for a sweet, pleasant — damned, mischievous son of a whore.

ACT II

An Old-Fashioned House

(HARDCASTLE, *followed by three or four awkward Servants.*)

Hardcastle. Well, I hope you're perfect in the table exercise I have been teaching you these three days. You all know your posts and your places, and can shew that you have been used to good company, without ever stirring from home.

Omnes. Ay, ay.

Hard. When company comes, you are not to pop out and stare, and then run in again, like frightened rabbits in a warren.

Omnes. No, no.

Hard. You, Diggory, whom I have taken from the barn, are to make a shew at the side-table; and you, Roger, whom I have advanced from the plough, are to place yourself behind my chair. But you're not to stand so, with your hands in your pockets. Take your hands from your pockets, Roger; and from your head, you blockhead, you. See how Diggory carries his hands. They're a little too stiff, indeed, but that's no great matter.

Diggory. Ay, mind how I hold them. I learned to hold my hands this way, when I was upon drill for the militia. And so being upon drill –

Hard. You must not be so talkative, Diggory. You must be all attention to the guests. You must hear us talk, and not think of talking; you must see us drink, and not think of drinking; you must see us eat, and not think of eating.

Diggory. By the laws, your worship, that's parfectly unpossible. Whenever Diggory sees yeating going forward, ecod, he's always wishing for a mouthful himself.

Hard. Blockhead! Is not a bellyful in the kitchen as good

as a bellyful in the parlour? Stay your stomach with that reflection.

Diggory. Ecod. I thank your worship, I'll make a shift to stay my stomach with a slice of cold beef in the pantry.

Hard. Diggory, you are too talkative. – Then, if I happen to say a good thing, or tell a good story at table, you must not all burst out a-laughing, as if you made part of the company.

Diggory. Then, ecod, your worship must not tell the story of old Grouse in the gun-room: I can't help laughing at that – he! he! he! – for the soul of me! We have laughed at that these twenty years – ha! ha! ha!

Hard. Ha! ha! ha! The story is a good one. Well, honest Diggory, you may laugh at that – but still remember to be attentive. Suppose one of the company should call for a glass of wine, how will you behave? A glass of wine, sir, if you please (*to Diggory*) – Eh, why don't you move?

Diggory. Ecod, your worship, I never have courage till I see the eatables and drinkables brought upo' the table, and then I'm as bauld as a lion.

Hard. What, will nobody move?

First Servant. I'm not to leave this pleace.

Second Servant. I'm sure it's no pleace of mine.

Third Servant. Nor mine, for sartain.

Diggory. Wauns, and I'm sure it canna be mine.

Hard. You numskulls! and so while, like your betters, you are quarrelling for places, the guests must be starved. Oh, you dunces! I find I must begin all over again. – But don't I hear a coach drive into the yard? To your posts, you blockheads. I'll go in the meantime and give my old friend's son a hearty reception at the gate.   [*Exit Hardcastle.*

Diggory. By the elevens, my pleace is gone quite out of my head.

Roger. I know that my pleace is to be everywhere!

First Servant. Where the devil is mine?

Second Servant. My pleace is to be nowhere at all; and so I'ze go about my business!

> [*Exeunt Servants, running about as if frighted, different ways.*

Enter Servant with lighted candles, showing in MARLOW *and* HASTINGS

Servant. Welcome, gentlemen, very welcome! This way.

Hastings. After the disappointments of the day, welcome once more, Charles, to the comforts of a clean room and a good fire. Upon my word, a very well-looking house; antique but creditable.

Marlow. The usual fate of a large mansion. Having first ruined the master by good house-keeping, it at last comes to levy contributions as an inn.

Hastings. As you say, we passengers are to be taxed to pay for all these fineries. I have often seen a good sideboard, or a marble chimney-piece, though not actually put in the bill, inflame a reckoning confoundedly.

Marlow. Travellers, George, must pay in all places. The only difference is, that in good inns you pay dearly for luxuries, in bad inns, you are fleeced and starved.

Hastings. You have lived pretty much among them. In truth, I have been often surprised, that you who have seen so much of the world, with your natural good sense, and your many opportunities, could never yet acquire a requisite share of assurance.

Marlow. The Englishman's malady. But tell me, George, where could I have learned that assurance you talk of? My life has been chiefly spent in a college or an inn, in seclusion from that lovely part of the creation that chiefly teach men confidence. I don't know that I was ever familiarly acquainted with a single modest woman – except my mother – but among females of another class, you know –

Hastings. Ay, among them you are impudent enough of all conscience!

Marlow. They are of *us*, you know.

Hastings. But in the company of women of reputation I never saw such an idiot, such a trembler; you look for all the world as if you wanted an opportunity of stealing out of the room.

Marlow. Why, man, that's because I do want to steal out of the room. Faith, I have often formed a resolution to break the ice, and rattle away at any rate. But I don't know how, a single glance from a pair of fine eyes has totally overset my resolution. An impudent fellow may counterfeit modesty, but I'll be hanged if a modest man can ever counterfeit impudence.

Hastings. If you could but say half the fine things to them, that I have heard you lavish upon the barmaid of an inn, or even a college bed-maker –

Marlow. Why, George, I can't say fine things to them. They freeze, they petrify me. They may talk of a comet, or a burning mountain, or some such bagatelle; but to me, a modest woman, drest out in all her finery, is the most tremendous object of the whole creation.

Hastings. Ha! ha! ha! At this rate, man, how can you ever expect to marry!

Marlow. Never; unless, as among kings and princes, my bride were to be courted by proxy. If, indeed, like an eastern bridegroom, one were to be introduced to a wife he never saw before, it might be endured. But to go through all the terrors of a formal courtship, together with the episode of aunts, grandmothers, and cousins, and at last to blurt out the broad staring question of, Madam, will you marry me? No, no, that's a strain much above me, I assure you!

Hastings. I pity you. But how do you intend behaving to the lady you are come down to visit at the request of your father?

Marlow. As I behave to all other ladies. Bow very low; answer yes, or no, to all her demands. – But for the rest,

I don't think I shall venture to look in her face, till I
see my father's again.

Hastings. I'm surprised that one who is so warm a friend
can be so cool a lover.

Marlow. To be explicit, my dear Hastings, my chief in-
ducement down was to be instrumental in forwarding
your happiness, not my own. Miss Neville loves you,
the family don't know you; as my friend you are sure
of a reception, and let honour do the rest.

Hastings. My dear Marlow! But I'll suppress the emotion. Were I a wretch, meanly seeking to carry off a
fortune, you should be the last man in the world I
would apply to for assistance. But Miss Neville's person is all I ask, and that is mine, both from her deceased father's consent, and her own inclination.

Marlow. Happy man! You have talents and art to
captivate any woman. I'm doomed to adore the sex,
and yet converse with the only part of it I despise.
This stammer in my address, and this awkward un-
prepossessing visage of mine, can never permit me to
soar above the reach of a milliner's apprentice, or one
of the duchesses of Drury-Lane. Pshaw! this fellow
here to interrupt us.

Enter HARDCASTLE

Hard. Gentlemen, once more you are heartily welcome.
Which is Mr Marlow? Sir, you're heartily welcome.
It's not my way, you see, to receive my friends with
my back to the fire. I like to give them a hearty reception in the old style at my gate. I like to see their
horses and trunks taken care of.

Marlow. (*Aside.*) He has got our names from the servants
already. (*To him.*) We approve your caution and
hospitality, sir. (*To Hastings.*) I have been thinking,
George, of changing our travelling dresses in the
morning. I am grown confoundedly ashamed of
mine.

Hard. I beg, Mr Marlow, you'll use no ceremony in this
   house.   [*Both ignore him.*

Hastings. I fancy, George, you're right: the first blow is
   half the battle. I intend opening the campaign with
   the white and gold.

Hard. Mr Marlow – Mr Hastings – gentlemen – pray
   be under no constraint in this house. This is Liberty
   Hall, gentlemen. You may do just as you please here.

Marlow. Yet, George, if we open the campaign too
   fiercely at first, we may want ammunition before it is
   over. I think to reserve the embroidery to secure a retreat.

Hard. Your talking of a retreat, Mr Marlow, puts me in
   mind of the Duke of Marlborough, when we went to
   besiege Denain. He first summoned the garrison –

Marlow. Don't you think the *ventre d'or* waistcoat will do
   with the plain brown?

Hard. He first summoned the garrison, which might consist of about five thousand men –

Hastings. I think not: brown and yellow mix but very
   poorly.

Hard. I say, gentlemen, as I was telling you, he summoned the garrison, which might consist of about five
   thousand men –

Marlow. The girls like finery.

Hard. Which might consist of about five thousand men,
   well appointed with stores, ammunition, and other
   implements of war. 'Now,' says the Duke of Marlborough to George Brooks, that stood next to him –
   you must have heard of George Brooks; 'I'll pawn my
   Dukedom,' says he, 'but I take that garrison without
   spilling a drop of blood.' So –

Marlow. What, my good friend, if you gave us a glass of
   punch in the meantime, it would help us to carry on
   the siege with vigour.

Hard. Punch, sir! (*Aside.*) This is the most unaccountable
   kind of modesty I ever met with.

Marlow. Yes, sir, punch! A glass of warm punch, after our journey, will be comfortable. This is Liberty Hall, you know.

Hard. Here's a cup, sir.

Marlow. (*Aside.*) So this fellow, in his Liberty Hall, will only let us have just what he pleases.

Hard. (*Taking the cup.*) I hope you'll find it to your mind. I have prepared it with my own hands, and I believe you'll own the ingredients are tolerable. Will you be so good as to pledge me, sir? Here, Mr Marlow, here is our better acquaintance!   [*Drinks.*

Marlow. (*Aside.*) A very impudent fellow this! but he's a character, and I'll humour him a little. Sir, my service to you.   [*Drinks.*

Hastings. (*Aside.*) I see this fellow wants to give us his company, and forgets that he's an innkeeper, before he has learned to be a gentleman.

Marlow. From the excellence of your cup, my old friend, I suppose you have a good deal of business in this part of the country. Warm work, now and then, at elections, I suppose?

Hard. No, sir, I have long given that work over. Since our betters have hit upon the expedient of electing each other, there's no business 'for us that sell ale'.

Hastings. So, then you have no turn for politics, I find.

Hard. Not in the least. There was a time, indeed, I fretted myself about the mistakes of government, like other people; but, finding myself every day grow more angry, and the government growing no better, I left it to mend itself. Since that, I no more trouble my head about Heyder Ally or Ally Cawn, than about Ally Croaker. Sir, my service to you.

Hastings. So that, with eating above stairs, and drinking below, with receiving your friends within, and amusing them without, you lead a good pleasant bustling life of it.

Hard. I do stir about a great deal, that's certain. Half the differences of the parish are adjusted in this very parlour.

Marlow. (*After drinking.*) And you have an argument in your cup, old gentleman, better than any in Westminster Hall.

Hard. Ay, young gentleman, that, and a little philosophy.

Marlow. (*Aside.*) Well, this is the first time I ever heard of an innkeeper's philosophy.

Hastings. So then, like an experienced general, you attack them on every quarter. If you find their reason manageable, you attack it with your philosophy; if you find they have no reason, you attack them with this. Here's your health, my philosopher.   [*Drinks.*

Hard. Good, very good, thank you; ha! ha! Your generalship puts me in mind of Prince Eugene, when he fought the Turks at the battle of Belgrade. You shall hear.

Marlow. Instead of the battle of Belgrade, I believe it's almost time to talk about supper. What has your philosophy got in the house for supper?

Hard. For supper, sir! (*Aside.*) Was ever such a request to a man in his own house!

Marlow. Yes, sir, supper, sir; I begin to feel an appetite. I shall make devilish work tonight in the larder, I promise you.

Hard. (*Aside.*) Such a brazen dog sure never my eyes beheld. (*To him.*) Why, really, sir, as for supper I can't well tell. My Dorothy, and the cook-maid, settle these things between them. I leave these kind of things entirely to them.

Marlow. You do, do you?

Hard. Entirely. By the by, I believe they are in actual consultation upon what's for supper this moment in the kitchen.

Marlow. Then I beg they'll admit me as one of their privy council. It's a way I have got. When I travel I always choose to regulate my own supper. Let the cook be called. No offence, I hope, sir.

Hard. Oh no, sir, none in the least; yet, I don't know how: our Bridget, the cook maid, is not very communicative upon these occasions. Should we send for her, she might scold us all out of the house.

Hastings. Let's see your list of the larder, then. I ask it as a favour. I always match my appetite to my bill of fare.

Marlow. (*To Hardcastle, who looks at them with surprise.*) Sir, he's very right, and it's my way, too.

Hard. Sir, you have a right to command here. Here, Roger, bring us the bill of fare for tonight's supper. I believe it's drawn out. – Your manner, Mr Hastings, puts me in mind of my uncle, Colonel Wallop. It was a saying of his, that no man was sure of his supper till he had eaten it.

Hastings. (*Aside.*) All upon the high rope! His uncle a colonel! We shall soon hear of his mother being a justice of peace. (*Hardcastle gives the paper to Marlow.*) But let's hear the bill of fare.

Marlow. (*Perusing.*) What's here? For the first course; for the second course; for the desert. The devil, sir, do you think we have brought down the whole Joiners' Company, or the Corporation of Bedford, to eat up such a supper? Two or three little things, clean and comfortable, will do.

Hastings. But let's hear it.

Marlow. (*Reading.*) For the first course at the top, a pig, and pruin sauce.

Hastings. Damn your pig, I say!

Marlow. And damn your pruin sauce, say I!

Hard. And yet, gentlemen, to men that are hungry, pig with pruin sauce is very good eating.

Marlow. At the bottom a calf's tongue and brains.

Hastings. Let your brains be knocked out, my good sir, I don't like them.

Marlow. Or you may clap them on a plate by themselves. I do.

Hard. (*Aside.*) Their impudence confounds me. (*To them.*)

Gentlemen, you are my guests, make what alterations you please. Is there anything else you wish to retrench or alter, gentlemen?

Marlow. A pork pie, a boiled rabbit and sausages, a Florentine, a shaking pudding, and a dish of tiff – taff – taffety cream!

Hastings. Confound your made dishes; I shall be as much at a loss in this house as at a green and yellow dinner at the French ambassador's table, I'm for plain eating.

Hard. I'm sorry, gentlemen, that I have nothing you like, but if there be anything you have a particular fancy to –

Marlow. Why really, sir, your bill of fare is so exquisite, that any one part of it is full as good as another. Send us what you please. So much for supper. And now to see that our beds are aired, and properly taken care of.

Hard. I entreat you'll leave all that to me. You shall not stir a step.

Marlow. Leave that to you! I protest, sir, you must excuse me, I always look to these things myself.

Hard. I must insist, sir, you'll make yourself easy on that head.

Marlow. You see I'm resolved on it. (*Aside.*) A very troublesome fellow this, as ever I met with.

Hard. Well, sir, I'm resolved at least to attend you. (*Aside.*) This may be modern modesty, but I never saw anything look so like old-fashioned impudence.

[*Exeunt Marlow and Hardcastle.*

Hastings. (*Alone*). So I find this fellow's civilities begin to grow troublesome. But who can be angry at those assiduities which are meant to please him? Ha! what do I see! Miss Neville, by all that's happy!

Enter MISS NEVILLE

Miss Neville. My dear Hastings! To what unexpected good fortune, to what accident, am I to ascribe this happy meeting?

Hastings. Rather let me ask the same question, as I could never have hoped to meet my dearest Constance at an inn.

Miss Neville. An inn! sure you mistake: my aunt, my guardian, lives here. What could induce you to think this house an inn?

Hastings. My friend, Mr Marlow, with whom I came down, and I, have been sent here as to an inn, I assure you. A young fellow, whom we accidentally met at a house hard by, directed us thither.

Miss Neville. Certainly it must be one of my hopeful cousin's tricks, of whom you have heard me talk so often: ha! ha! ha!

Hastings. He whom your aunt intends for you? He of whom I have such just apprehensions?

Miss Neville. You have nothing to fear from him, I assure you. You'd adore him if you knew how heartily he despises me. My aunt knows it, too, and has undertaken to court me for him, and actually begins to think she has made a conquest.

Hastings. Thou dear dissembler! You must know, my Constance, I have just seized this happy opportunity of my friend's visit here to get admittance into the family. The horses that carried us down are now fatigued with their journey, but they'll soon be refreshed; and then, if my dearest girl will trust in her faithful Hastings, we shall soon be landed in France, where even among slaves the laws of marriage are respected.

Miss Neville. I have often told you, that though ready to obey you, I yet should leave my little fortune behind with reluctance. The greatest part of it was left me by my uncle, the India Director, and chiefly consists in jewels. I have been for some time persuading my aunt to let me wear them. I fancy I'm very near succeeding. The instant they are put into my possession you shall find me ready to make them and myself yours.

Hastings. Perish the baubles! Your person is all I desire. In the meantime, my friend Marlow must not be let into his mistake. I know the strange reserve of his temper is such that, if abruptly informed of it, he would instantly quit the house before our plan was ripe for execution.

Miss Neville. But how shall we keep him in the deception? Miss Hardcastle is just returned from walking; what if we still continue to deceive him? – This, this way –

[*They confer.*

Enter MARLOW

Marlow. The assiduities of these good people tease me beyond bearing. My host seems to think it ill manners to leave me alone, and so he claps not only himself, but his old-fashioned wife on my back. They talk of coming to sup with us, too; and then, I suppose, we are to run the gauntlet through all the rest of the family. – What have we got here? –

Hastings. My dear Charles! Let me congratulate you! – The most fortunate accident! – Who do you think is just alighted?

Marlow. Cannot guess.

Hastings. Our mistresses, boy, Miss Hardcastle and Miss Neville. Give me leave to introduce Miss Constance Neville to your acquaintance. Happening to dine in the neighbourhood, they called, on their return, to take fresh horses here. Miss Hardcastle has just stepped into the next room, and will be back in an instant. Wasn't it lucky? eh!

Marlow. (*Aside.*) I have just been mortified enough of all conscience, and here comes something to complete my embarrassment.

Hastings. Well! but wasn't it the most fortunate thing in the world?

Marlow. Oh! yes. Very fortunate – a most joyful encounter. – But our dresses, George, you know, are in disorder. – What if we should postpone the happiness till tomorrow? – Tomorrow at her own house. – It will be every bit as convenient – and rather more respectful. – Tomorrow let it be.   [*Offering to go.*

Miss Neville. By no means, sir. Your ceremony will displease her. The disorder of your dress will shew the ardour of your impatience. Besides, she knows you are in the house, and will permit you to see her.

Marlow. Oh! the devil! how shall I support it? Hem! hem! Hastings, you must not go. You are to assist me, you know. I shall be confoundedly ridiculous. Yet, hang it! I'll take courage. Hem!

Hastings. Pshaw, man! it's but the first plunge, and all's over. She's but a woman, you know.

Marlow. And of all women, she that I dread most to encounter!

Enter MISS HARDCASTLE, *as returned from walking*

Hastings. (*Introducing them.*) Miss Hardcastle. Mr Marlow. I'm proud of bringing two persons of such merit together, that only want to know, to esteem each other.

Miss Hard. (*Aside.*) Now, for meeting my modest gentleman with a demure face, and quite in his own manner. (*After a pause, in which he appears very uneasy and disconcerted.*) I'm glad of your safe arrival, sir – I'm told you had some accidents by the way.

Marlow. Only a few, madam. Yes, we had some. Yes, madam, a good many accidents, but should be sorry – madam – or rather glad of any accidents – that are so agreeably concluded. Hem!

Hastings. (*To him.*) You never spoke better in your whole life. Keep it up, and I'll insure you the victory.

Miss Hard. I'm afraid you flatter, sir. You that have seen so much of the finest company can find little entertainment in an obscure corner of the country.

Marlow. (*Gathering courage.*) I have lived, indeed, in the world, madam; but I have kept very little company.

I have been but an observer upon life, madam, while others were enjoying it.

Miss Neville. But that, I am told, is the way to enjoy it at last.

Hastings. (*To him.*) Cicero never spoke better. Once more, and you are confirmed in assurance for ever.

Marlow. (*To him.*) Hem! Stand by me, then, and when I'm down, throw in a word or two to set me up again.

Miss Hard. An observer, like you, upon life, were, I fear, disagreeably employed, since you must have had much more to censure than to approve.

Marlow. Pardon me, madam. I was always willing to be amused. The folly of most people is rather an object of mirth than uneasiness.

Hastings. (*To him.*) Bravo, bravo. Never spoke so well in your whole life. Well, Miss Hardcastle, I see that you and Mr Marlow are going to be very good company. I believe our being here will but embarrass the interview.

Marlow. Not in the least, Mr Hastings. We like your company of all things. (*To him.*) Zounds! George, sure you won't go? How can you leave us?

Hastings. Our presence will but spoil conversation, so we'll retire to the next room. (*To him.*) You don't consider, man, that we are to manage a little *tête-à-tête* of our own. [*Exeunt.*

Miss Hard. (*After a pause.*) But you have not been wholly an observer, I presume, sir: the ladies, I should hope, have employed some part of your addresses.

Marlow. (*Relapsing into timidity.*) Pardon me, madam, I – I – I – as yet have studied – only – to – deserve them.

Miss Hard. And that some say is the very worst way to obtain them.

Marlow. Perhaps so, madam. But I love to converse only with the more grave and sensible part of the sex. – But I'm afraid I grow tiresome.

Miss Hard. Not at all, sir; there is nothing I like so much as grave conversation myself: I could hear it for ever.

Indeed, I have often been surprised how a man of
sentiment could ever admire those light airy pleasures,
where nothing reaches the heart.

Marlow. It's – a disease – of the mind, madam. In the
variety of tastes there must be some who, wanting a
relish for – um-a-um.

Miss Hard. I understand you, sir. There must be some,
who, wanting a relish for refined pleasures, pretend
to despise what they are incapable of tasting.

Marlow. My meaning, madam, but infinitely better
expressed. And I can't help observing – a –

Miss Hard. (*Aside.*) Who could ever suppose this fellow
impudent upon some occasions. (*To him.*) You were
going to observe, sir –

Marlow. I was observing, madam – I protest, madam, I
forget what I was going to observe.

Miss Hard. (*Aside.*) I vow and so do I. (*To him.*) You were
observing, sir, that in this age of hypocrisy – something about hypocrisy, sir.

Marlow. Yes, madam. In this age of hypocrisy, there are
few who upon strict inquiry do not – a – a – a –

Miss Hard. I understand you perfectly, sir.

Marlow. (*Aside.*) Egad! and that's more than I do myself!

Miss Hard. You mean that in this hypocritical age there
are few that do not condemn in public what they
practise in private, and think they pay every debt to
virtue when they praise it.

Marlow. True, madam; those who have most virtue in
their mouths, have least of it in their bosoms. But I'm
sure I tire you, madam.

Miss Hard. Not in the least, sir; there's something so
agreeable and spirited in your manner, such life and
force – pray, sir, go on.

Marlow. Yes, madam. I was saying – that there are some
occasions – when a total want of courage, madam,
destroys all the – and puts us – upon a – a – a –

Miss Hard. I agree with you entirely, a want of courage

upon some occasions assumes the appearance of ignorance, and betrays us when we most want to excel. I beg you'll proceed.

Marlow. Yes, madam. Morally speaking, madam – but I see Miss Neville expecting us in the next room. I would not intrude for the world.

Miss Hard. I protest, sir, I never was more agreeably entertained in all my life. Pray go on.

Marlow. Yes, madam. I was – but she beckons us to join her. Madam, shall I do myself the honour to attend you?

Miss Hard. Well then, I'll follow.

Marlow. (*Aside.*) This pretty smooth dialogue has done for me. [*Exit.*

Miss Hard. (*Alone.*) Ha! ha! ha! Was there ever such a sober sentimental interview? I'm certain he scarce looked in my face the whole time. Yet the fellow, but for his unaccountable bashfulness, is pretty well, too. He has good sense, but then so buried in his fears, that it fatigues one more than ignorance. If I could teach him a little confidence, it would be doing somebody that I know of a piece of service. But who is that somebody? – that, faith, is a question I can scarce answer. [*Exit.*

Enter TONY *and* MISS NEVILLE, *followed by* MRS HARDCASTLE *and* HASTINGS

Tony. What do you follow me for, cousin Con? I wonder you're not ashamed to be so very engaging.

Miss Neville. I hope, cousin, one may speak to one's own relations, and not be to blame.

Tony. Ay, but I know what sort of a relation you want to make me, though; but it won't do. I tell you, cousin Con, it won't do; so I beg you'll keep your distance, I want no nearer relationship.

[*She follows, coquetting him to the back scene.*

Mrs Hard. Well! I vow, Mr Hastings, you are very entertaining. There's nothing in the world I love to talk of

so much as London, and the fashions, though I was
never there myself.

Hastings. Never there! You amaze me! From your air
and manner, I concluded you had been bred all your
life either at Ranelagh, St James's, or Tower Wharf.

Mrs Hard. Oh! sir, you're only pleased to say so. We
country persons can have no manner at all. I'm in love
with the town, and that serves to raise me above some
of our neighbouring rustics; but who can have a
manner, that has never seen the Pantheon, the Grotto
Gardens, the Borough, and such places where the
nobility chiefly resort? All I can do is to enjoy London
at second-hand. I take care to know every *tête-à-tête*
from the Scandalous Magazine, and have all the
fashions as they come out, in a letter from the two
Miss Rickets of Crooked Lane. Pray how do you like
this head, Mr Hastings?

Hastings. Extremely elegant and *dégagée*, upon my word,
madam. Your friseur is a Frenchman, I suppose?

Mrs Hard. I protest. I dressed it myself from a print in
the Ladies' Memorandum-book for the last year.

Hastings. Indeed. Such a head in a side-box, at the play-
house, would draw as many gazers as my Lady
Mayoress at a city ball.

Mrs Hard. I vow, since inoculation began, there is no
such thing to be seen as a plain woman; so one must
dress a little particular, or one may escape in the
crowd.

Hastings. But that can never be your case, madam, in any
dress! (*Bowing.*)

Mrs Hard. Yet, what signifies my dressing when I have
such a piece of antiquity by my side as Mr Hardcastle:
all I can say will never argue down a single button
from his clothes. I have often wanted him to throw off
his great flaxen wig, and where he was bald, to plaster
it over like my Lord Pately, with powder.

Hastings. You are right, madam; for, as among the ladies

there are none ugly, so among the men there are none old.

Mrs Hard. But what do you think his answer was? Why, with his usual Gothic vivacity, he said I only wanted him to throw off his wig to convert it into a *tête* for my own wearing!

Hastings. Intolerable! At your age you may wear what you please, and it must become you.

Mrs Hard. Pray, Mr Hastings, what do you take to be the most fashionable age about town?

Hastings. Some time ago forty was all the mode; but I'm told the ladies intend to bring up fifty for the ensuing winter.

Mrs Hard. Seriously? Then I shall be too young for the fashion!

Hastings. No lady begins now to put on jewels till she's past forty. For instance, Miss there, in a polite circle, would be considered as a child, as a mere maker of samplers.

Mrs Hard. And yet Mrs Niece thinks herself as much a woman, and is as fond of jewels as the oldest of us all.

Hastings. Your niece, is she? And that young gentleman, a brother of yours, I should presume?

Mrs Hard. My son, sir. They are contracted to each other. Observe their little sports. They fall in and out ten times a day, as if they were man and wife already. (*To them.*) Well, Tony child, what soft things are you saying to your cousin Constance this evening?

Tony. I have been saying no soft things; but that it's very hard to be followed about so! Ecod! I've not a place in the house now that's left to myself but the stable.

Mrs Hard. Never mind him, Con, my dear. He's in another story behind your back.

Miss Neville. There's something generous in my cousin's manner. He falls out before faces to be forgiven in private.

Tony. That's a damned confounded – crack.

Mrs Hard. Ah! he's a sly one. Don't you think they're like each other about the mouth, Mr Hastings? The Blenkinsop mouth to a T. They're of a size, too. Back to back, my pretties, that Mr Hastings may see you. Come, Tony.

Tony. You had as good not make me, I tell you.

                                              [*Measuring.*

Miss Neville. Oh lud! he has almost cracked my head.

Mrs Hard. Oh, the monster! For shame, Tony. You a man, and behave so!

Tony. If I'm a man, let me have my fortin. Ecod! I'll not be made a fool of no longer.

Mrs Hard. Is this, ungrateful boy, all that I'm to get for the pains I have taken in your education? I that have rocked you in your cradle, and fed that pretty mouth with a spoon! Did not I work that waistcoat to make you genteel? Did not I prescribe for you every day, and weep while the receipt was operating?

Tony. Ecod! you had reason to weep, for you have been dosing me ever since I was born. I have gone through every receipt in the complete housewife ten times over; and you have thoughts of coursing me through Quincy next spring. But, ecod! I tell you, I'll not be made a fool of no longer.

Mrs Hard. Wasn't it all for your good, viper? Wasn't it all for your good?

Tony. I wish you'd let me and my good alone, then. Snubbing this way when I'm in spirits. If I'm to have any good, let it come of itself; not to keep dinging it, dinging it into one so.

Mrs Hard. That's false; I never see you when you're in spirits. No, Tony, you then go to the alehouse or kennel. I'm never to be delighted with your agreeable wild notes, unfeeling monster!

Tony. Ecod! Mamma, your own notes are the wildest of the two.

Mrs Hard. Was ever the like? But I see he wants to break my heart, I see he does.

Hastings. Dear Madam, permit me to lecture the young gentleman a little. I'm certain I can persuade him to his duty.

Mrs Hard. Well, I must retire. Come, Constance, my love. You see, Mr Hastings, the wretchedness of my situation. Was ever poor woman so plagued with a dear, sweet, pretty, provoking, undutiful boy.

[*Exeunt Mrs Hardcastle and Miss Neville,*
Hastings, Tony

Tony. (*Singing.*) 'There was a young man riding by, and fain would have his will. Rang do didlo dee.'
Don't mind her. Let her cry. It's the comfort of her heart. I have seen her and sister cry over a book for an hour together, and they said they liked the book the better the more it made them cry.

Hastings. Then you're no friend to the ladies, I find, my pretty young gentleman?

Tony. That's as I find 'um.

Hastings. Not to her of your mother's choosing, I dare answer! And yet she appears to me a pretty, well-tempered girl.

Tony. That's because you don't know her as well as I. Ecod! I know every inch about her; and there's not a more bitter cantankerous toad in all Christendom!

Hastings. (*Aside.*) Pretty encouragement this for a lover!

Tony. I have seen her since the height of that. She has as many tricks as a hare in a thicket, or a colt the first day's breaking.

Hastings. To me she appears sensible and silent.

Tony. Ay, before company. But when she's with her playmates, she's as loud as a hog in a gate.

Hastings. But there is a meek modesty about her that charms me.

Tony. Yes, but curb her never so little, she kicks up, and you're flung in a ditch.

Hastings. Well, but you must allow her a little beauty. — Yes, you must allow her some beauty.

Tony. Bandbox! She's all a made-up thing, mun. Ah! could you but see Bet Bouncer of these parts, you might then talk of beauty. Ecod, she has two eyes as black as sloes, and cheeks as broad and red as a pulpit cushion. She'd make two of she.

Hastings. Well, what say you of a friend that would take this bitter bargain off your hands?

Tony. Anon?

Hastings. Would you thank him that would take Miss Neville, and leave you to happiness and your dear Betsy?

Tony. Ay; but where is there such a friend, for who would take her?

Hastings. I am he. If you but assist me, I'll engage to whip her off to France, and you shall never hear more of her.

Tony. Assist you! Ecod, I will, to the last drop of my blood. I'll clap a pair of horses to your chaise that shall trundle you off in a twinkling, and may be get you a part of her fortin beside in jewels that you little dream of.

Hastings. My dear 'squire, this looks like a lad of spirit.

Tony. Come along then, and you shall see more of my spirit before you have done with me.

   (*Singing.*)

      We are the boys
      That fears no noise
      Where the thundering cannons roar.

                              [*Exeunt.*

ACT III

Enter HARDCASTLE *alone*

Hard. What could my old friend Sir Charles mean by recommending his son as the modestest young man in town? To me he appears the most impudent piece of brass that ever spoke with a tongue. He has taken possession of the easy chair by the fireside already. He took off his boots in the parlour, and desired me to see them taken care of. I'm desirous to know how his impudence affects my daughter. – She will certainly be shocked at it.

Enter MISS HARDCASTLE *plainly dressed*

Hard. Well, my Kate, I see you have changed your dress, as I bid you; and yet, I believe, there was no great occasion.

Miss Hard. I find such a pleasure, sir, in obeying your commands, that I take care to observe them without ever debating their propriety.

Hard. And yet, Kate, I sometimes give you some cause, particularly when I recommended my modest gentleman to you as a lover today.

Miss Hard. You taught me to expect something extraordinary, and I find the original exceeds the description!

Hard. I was never so surprised in my life! He has quite confounded all my faculties!

Miss Hard. I never saw anything like it: and a man of the world, too!

Hard. Ay, he learned it all abroad, – what a fool was I, to think a young man could learn modesty by travelling. He might as soon learn wit at a masquerade.

Miss Hard. It seems all natural to him.

Hard. A good deal assisted by bad company and a French dancing-master.

Miss Hard. Sure, you mistake, papa! A French dancing-master could never have taught him that timid look – that awkward address – that bashful manner –

Hard. Whose look? whose manner, child?

Miss Hard. Mr Marlow's: his *mauvaise honte,* his timidity, struck me at the first sight.

Hard. Then your first sight deceived you; for I think him one of the most brazen first sights that ever astonished my senses!

Miss Hard. Sure, sir, you rally! I never saw anyone so modest.

Hard. And can you be serious! I never saw such a bouncing swaggering puppy since I was born. Bully Dawson was but a fool to him.

Miss Hard. Surprising! He met me with a respectful bow, a stammering voice, and a look fixed on the ground.

Hard. He met me with a loud voice, a lordly air, and a familiarity that made my blood freeze again.

Miss Hard. He treated me with diffidence and respect; censured the manners of the age; admired the prudence of girls that never laughed; tired me with apologies for being tiresome; then left the room with a bow, and 'Madam, I would not for the world detain you.'

Hard. He spoke to me as if he knew me all his life before; asked twenty questions, and never waited for an answer; interrupted my best remarks with some silly pun, and when I was in my best story of the Duke of Marlborough and Prince Eugene, he asked if I had not a good hand at making punch. Yes, Kate, he asked your father if he was a maker of punch!

Miss Hard. One of us must certainly be mistaken.

Hard. If he be what he has shown himself, I'm determined he shall never have my consent.

Miss Hard. And if he be the sullen thing I take him, he shall never have mine.

Hard. In one thing then we are agreed – to reject him.

Miss Hard. Yes: but upon conditions. For if you should find him less impudent, and I more presuming; if you find him more respectful, and I more importunate – I don't know – the fellow is well enough for a man. – Certainly we don't meet many such at a horse-race in the country.

Hard. If we should find him so – but that's impossible. The first appearance has done my business. I'm seldom deceived in that.

Miss Hard. And yet there may be many good qualities under that first appearance.

Hard. Ay, when a girl finds a fellow's outside to her taste, she then sets about guessing the rest of his furniture. With her, a smooth face stands for good sense, and a genteel figure for every virtue.

Miss Hard. I hope, sir, a conversation begun with a compliment to my good sense won't end with a sneer at my understanding?

Hard. Pardon me, Kate. But if young Mr Brazen can find the art of reconciling contradictions, he may please us both, perhaps.

Miss Hard. And as one of us must be mistaken, what if we go to make further discoveries?

Hard. Agreed. But depend on't I'm in the right.

Miss Hard. And depend on't I'm not much in the wrong.   [*Exeunt.*

Enter TONY, *running in with a casket*

Tony. Ecod! I have got them. Here they are. My cousin Con's necklaces, bobs and all. My mother shan't cheat the poor souls out of their fortin neither. Oh! my genius, is that you?

Enter HASTINGS

Hastings. My dear friend, how have you managed with your mother? I hope you have amused her with

pretending love for your cousin, and that you are
willing to be reconciled at last? Our horses will be
refreshed in a short time, and we shall soon be ready
to set off.

Tony. And here's something to bear your charges by the
way. (*Giving the casket.*) Your sweetheart's jewels. Keep
them, and hang those, I say, that would rob you of
one of them.

Hastings. But how have you procured them from your
mother?

Tony. Ask me no questions, and I'll tell you no fibs. I
procured them by the rule of thumb. If I had not a
key to every drawer in mother's bureau, how could
I go to the alehouse so often as I do? An honest man
may rob himself of his own at any time.

Hastings. Thousands do it every day. But to be plain with
you, Miss Neville is endeavouring to procure them
from her aunt this very instant. If she succeeds, it
will be the most delicate way at least of obtaining
them.

Tony. Well, keep them, till you know how it will be.
But I know how it will be well enough; she'd as soon
part with the only sound tooth in her head!

Hastings. But I dread the effects of her resentment, when
she finds she has lost them.

Tony. Never you mind her resentment, leave *me* to
manage that. I don't value her resentment the bounce
of a cracker. Zounds! here they are! Morrice! prance!
                                                    [*Exit Hastings.*

TONY, MRS HARDCASTLE, *and* MISS NEVILLE

Mrs Hard. Indeed, Constance, you amaze me. Such a
girl as you want jewels? It will be time enough for
jewels, my dear, twenty years hence, when your beauty
begins to want repairs.

Miss Neville. But what will repair beauty at forty, will
certainly improve it at twenty, madam.

Mrs Hard. Yours, my dear, can admit of none. That natural blush is beyond a thousand ornaments. Besides, child, jewels are quite out at present. Don't you see half the ladies of our acquaintance, my Lady Kill-daylight, and Mrs Crump, and the rest of them, carry their jewels to town, and bring nothing but paste and marcasites back?

Miss Neville. But who knows, madam, but somebody that shall be nameless would like me best with all my little finery about me?

Mrs Hard. Consult your glass, my dear, and then see, if with such a pair of eyes, you want any better sparklers. What do you think, Tony, my dear, does your cousin Con want any jewels, in your eyes, to set off her beauty?

Tony. That's as thereafter may be.

Miss Neville. My dear aunt, if you knew how it would oblige me.

Mrs Hard. A parcel of old-fashioned rose and table-cut things. They would make you look like the court of King Solomon at a puppet-show. Besides, I believe I can't readily come at them. They may be missing, for aught I know to the contrary.

Tony. (*Apart to Mrs Hard.*) Then why don't you tell her so at once, as she's so longing for them. Tell her they're lost. It's the only way to quiet her. Say they're lost, and call me to bear witness.

Mrs Hard. (*Apart to Tony.*) You know, my dear, I'm only keeping them for you. So if I say they're gone, you'll bear me witness, will you? He! he! he!

Tony. Never fear me. Ecod! I'll say I saw them taken out with my own eyes.

Miss Neville. I desire them but for a day, madam. Just to be permitted to shew them as relics, and then they may be locked up again.

Mrs Hard. To be plain with you, my dear Constance, if I could find them, you should have them. They're

missing, I assure you. Lost, for aught I know; but we
must have patience wherever they are.

Miss Neville. I'll not believe it; this is but a shallow
pretence to deny me. I know they're too valuable to
be so slightly kept, and as you are to answer for the
loss –

Mrs Hard. Don't be alarmed, Constance. If they be lost,
I must restore an equivalent. But my son knows they
are missing, and not to be found.

Tony. That I can bear witness to. They are missing, and
not to be found, I'll take my oath on't.

Mrs Hard. You must learn resignation, my dear; for
though we lose our fortune, yet we should not lose our
patience. See me, how calm I am.

Miss Neville. Ay, people are generally calm at the
misfortunes of others.

Mrs Hard. Now, I wonder a girl of your good sense
should waste a thought upon such trumpery. We shall
soon find them; and, in the meantime, you shall make
use of my garnets till your jewels be found.

Miss Neville. I detest garnets.

Mrs Hard. The most becoming things in the world to set
off a clear complexion. You have often seen how well
they look upon me. You shall have them.   [*Exit.*

Miss Neville. (*Trying to detain her.*) I dislike them of all
things. You shan't stir. Was ever anything so provoking to mislay my own jewels, and force me to wear
her trumpery.

Tony. Don't be a fool. If she gives you the garnets, take
what you can get. The jewels are your own already.
I have stolen them out of her bureau, and she does
not know it. Fly to your spark, he'll tell you more of
the matter. Leave me to manage her.

Miss Neville. My dear cousin!

Tony. Vanish. She's here, and has missed them already.
Zounds! how she fidgets and spits about like a cath-
erine wheel!

Enter MRS HARDCASTLE

Mrs Hard. Confusion! thieves! robbers! We are cheated, plundered, broke open, undone!

Tony. What's the matter, what's the matter, mamma? I hope nothing has happened to any of the good family!

Mrs Hard. We are robbed. My bureau has been broke open, the jewels taken out, and I'm undone!

Tony. Oh! is that all? Ha! ha! ha! By the laws, I never saw it better acted in my life. Ecod, I thought you was ruined in earnest, ha, ha, ha!

Mrs Hard. Why, boy, I am ruined in earnest. My bureau has been broke open, and all taken away.

Tony. Stick to that; ha, ha, ha! stick to that. I'll bear witness, you know, call me to bear witness.

Mrs Hard. I tell you, Tony, by all that's precious, the jewels are gone, and I shall be ruined for ever.

Tony. Sure I know they're gone, and I am to say so.

Mrs Hard. My dearest Tony, but hear me. They're gone, I say.

Tony. By the laws, mamma, you make me for to laugh, ha! ha! I know who took them well enough, ha! ha! ha!

Mrs Hard. Was there ever such a blockhead, that can't tell the difference between jest and earnest. I tell you I'm not in jest, booby!

Tony. That's right, that's right: you must be in a bitter passion, and then nobody will suspect either of us. I'll bear witness that they are gone.

Mrs Hard. Was there ever such a cross-grained brute, that won't hear me! Can you bear witness that you're no better than a fool? Was ever poor woman so beset with fools on one hand, and thieves on the other?

Tony. I can bear witness to that.

Mrs Hard. Bear witness again, you blockhead you, and I'll turn you out of the room directly. My poor niece, what will become of her? Do you laugh, you unfeeling brute, as if you enjoyed my distress?

Tony. I can bear witness to that.

Mrs Hard. Do you insult me, monster? I'll teach you to vex your mother, I will.

Tony. I can bear witness to that.

> [*He runs off, she follows him.*

Enter MISS HARDCASTLE *and Maid*

Miss Hard. What an unaccountable creature is that brother of mine, to send them to the house as an inn, ha! ha! I don't wonder at his impudence.

Maid. But what is more, madam, the young gentleman as you passed by in your present dress, asked me if you were the barmaid. He mistook you for the barmaid, madam!

Miss Hard. Did he? Then as I live I'm resolved to keep up the delusion. Tell me, Pimple, how do you like my present dress? Don't you think I look something like Cherry in the *Beaux' Stratagem*?

Maid. It's the dress, madam, that every lady wears in the country, but when she visits or receives company.

Miss Hard. And are you sure he does not remember my face or person?

Maid. Certain of it.

Miss Hard. I vow, I thought so; for though we spoke for some time together, yet his fears were such, that he never once looked up during the interview. Indeed, if he had, my bonnet would have kept him from seeing me.

Maid. But what do you hope from keeping him in his mistake?

Miss Hard. In the first place, I shall be seen, and that is no small advantage to a girl who brings her face to market. Then I shall perhaps make an acquaintance, and that's no small victory gained over one who never addresses any but the wildest of her sex. But my chief aim is to take my gentleman off his guard, and like an invisible champion of romance, examine the giant's force before I offer to combat.

Maid. But you are sure you can act your part, and disguise your voice, so that he may mistake that, as he
has already mistaken your person?

Miss Hard. Never fear me. I think I have got the true
bar cant. Did your honour call? – Attend the Lion
there. – Pipes and tobacco for the Angel. – The Lamb
has been outrageous this half-hour.

Maid. It will do, madam. But he's here.   [*Exit Maid.*

Enter MARLOW

Marlow. What a bawling in every part of the house; I
have scarce a moment's repose. If I go to the best
room, there I find my host and his story. If I fly to
the gallery, there we have my hostess with her curtsy
down to the ground. I have at last got a moment to
myself, and now for recollection.   [*Walks and muses.*

Miss Hard. Did you call, sir? Did your honour call?

Marlow. (*Musing.*) As for Miss Hardcastle, she's too grave
and sentimental for me.   [*Paces to left.*

Miss Hard. Did your honour call?

        [*She still places herself before him, he turning away.*

Marlow. No, child. (*Musing.*) Besides from the glimpse I
had of her, I think she squints.

Miss Hard. I'm sure, sir, I heard the bell ring.

Marlow. No, no. (*Musing.*) I have pleased my father,
however, by coming down, and I'll tomorrow please
myself by returning.

              [*Taking out his tablets, and perusing.*

Miss Hard. Perhaps the other gentleman called, sir?

Marlow. I tell you, no.

Miss Hard. I should be glad to know, sir. We have such a
parcel of servants.

Marlow. No, no, I tell you. (*Looks full in her face.*) Yes,
child, I think I did call. I wanted – I wanted – I vow,
child, you are vastly handsome.

Miss Hard. O la, sir, you'll make one ashamed.

Marlow. Never saw a more sprightly malicious eye. Yes,

yes, my dear, I did call. Have you got any of your –
a – what d'ye call it in the house?

Miss Hard. No, sir, we have been out of that these ten
days.

Marlow. One may call in this house, I find, to very little
purpose. Suppose I should call for a taste, just by
way of trial, of the nectar of your lips; perhaps I might
be disappointed in that, too.

Miss Hard. Nectar! nectar! that's a liquor there's no
call for in these parts. French, I suppose. We keep no
French wines here, sir.

Marlow. Of true English growth, I assure you.

Miss Hard. Then it's odd I should not know it. We brew
all sorts of wines in this house, and I have lived here
these eighteen years.

Marlow. Eighteen years! Why one would think, child, you
kept the bar before you were born. How old are you?

Miss Hard. O! sir, I must not tell my age. They say
women and music should never be dated.

Marlow. To guess at this distance, you can't be much
above forty. (*Approaching.*) Yet nearer I don't think so
much. (*Approaching.*) By coming close to some women
they look younger still; but when we come very close
indeed –   [*Attempting to kiss her.*

Miss Hard. Pray, sir, keep your distance. One would
think you wanted to know one's age as they do horses,
by mark of mouth.

Marlow. I protest, child, you use me extremely ill. If you
keep me at this distance, how is it possible you and I
can ever be acquainted?

Miss Hard. And who wants to be acquainted with you?
I want no such acquaintance, not I. I'm sure you
did not treat Miss Hardcastle that was here awhile ago
in this obstropalous manner. I'll warrant me, before
her you looked dashed, and kept bowing to the ground,
and talked, for all the world, as if you was before a
justice of peace.

Marlow. (*Aside.*) Egad! she has hit it, sure enough. (*To her.*) In awe of her, child? Ha! ha! ha! A mere awkward, squinting thing, no, no. I find you don't know me. I laughed, and rallied her a little; but I was unwilling to be too severe. No, I could not be too severe, curse me!

Miss Hard. Oh! then, sir, you are a favourite, I find, among the ladies?

Marlow. Yes, my dear, a great favourite. And yet, hang me, I don't see what they find in me to follow. At the ladies' club in town I'm called their agreeable Rattle. Rattle, child, is not my real name, but one I'm known by. My name is Solomons. Mr Solomons, my dear, at your service.   [*Offering to salute her.*

Miss Hard. Hold, sir; you are introducing me to your club, not to yourself. And you're so great a favourite there, you say?

Marlow. Yes, my dear. There's Mrs Mantrap, Lady Betty Blackleg, the Countess of Sligo, Mrs Langhorns, old Miss Biddy Buckskin and your humble servant, keep up the spirit of the place.

Miss Hard. Then it's a very merry place, I suppose?

Marlow. Yes, as merry as cards, suppers, wine, and old women can make us.

Miss Hard. And their agreeable Rattle, ha! ha! ha!

Marlow. (*Aside.*) Egad! I don't quite like this chit. She looks knowing, methinks. You laugh, child!

Miss Hard. I can't but laugh to think what time they all have for minding their work or their family.

Marlow. (*Aside.*) All's well, she don't laugh at me. (*To her.*) Do you ever work, child?

Miss Hard. Ay, sure. There's not a screen or a quilt in the whole house but what can bear witness to that.

Marlow. Odso! Then you must show me your embroidery. I embroider and draw patterns myself a little. If you want a judge of your work you must apply to me.

[*Seizing her hand.*

Miss Hard. Ay, but the colours don't look well by candle-light. You shall see all in the morning.   [*Struggling.*

Marlow. And why not now, my angel? Such beauty fires beyond the power of resistance. – Pshaw! the father here! My old luck: I never nicked seven that I did not throw ames-ace three times following.

[*Exit Marlow.*

Enter HARDCASTLE, *who stands in surprise*

Hard. So, madam. So I find this is your modest lover. This is your humble admirer that kept his eyes fixed on the ground, and only adored at humble distance. Kate, Kate, art thou not ashamed to deceive your father so?

Miss Hard. Never trust me, dear papa, but he's still the modest man I first took him for, you'll be convinced of it as well as I.

Hard. By the hand of my body. I believe his impudence is infectious! Didn't I see him seize your hand? Didn't I see him haul you about like a milkmaid? and now you talk of his respect and his modesty, forsooth!

Miss Hard. But if I shortly convince you of his modesty, that he has only the faults that will pass off with time, and the virtues that will improve with age, I hope you'll forgive him.

Hard. The girl would actually make one run mad! I tell you I'll not be convinced. I am convinced. He has scarcely been three hours in the house, and he has already encroached on all my prerogatives. You may like his impudence, and call it modesty. But my son-in-law, madam, must have very different qualifications.

Miss Hard. Sir, I ask but this night to convince you.

Hard. You shall not have half the time, for I have thoughts of turning him out this very hour.

Miss Hard. Give me that hour then, and I hope to satisfy you.

Hard. Well, an hour let it be then. But I'll have no trifling with your father. All fair and open, do you mind me?

Miss Hard. I hope, sir, you have ever found that I considered your commands as my pride; for your kindness is such, that my duty as yet has been inclination.

ACT IV

Enter HASTINGS *and* MISS NEVILLE

Hastings. You surprise me! Sir Charles Marlow expected here this night? Where have you had your information?

Miss Neville. You may depend upon it. I just saw his letter to Mr Hardcastle, in which he tells him he intends setting out a few hours after his son.

Hastings. Then, my Constance, all must be completed before he arrives. He knows me; and should he find me here, would discover my name, and perhaps my designs, to the rest of the family.

Miss Neville. The jewels, I hope, are safe.

Hastings. Yes, yes. I have sent them to Marlow, who keeps the keys of our baggage. In the meantime, I'll go to prepare matters for our elopement. I have had the 'squire's promise of a fresh pair of horses; and, if I should not see him again, will write him further directions. [*Exit.*

Miss Neville. Well! success attend you. In the meantime, I'll go amuse my aunt with the old pretence of a violent passion for my cousin. [*Exit.*

Enter MARLOW *followed by servant*

Marlow. I wonder what Hastings could mean by sending me so valuable a thing as a casket to keep for him, when he knows the only place I have is the seat of a post-coach at an inn-door. Have you deposited the casket with the landlady, as I ordered you? Have you put it into her own hands?

Servant. Yes, your honour.

Marlow. She said she'd keep it safe, did she?

Servant. Yes, she said she'd keep it safe enough; she asked me how I came by it, and she said she had a great mind to make me give an account of myself. [*Exit Servant.*

Marlow. Ha! ha! ha! They're safe, however. What an

unaccountable set of beings have we got amongst!
This little barmaid, though, runs in my head most
strangely, and drives out the absurdities of all the rest
of the family. She's mine, she must be mine, or I'm
greatly mistaken.

Enter HASTINGS

Hastings. Bless me! I quite forgot to tell her that I intended to prepare at the bottom of the garden.
Marlow here, and in spirits too!

Marlow. Give me joy, George! Crown me, shadow me
with laurels! Well, George, after all, we modest
fellows don't want for success among the women.

Hastings. Some women, you mean. But what success has
your honour's modesty been crowned with now, that
it grows so insolent upon us?

Marlow. Didn't you see the tempting, brisk, lovely little
thing that runs about the house with a bunch of keys
to its girdle?

Hastings. Well! and what then?

Marlow. She's mine, you rogue you. Such fire, such
motions, such eyes, such lips – but, egad! she would
not let me kiss them though.

Hastings. But are you so sure, so very sure of her?

Marlow. Why man, she talked of showing me her work
above stairs and I am to improve the pattern.

Hastings. But how can you, Charles, go about to rob a
woman of her honour?

Marlow. Pshaw! pshaw! We all know the honour of a
barmaid of an inn. I don't intend to rob her, take
my word for it, there's nothing in this house I shan't
honestly pay for.

Hastings. I believe the girl has virtue.

Marlow. And if she has, I should be the last man in the
world that would attempt to corrupt it.

Hastings. You have taken care, I hope, of the casket I
sent you to lock up? It's in safety?

Marlow. Yes, yes. It's safe enough. I have taken care of it. But how could you think the seat of a post-coach at an inn-door a place of safety? Ah! numbskull! I have taken better precautions for you than you did for yourself. – I have –

Hastings. What?

Marlow. I have sent it to the landlady to keep for you.

Hastings. To the landlady!

Marlow. The landlady.

Hastings. You did?

Marlow. I did. She's to be answerable for its forthcoming, you know.

Hastings. Yes, she'll bring it forth with a witness.

Marlow. Wasn't I right? I believe you'll allow that I acted prudently upon this occasion?

Hastings. (*Aside.*) He must not see my uneasiness.

Marlow. You seem a little disconcerted, though, methinks. Sure nothing has happened?

Hastings. No, nothing. Never was in better spirits in all my life. And so you left it with the landlady, who, no doubt, very readily undertook the charge?

Marlow. Rather too readily. For she not only kept the casket, but, through her great precaution, was going to keep the messenger too. Ha! ha! ha!

Hastings. He! he! he! They're safe, however.

Marlow. As a guinea in a miser's purse.

Hastings. (*Aside.*) So now all hopes of fortune are at an end, and we must set off without it. (*To him.*) Well, Charles, I'll leave you to your meditations on the pretty barmaid, and, he! he! he! may you be as successful for yourself as you have been for me. [*Exit.*

Marlow. Thank ye, George! I ask no more. Ha! ha! ha!

Enter HARDCASTLE

Hard. I no longer know my own house. It's turned all topsy-turvy. His servants have got drunk already. I'll bear it no longer, and yet, from my respect for his father, I'll be calm. (*To him.*) Mr Marlow, your servant. I'm your very humble servant. [*Bowing low.*

Marlow. Sir, your humble servant. (*Aside.*) What's to be the wonder now?

Hard. I believe, sir, you must be sensible, sir, that no man alive ought to be more welcome than your father's son, sir. I hope you think so?

Marlow. I do, from my soul, sir. I don't want much entreaty. I generally make my father's son welcome wherever he goes.

Hard. I believe you do, from my soul, sir. But though I say nothing to your own conduct, that of your servants is insufferable. Their manner of drinking is setting a very bad example in this house, I assure you.

Marlow. I protest, my very good sir, that's no fault of mine. If they don't drink as they ought they are to blame. I ordered them not to spare the cellar. I did, I assure you. (*To the side scene.*) Here, let one of my servants come up. (*To him.*) My positive directions were, that as I did not drink myself, they should make up for my deficiencies below.

Hard. Then they had your orders for what they do! I'm satisfied!

Marlow. They had, I assure you. You shall hear from one of themselves.

Enter SERVANT, *drunk*

Marlow. You, Jeremy! Come forward, sirrah! What were my orders? Were you not told to drink freely, and call for what you thought fit, for the good of the house?

Hard. (*Aside.*) I begin to lose my patience.

Jeremy. (*Staggering forward.*) Please your honour, liberty and Fleet Street for ever! Though I'm but a servant, I'm as good as another man. I'll drink for no man before supper, sir, dammy! Good liquor will sit upon

a good supper, but a good supper will not sit upon –
hiccup – upon my conscience, sir.

Marlow. You see, my old friend, the fellow is as drunk
as he can possibly be. I don't know what you'd have
more, unless you'd have the poor devil soused in a
beer-barrel.

Hard. Zounds! He'll drive me distracted if I contain
myself any longer. Mr Marlow, Sir; I have submitted
to your insolence for more than four hours, and I see
no likelihood of its coming to an end. I'm now resolved
to be master here, sir, and I desire that you and your
drunken pack may leave my house directly.

Marlow. Leave your house! – Sure, you jest, my good
friend! What, when I'm doing what I can to please
you!

Hard. I tell you, sir, you don't please me; so I desire
you'll leave my house.

Marlow. Sure, you cannot be serious! At this time o'
night, and such a night! You only mean to banter
me!

Hard. I tell you, sir, I'm serious; and, now that my
passions are roused, I say this house is mine, sir;
this house is mine, and I command you to leave it
directly.

Marlow. Ha! ha! ha! A puddle in a storm. I shan't stir
a step, I assure you. (*In a serious tone.*) This your house,
fellow! It's my house. This is my house. Mine, while
I choose to stay. What right have you to bid me leave
this house, sir? I never met with such impudence,
curse me, never in my whole life before.

Hard. Nor I, confound me if ever I did! To come to my
house, to call for what he likes, to turn me out of my
own chair, to insult the family, to order his servants
to get drunk, and then to tell me *This house is mine, sir.*
By all that's impudent, it makes me laugh. Ha! ha!
ha! Pray sir, (*bantering*) as you take the house, what
think you of taking the rest of the furniture? There's

a pair of silver candlesticks, and there's a firescreen, and here's a pair of brazen-nosed bellows, perhaps you may take a fancy to them?

Marlow. Bring me your bill, sir, bring me your bill, and let's make no more words about it.

Hard. There are a set of prints, too. What think you of the Rake's Progress for your own apartment?

Marlow. Bring me your bill, I say; and I'll leave you and your infernal house directly.

Hard. Then there's a mahogany table, that you may see your own face in.

Marlow. My bill, I say.

Hard. I had forgot the great chair, for your own particular slumbers, after a hearty meal.

Marlow. Zounds! bring me my bill, I say, and let's hear no more on't.

Hard. Young man, young man, from your father's letter to me, I was taught to expect a well-bred modest man, as a visitor here, but now I find him no better than a coxcomb and a bully; but he will be down here presently, and shall hear more of it.   [*Exit.*

Marlow. How's this! Sure I have not mistaken the house! Everything looks like an inn. The servants cry 'coming'. The attendance is awkward; the barmaid, too, to attend us. But she's here, and will further inform me. Whither so fast, child? A word with you.

Enter MISS HARDCASTLE

Miss Hard. Let it be short, then. I'm in a hurry. (*Aside.*) I believe he begins to find out his mistake, but it's too soon quite to undeceive him.

Marlow. Pray, child, answer me one question. What are you, and what may your business in this house be?

Miss Hard. A relation of the family, sir.

Marlow. What, a poor relation?

Miss Hard. Yes, sir. A poor relation appointed to keep

the keys, and to see that the guests want nothing in my power to give them.

Marlow. That is, you act as the barmaid of this inn.

Miss Hard. Inn. O law! – What brought that in your head? One of the best families in the country keep an inn! Ha, ha, ha, old Mr Hardcastle's house an inn!

Marlow. Mr Hardcastle's house! Is this house Mr Hardcastle's house, child?

Miss Hard. Ay, sure. Whose else should it be?

Marlow. So then all's out, and I have been damnably imposed on. O, confound my stupid head, I shall be laughed at over the whole town. I shall be stuck up in caricatura in all the print-shops. The Dullissimo Maccaroni. To mistake this house of all others for an inn, and my father's old friend for an innkeeper. What a swaggering puppy must he take me for. What a silly puppy do I find myself. There again, may I be hanged, my dear, but I mistook you for the barmaid.

Miss Hard. Dear me! dear me! I'm sure there's nothing in my behaviour to put me upon a level with one of that stamp.

Marlow. Nothing, my dear, nothing. But I was in for a list of blunders, and could not help making you a subscriber. My stupidity saw everything the wrong way. I mistook your assiduity for assurance, and your simplicity for allurement. But it's over. – This house I no more show my face in!

Miss Hard. I hope, sir, I have done nothing to disoblige you. I'm sure I should be sorry to affront any gentleman who has been so polite, and said so many civil things to me. I'm sure I should be sorry (*pretending to cry*) if he left the family upon my account. I'm sure I should be sorry people said anything amiss, since I have no fortune but my character.

Marlow. (*Aside.*) By heaven, she weeps. This is the first mark of tenderness I ever had from a modest woman, and it touches me. (*To her.*) Excuse me, my lovely girl,

you are the only part of the family I leave with reluctance. But to be plain with you, the difference of
our birth, fortune and education, make an honourable
connexion impossible.

Miss Hard. (*Aside.*) Generous man! I now begin to
admire him. (*To him.*) But I'm sure my family is as
good as Miss Hardcastle's, and though I'm poor, that's
no great misfortune to a contented mind, and, until this
moment, I never thought that it was bad to want fortune.

Marlow. And why now, my pretty simplicity?

Miss Hard. Because it puts me at a distance from one,
that if I had a thousand pound I would give it all to.

Marlow (*Aside.*) This simplicity bewitches me, so that if
I stay I'm undone. I must make one bold effort, and
leave her. (*To her.*) Your partiality in my favour, my
dear, touches me most sensibly, and were I to live for
myself alone, I could easily fix my choice. But I owe
too much to the opinion of the world, too much to the
authority of a father, so that – I can scarcely speak it –
it affects me. Farewell.   [*Exit.*

Miss Hard. I never knew half his merit till now. He shall
not go, if I have power or art to detain him. I'll still
preserve the character in which I stooped to conquer,
but will undeceive my papa, who, perhaps, may laugh
him out of his resolution.   [*Exit.*

Enter TONY, MISS NEVILLE

Tony. Ay, you may steal for yourselves the next time. I
have done my duty. She has got the jewels again,
that's a sure thing; but she believes it was all a mistake of the servants.

Miss Neville. But, my dear cousin, sure, you won't forsake
us in this distress. If she in the least suspects that I am
going off, I shall certainly be locked up, or sent to my
Aunt Pedigree's which is ten times worse.

Tony. To be sure, aunts of all kinds are damned bad
things. But what can I do? I have got you a pair of

horses that will fly like Whistlejacket, and I'm sure
you can't say but I have courted you nicely before her
face. Here she comes, we must court a bit or two
more, for fear she should suspect us.

> [*They retire, and seem to fondle.*

Enter MRS HARDCASTLE

Mrs Hard. Well, I was greatly fluttered, to be sure. But
my son tells me it was all a mistake of the servants.
I shan't be easy, however, till they are fairly married,
and then let her keep her own fortune. But what do
I see? Fondling together, as I'm alive! I never saw
Tony so sprightly before. Ah! have I caught you, my
pretty doves! What, billing, exchanging stolen glances,
and broken murmurs! Ah!

Tony. As for murmurs, mother, we grumble a little now
and then, to be sure. But there's no love lost between us.

Mrs Hard. A mere sprinkling, Tony, upon the flame,
only to make it burn brighter.

Miss Neville. Cousin Tony promises to give us more of
his company at home. Indeed, he shan't leave us any
more. It won't leave us, cousin Tony, will it?

Tony. O! it's a pretty creature. No, I'd sooner leave my
horse in a pound, than leave you when you smile
upon one so. Your laugh makes you so becoming.

Miss Neville. Agreeable cousin! Who can help admiring
that natural humour, that pleasant, broad, red,
thoughtless (*patting his cheek*) ah! it's a bold face.

Mrs Hard. Pretty innocence!

Tony. I'm sure I always loved cousin Con's hazel eyes,
and her pretty long fingers, that she twists this way and
that, over the haspicholls, like a parcel of bobbins.

Mrs Hard. Ah, he would charm the bird from the tree.
I was never so happy before. My boy takes after his
father, poor Mr Lumpkin, exactly. The jewels, my
dear Con, shall be yours incontinently. You shall have
them. Isn't he a sweet boy, my dear? You shall be

married tomorrow, and we'll put off the rest of his education, like Dr Drowsy's sermons, to a fitter opportunity.

Enter DIGGORY

Diggory. Where's the 'Squire? I have got a letter for your worship.

Tony. Give it to my mamma. She reads all my letters first.

Diggory. I had orders to deliver it into your own hands.

Tony. Who does it come from?

Diggory. Your worship mun ask that o' the letter itself.

Tony. I could wish to know, though.

[*Turning the letter, and gazing on it.*

Miss Neville. (*Aside.*) Undone, undone. A letter to him from Hastings. I know the hand. If my aunt sees it we are ruined for ever. I'll keep her employed a little if I can. (*To Mrs Hardcastle.*) But I have not told you, madam, of my cousin's smart answer just now to Mr Marlow. We so laughed. – You must know, madam – This way a little, for he must not hear us. [*They confer.*

Tony. (*Still gazing*) A damned cramp piece of penmanship, as ever I saw in my life. I can read your printhand very well. But here there are such handles, and shakes, and dashes, that one can scarce tell the head from the tail. 'To Anthony Lumpkin, Esquire.' It's very odd, I can read the outside of my letters, where my own name is, well enough. But when I come to open it, it's all – buzz. That's hard, very hard; for the inside of the letter is always the cream of the correspondence.

Mrs Hard. Ha! ha! ha! Very well, very well. And so my son was too hard for the philosopher.

Miss Neville. Yes, madam; but you must hear the rest, madam. A little more this way, or he may hear us. You'll hear how he puzzled him again.

Mrs Hard. He seems strangely puzzled now himself, methinks.

Tony. (*Still gazing*) A damned up and down hand, as if it was disguised in liquor. (*Reading*) Dear Sir. Ay, that's that. Then there's an M, and a T, and an S, but whether the next be an izzard or an R, confound me, I cannot tell.

Mrs Hard. What's that, my dear? Can I give you any assistance?

Miss Neville. Pray, aunt, let me read it. Nobody reads a cramp hand better than I. (*twitching the letter from her*) Do you know who it is from?

Tony. Can't tell, except from Dick Ginger the feeder.

Miss Neville. Ay, so it is. (*pretending to read*) Dear 'Squire, Hoping that you're in health, as I am, at this present. The gentlemen of the Shakebag club has cut the gentlemen of Goose-green quite out of feather. The odds – um – odd battle – um – long fighting – um, here, here, it's all about cocks, and fighting; it's of no consequence, here, put it up, put it up.

[*Thrusting the crumpled letter upon him.*

Tony. But I tell you, miss, it's of all the consequence in the world. I would not lose the rest of it for a guinea. Here, mother, do you make it out? Of no consequence!

[*Giving Mrs Hardcastle the letter.*

Mrs Hard. How's this! (*reads*) 'Dear 'Squire, I'm now waiting for Miss Neville, with a post-chaise and pair, at the bottom of the garden but I find my horses yet unable to perform the journey. I expect you'll assist us with a pair of fresh horses, as you promised. Dispatch is necessary, as the hag' – ay, the hag – 'your mother, will otherwise suspect us. Yours, Hastings.' Grant me patience. I shall run distracted. My rage chokes me.

Miss Neville. I hope, madam, you'll suspend your resentment for a few moments, and not impute to me any impertinence, or sinister design, that belongs to another.

Mrs Hard. (*Curtsying very low.*) Fine spoken, madam, you are most miraculously polite and engaging, and quite the very pink of courtesy and circumspection, madam.

(*Changing her tone*) And you, you great ill-fashioned oaf, with scarce sense enough to keep your mouth shut. Were you, too, joined against me? But I'll defeat all your plots in a moment. As for you, madam, since you have got a pair of fresh horses ready, it would be cruel to disappoint them. So, if you please, instead of running away with your spark, prepare, this very moment, to run off with me. Your old Aunt Pedigree will keep you secure, I'll warrant me. You too, sir, may mount your horse, and guard us upon the way. Here, Thomas, Roger, Diggory, I'll show you that I wish you better than you do yourselves.   [*Exit*.

Miss Neville. So now I'm completely ruined.

Tony. Ay, that's a sure thing.

Miss Neville. What better could be expected from being connected with such a stupid fool, and after all the nods and signs I made him.

Tony. By the laws, miss, it was your own cleverness, and not my stupidity, that did your business. You were so nice and so busy with your Shake-bags and Goosegreens, that I thought you could never be making believe.

Enter HASTINGS

Hastings. So, sir, I find by my servant, that you have shown my letter, and betrayed us. Was this well done, young gentleman?

Tony. Here's another. Ask Miss there who betrayed you. Ecod, it was her doing, not mine.

Enter MARLOW

Marlow. So I have been finely used here among you. Rendered contemptible, driven into ill manners, despised, insulted, laughed at.

Tony. Here's another. We shall have old Bedlam broke loose presently.

Miss Neville. And there, sir, is the gentleman to whom we all owe every obligation.

Marlow. What can I say to him, a mere boy, an idiot, whose ignorance and age are a protection.

Hastings. A poor contemptible booby, that would but disgrace correction.

Miss Neville. Yet with cunning and malice enough to make himself merry with all our embarrassments.

Hastings. An insensible cub.

Marlow. Replete with tricks and mischief.

Tony. Baw! damme, but I'll fight you both one after the other – with baskets.

Marlow. As for him, he's below resentment. But your conduct, Mr Hastings, requires an explanation. You knew of my mistakes, yet would not undeceive me.

Hastings. Tortured as I am with my own disappointments, is this a time for explanations? It is not friendly, Mr Marlow.

Marlow. But, sir –

Miss Neville. Mr Marlow, we never kept on your mistake, till it was too late to undeceive you. Be pacified.

Enter SERVANT

Servant. My mistress desires you'll get ready immediately, madam. The horses are putting to. Your hat and things are in the next room. We are to go thirty miles before morning.   [*Exit Servant.*

Miss Neville. Well, well; I'll come presently.

Marlow. (*To Hastings*) Was it well done, sir, to assist in rendering me ridiculous? To hang me out for the scorn of all my acquaintance? Depend upon it, sir, I shall expect an explanation.

Hastings. Was it well done, sir, if you're upon that subject, to deliver what I entrusted to yourself, to the care of another, sir?

Miss Neville. Mr Hastings, Mr Marlow. Why will you increase my distress by this groundless dispute? I implore, I entreat you –

Enter SERVANT

Servant. Your cloak, madam. My mistress is impatient.

[*Exit Servant.*

Miss Neville. I come. Pray be pacified. If I leave you thus, I shall die with apprehension!

Enter SERVANT

Servant. Your fan, muff, and gloves, madam. The horses are waiting.

Miss Neville. O, Mr Marlow! if you knew what a scene of constraint and ill-nature lies before me, I'm sure it would convert your resentment into pity.

Marlow. I'm so distracted with a variety of passions, that I don't know what I do. Forgive me, madam. George, forgive me. You know my hasty temper, and should not exasperate it.

Hastings. The torture of my situation is my only excuse.

Miss Neville. Well, my dear Hastings, if you have that esteem for me that I think, that I am sure you have, your constancy for three years will but increase the happiness of our future connexion. If –

Mrs Hard. (*Within.*) Miss Neville. Constance, why, Constance, I say.

Miss Neville. I'm coming. Well, constancy. Remember, constancy is the word. [*Exit*

Hastings. My heart! How can I support this? To be so near happiness, and such happiness!

Marlow. (*To Tony.*) You see now, young gentleman, the effects of your folly. What might be amusement to you, is here disappointment, and even distress.

Tony. (*From a reverie.*) Ecod, I have hit it. It's here. Your hands. Yours and yours, my poor Sulky. My boots there, ho! Meet me two hours hence at the bottom of the garden; and if you don't find Tony Lumpkin a more good-natur'd fellow than you thought for, I'll give you leave to take my best horse, and Bet Bouncer into the bargain. Come along. My boots, ho! [*Exeunt.*

ACT V

Scene Continues

Enter HASTINGS *and* SERVANT

Hastings. You saw the old lady and Miss Neville drive off, you say?

Servant. Yes, your honour. They went off in a post coach, and the young 'squire went on horseback. They're thirty miles off by this time.

Hastings. Then all my hopes are over.

Servant. Yes, sir. Old Sir Charles is arrived. He and the old gentleman of the house have been laughing at Mr Marlow's mistake this half-hour. They are coming this way.

Hastings. Then I must not be seen. So now to my fruitless appointment at the bottom of the garden. This is about the time. [*Exit.*

Enter SIR CHARLES *and* HARDCASTLE

Hard. Ha! ha! ha! The peremptory tone in which he sent forth his sublime commands.

Sir Charles. And the reserve with which I suppose he treated all your advances.

Hard. And yet he might have seen something in me above a common innkeeper, too.

Sir Charles. Yes, Dick, but he mistook you for an uncommon innkeeper, ha! ha! ha!

Hard. Well, I'm in too good spirits to think of anything but joy. Yes, my dear friend, this union of our families will make our personal friendships hereditary: and though my daughter's fortune is but small —

Sir Charles. Why, Dick, will you talk of fortune to me? My son is possessed of more than a competence already, and can want nothing but a good and virtuous girl to share his happiness and increase it. If they like each other, as you say they do —

Hard. If, man! I tell you they do like each other. My daughter as good as told me so.

Sir Charles. But girls are apt to flatter themselves, you know.

Hard. I saw him grasp her hand in the warmest manner myself; and here he comes to put you out of your ifs, I warrant him.

Enter MARLOW

Marlow. I come, sir, once more, to ask pardon for my strange conduct. I can scarce reflect on my insolence without confusion.

Hard. Tut, boy, a trifle. You take it too gravely. An hour or two's laughing with my daughter will set all to rights again. She'll never like you the worse for it.

Marlow. Sir, I shall be always proud of her approbation.

Hard. Approbation is but a cold word, Mr Marlow; if I am not deceived, you have something more than approbation thereabouts. You take me.

Marlow. Really, sir, I have not that happiness.

Hard. Come, boy, I'm an old fellow, and know what's what, as well as you that are younger. I know what has past between you; but mum.

Marlow. Sure, sir, nothing has passed between us but the most profound respect on my side, and the most distant reserve on hers. You don't think, sir, that my impudence has been passed upon all the rest of the family.

Hard. Impudence! No, I don't say that – not quite impudence – though girls like to be played with, and rumpled a little too, sometimes. But she has told no tales, I assure you.

Marlow. I never gave her the slightest cause.

Hard. Well, well, I like modesty in its place well enough. But this is over-acting, young gentleman. You may be open. Your father and I will like you the better for it.

Marlow. May I die, sir, if I ever –

Hard. I tell you, she don't dislike you; and as I'm sure you like her –

Marlow. Dear sir – I protest, sir –

Hard. I see no reason why you should not be joined as fast as the parson can tie you.

Marlow. But hear me, sir –

Hard. Your father approves the match, I admire it, every moment's delay will be doing mischief, so –

Marlow. But why won't you hear me? By all that's just and true, I never gave Miss Hardcastle the slightest mark of my attachment, or even the most distant hint to suspect me of affection. We had but one interview, and that was formal, modest, and uninteresting.

Hard. (*Aside.*) This fellow's formal modest impudence is beyond bearing.

Sir Charles. And you never grasped her hand, or made any protestations!

Marlow. As heaven is my witness, I came down in obedience to your commands. I saw the lady without emotion, and parted without reluctance. I hope you'll exact no further proofs of my duty, nor prevent me from leaving a house in which I suffer so many mortifications.   [*Exit.*

Sir Charles. I'm astonished at the air of sincerity with which he parted.

Hard. And I'm astonished at the deliberate intrepidity of his assurance.

Sir Charles. I dare pledge my life and honour upon his truth.

Hard. (*Looking out to right.*) Here comes my daughter, and I would stake my happiness upon her veracity.

Enter Miss Hardcastle

Hard. Kate, come hither, child. Answer us sincerely, and without reserve; has Mr Marlow made you any professions of love and affection?

Miss Hard. The question is very abrupt, sir! But since you require unreserved sincerity, I think he has.

Hard. (*To Sir Charles.*) You see.

Sir Charles. And pray, madam, have you and my son had more than one interview?

Miss Hard. Yes, sir, several.

Hard. (*To Sir Charles.*) You see.

Sir Charles. But did he profess any attachment?

Miss Hard. A lasting one.

Sir Charles. Did he talk of love?

Miss Hard. Much, sir.

Sir Charles. Amazing! And all this formally?

Miss Hard. Formally.

Hard. Now, my friend, I hope you are satisfied.

Sir Charles. And how did he behave, madam?

Miss Hard. As most professed admirers do. Said some civil things of my face, talked much of his want of merit, and the greatness of mine; mentioned his heart, gave a short tragedy speech, and ended with pretended rapture.

Sir Charles. Now I'm perfectly convinced, indeed. I know his conversation among women to be modest and submissive. This forward, canting, ranting manner by no means describes him, and I am confident he never sat for the picture.

Miss Hard. Then what, sir, if I should convince you to your face of my sincerity? If you and my papa, in about half an hour, will place yourselves behind that screen, you shall hear him declare his passion to me in person.

Sir Charles. Agreed. And if I find him what you describe, all my happiness in him must have an end.   [*Exit.*

Miss Hard. And if you don't find him what I describe – I fear my happiness must never have a beginning.

[*Exeunt.*

Scene changes to the back of the garden.

Enter HASTINGS

Hastings. What an idiot am I, to wait here for a fellow,

who probably takes a delight in mortifying me. He never intended to be punctual, and I'll wait no longer. What do I see? It is he, and perhaps with news of my Constance.

Enter TONY, *booted and spattered*

Hastings. My honest 'Squire! I now find you a man of your word. This looks like friendship.

Tony. Ay, I'm your friend, and the best friend you have in the world, if you knew but all. This riding by night, by the by, is cursedly tiresome. It has shook me worse than the basket of a stage-coach.

Hastings. But how? Where did you leave your fellow-travellers? Are they in safety? Are they housed?

Tony. Five and twenty miles in two hours and a half is no such bad driving. The poor beasts have smoked for it: rabbit me, but I'd rather ride forty miles after a fox, than ten with such varmint.

Hastings. Well, but where have you left the ladies? I die with impatience.

Tony. Left them? Why, where should I leave them, but where I found them?

Hastings. This is a riddle.

Tony. Riddle me this, then. What's that goes round the house, and round the house, and never touches the house?

Hastings. I'm still astray.

Tony. Why, that's it, mon. I have led them astray. By jingo, there's not a pond or slough within five miles of the place but they can tell the taste of.

Hastings. Ha, ha, ha, I understand; you took them in a round, while they supposed themselves going forward. And so you have at last brought them home again.

Tony. You shall hear. I first took them down Feather-Bed Lane, where we stuck fast in the mud. I then rattled them crack over the stones of Up-and-Down Hill – I then introduced them to the gibbet on Heavy-Tree

Heath, and from that, with a circumbendibus, I fairly lodged them in the horsepond at the bottom of the garden.

Hastings. But no accident, I hope.

Tony. No, no. Only mother is confoundedly frightened. She thinks herself forty miles off. She's sick of the journey, and the cattle can scarce crawl. So, if your own horses be ready, you may whip off with cousin, and I'll be bound that no soul here can budge a foot to follow you.

Hastings. My dear friend, how can I be grateful?

Tony. Ay, now it's dear friend, noble 'Squire. Just now, it was all idiot, cub, and run me through the guts. Damn your way of fighting, I say. After we take a knock in this part of the country, we kiss and be friends. But if you had run me through the guts, then I should be dead, and you might go kiss the hangman.

Hastings. The rebuke is just. But I must hasten to relieve Miss Neville; if you keep the old lady employed, I promise to take care of the young one. [*Exit Hastings.*

Tony. Never fear me. Here she comes. Vanish. She's got from the pond, and draggled up to the waist like a mermaid.

Enter MRS HARDCASTLE

Mrs Hard. Oh, Tony, I'm killed. Shook. Battered to death. I shall never survive it. That last jolt that laid us against the quickset hedge has done my business.

Tony. Alack, mamma, it was all your own fault. You would be for running away by night, without knowing one inch of the way.

Mrs Hard. I wish we were at home again. I never met so many accidents in so short a journey. Drenched in the mud, overturned in a ditch, stuck fast in a slough, jolted to a jelly, and at last to lose our way. Whereabouts do you think we are, Tony?

Tony. By my guess we should be upon Crackskull Common, about forty miles from home.

Mrs Hard. O lud! O lud! the most notorious spot in all the country. We only want a robbery to make a complete night on't.

Tony. Don't be afraid, mamma, don't be afraid. Two of the five that kept here are hanged, and the other three may not find us. Don't be afraid. Is that a man that's galloping behind us? No; it's only a tree. Don't be afraid.

Mrs Hard. The fright will certainly kill me.

Tony. Do you see anything like a black hat moving behind the thicket?

Mrs Hard. O death!

Tony. No, it's only a cow. Don't be afraid, mamma, don't be afraid.

Mrs Hard. As I'm alive, Tony, I see a man coming towards us. Ah! I'm sure on't. If he perceives us, we are undone.

Tony. (*Aside.*) Father-in-law, by all that's unlucky, come to take one of his night walks. (*To her.*) Ah, it's a highwayman, with pistols as long as my arm. A damned ill-looking fellow.

Mrs Hard. Good Heaven defend us! He approaches.

Tony. Do you hide yourself in that thicket and leave me to manage him. If there be any danger I'll cough and cry hem. When I cough be sure to keep close.

[*Mrs Hardcastle hides behind a tree in the back scene.*

Enter HARDCASTLE

Hard. I'm mistaken, or I heard voices of people in want of help. Oh, Tony, is that you? I did not expect you so soon back. Are your mother and her charge in safety?

Tony. Very safe, sir, at my Aunt Pedigree's. Hem.

Mrs Hard. (*From behind.*) Ah! I find there's danger.

Hard. Forty miles in three hours; sure, that's too much, my youngster.

Tony. Stout horses and willing minds make short journeys, as they say. Hem.

Mrs Hard. (*From behind.*) Sure he'll do the dear boy no harm.

Hard. But I heard a voice here; I should be glad to know from whence it came?

Tony. It was I, sir, talking to myself, sir. I was saying that forty miles in four hours was very good going. Hem. As to be sure it was. Hem. I have got a sort of cold by being out in the air. We'll go in if you please. Hem.

Hard. But if you talked to yourself, you did not answer yourself. I am certain I heard two voices, and am resolved (*raising his voice*) to find the other out.

Mrs Hard. (*From behind.*) Oh! he's coming to find me out. Oh!

Tony. What need you go, sir, if I tell you? Hem. I'll lay down my life for the truth – hem – I'll tell you all, sir.
[*Detaining him.*

Hard. I tell you I will not be detained. I insist on seeing. It's in vain to expect I'll believe you.

Mrs Hard. (*Running forward from behind.*) O lud, he'll murder my poor boy, my darling. Here, good gentleman, whet your rage upon me. Take my money, my life, but spare that young gentleman, spare my child, if you have any mercy.

Hard. My wife! as I'm a Christian. From whence can she come, or what does she mean?

Mrs Hard. (*Kneeling.*) Take compassion on us, good Mr Highwayman. Take our money, our watches, all we have, but spare our lives. We will never bring you to justice, indeed we won't, good Mr Highwayman.

Hard. I believe the woman's out of her senses. What, Dorothy, don't you know me?

Mrs Hard. Mr Hardcastle, as I'm alive! My fears blinded me. But who, my dear, could have expected to meet you here, in this frightful place, so far from home. What has brought you to follow us?

Hard. Sure, Dorothy, you have not lost your wits. So far from home, when you are within forty yards of your own door! (*To him.*) This is one of your old tricks, you graceless rogue, you! (*To her.*) Don't you know the gate, and the mulberry-tree; and don't you remember the horsepond, my dear?

Mrs Hard. Yes, I shall remember the horsepond as long as I live; I have caught my death in it. (*To Tony.*) And it is to you, you graceless varlet, I owe all this? I'll teach you to abuse your mother, I will.

Tony. Ecod, mother, all the parish says you have spoiled me, and so you may take the fruits on't.

Mrs Hard. I'll spoil you, I will. [*Follows him off the stage.*

Hard. There's morality, however, in his reply.

[*Exit.*

Enter HASTINGS *and* MISS NEVILLE

Hastings. My dear Constance, why will you deliberate thus? If we delay a moment, all is lost for ever. Pluck up a little resolution, and we shall soon be out of the reach of her malignity.

Miss Neville. I find it impossible. My spirits are so sunk with the agitations I have suffered, that I am unable to face any new danger. Two or three years' patience will at last crown us with happiness.

Hastings. Such a tedious delay is worse than inconstancy. Let us fly, my charmer. Let us date our happiness from this very moment. Perish fortune. Love and content will increase what we possess beyond a monarch's revenue. Let me prevail.

Miss Neville. No, Mr Hastings; no. Prudence once more comes to my relief, and I will obey its dictates. In the moment of passion, fortune may be despised, but it ever produces a lasting repentance. I'm resolved to apply to Mr Hardcastle's compassion and justice for redress.

Hastings. But though he had the will, he has not the power to relieve you.

Miss Neville. But he has influence, and upon that I am resolved to rely.

Hastings. I have no hopes. But since you persist, I must reluctantly obey you.   [*Exeunt.*

Scene changes

Enter SIR CHARLES *and* MISS HARDCASTLE

Sir Charles. What a situation am I in. If what you say appears, I shall then find a guilty son. If what he says be true, I shall then lose one that, of all others, I most wished for a daughter.

Miss Hard. I am proud of your approbation, and, to show I merit it, if you place yourselves as I directed, you shall hear his explicit declaration. But he comes.

Sir Charles. I'll to your father, and keep him to the appointment.   [*Exit Sir Charles.*

Enter MARLOW

Marlow. Though prepared for setting out, I come once more to take leave, nor did I, till this moment, know the pain I feel in the separation.

Miss Hard. (*In her own natural manner.*) I believe sufferings cannot be very great, sir, which you can so easily remove. A day or two longer, perhaps, might lessen your uneasiness, by showing the little value of what you think proper to regret.

Marlow. (*Aside.*) This girl every moment improves upon me. (*To her.*) It must not be, madam. I have already trifled too long with my heart. My very pride begins to submit to my passion. The disparity of education and fortune, the anger of a parent, and the contempt of my equals, begin to lose their weight; and nothing can restore me to myself but this painful effort of resolution.

Miss Hard. Then go, sir. I'll urge nothing more to detain you. Though my family be as good as hers you came down to visit, and my education, I hope, not inferior, what are these advantages without equal affluence? I must remain contented with the slight approbation of imputed merit; I must have only the mockery of your addresses, while all your serious aims are fixed on fortune.

Enter HARDCASTLE *and* SIR CHARLES *from behind*

Sir Charles. Here, behind this screen.

Hard. Ay, ay, make no noise. I'll engage my Kate covers him with confusion at last.

Marlow. By heavens, madam, fortune was ever my smallest consideration. Your beauty at first caught my eye; for who could see that without emotion? But every moment that I converse with you, steals in some new grace, heightens the picture, and gives it stronger expression. What at first seemed rustic plainness, now appears refined simplicity. What seemed forward assurance, now strikes me as the result of courageous innocence, and conscious virtue.

Sir Charles. What can it mean! He amazes me!

Hard. I told you how it would be. Hush!

Marlow. I am now determined to stay, madam, and I have too good an opinion of my father's discernment, when he sees you, to doubt his approbation.

Miss Hard. No, Mr Marlow, I will not, cannot detain you. Do you think I could suffer a connexion, in which there is the smallest room for repentance? Do you think I would take the mean advantage of a transient passion, to load you with confusion? Do you think I could ever relish that happiness, which was acquired by lessening yours!

Marlow. By all that's good, I can have no happiness but what's in your power to grant me. Nor shall I ever feel repentance, but in not having seen your merits before. I will stay, even contrary to your wishes; and though you should persist to shun me, I will make my respectful assiduities atone for the levity of my past conduct.

Miss Hard. Sir, I must entreat you'll desist. As our acquaintance began, so let it end, in indifference. I might have given an hour or two to levity; but, seriously, Mr Marlow, do you think I could ever submit to a connexion, where I must appear mercenary, and you imprudent? Do you think, I could ever catch at the confident addresses of a secure admirer?

Marlow. (*Kneeling.*) Does this look like security? Does this look like confidence? No, madam, every moment that shows me your merit, only serves to increase my diffidence and confusion. Here let me continue –

Sir Charles. I can hold it no longer. Charles, Charles, how hast thou deceived me! Is this your indifference, your uninteresting conversation!

Hard. Your cold contempt; your formal interview. What have you to say now?

Marlow. That I'm all amazement! What can it mean!

Hard. It means that you can say and unsay things at pleasure. That you can address a lady in private, and deny it in public; that you have one story for us, and another for my daughter!

Marlow. Daughter! this lady your daughter!

Hard. Yes, sir, my only daughter. My Kate, whose else should she be?

Marlow. Oh, the devil!

Miss Hard. Yes, sir, that very identical tall squinting lady you were pleased to take me for. (*Curtsying.*) She that you addressed as the mild, modest, sentimental man of gravity, and the bold, forward, agreeable Rattle of the Ladies' Club: ha, ha, ha.

Marlow. Zounds, there's no bearing this; it's worse than death.

Miss Hard. In which of your characters, sir, will you give us leave to address you? As the faltering gentleman, with looks on the ground, that speaks just to be heard, and hates hypocrisy: or the loud confident creature,

that keeps it up with Mrs Mantrap, and old Miss
Biddy Buckskin, till three in the morning; ha, ha, ha!

Marlow. Oh, curse on my noisy head. I never attempted
to be imprudent yet, that I was not taken down. I
must be gone.   [*Going.*

Hard. By the hand of my body, but you shall not. I see
it was all a mistake, and I am rejoiced to find it. You
shall not, sir, I tell you. I know she'll forgive you.
Won't you forgive him, Kate? We'll all forgive you.
Take courage, man.

[*They retire, she tormenting him, to the back scene.*

Enter MRS HARDCASTLE, TONY

Mrs Hard. So, so, they're gone off. Let them go, I care not.

Hard. Who gone?

Mrs Hard. My dutiful niece and her gentleman, Mr
Hastings, from town. He who came down with our
modest visitor here.

Sir Charles. Who, my honest George Hastings? As worthy
a fellow as lives, and the girl could not have made a
more prudent choice.

Hard. Then, by the hand of my body, I'm proud of the
connexion.

Mrs Hard. Well, if he has taken away the lady, he has
not taken her fortune, that remains in this family to
console us for her loss.

Hard. Sure, Dorothy, you would not be so mercenary?

Mrs Hard. Ay, that's my affair, not yours.

Hard. But you know, if your son, when of age, refuses to
marry his cousin, her whole fortune is then at her own
disposal.

Mrs Hard. Ah, but he's not of age, and she has not thought
proper to wait for his refusal.

Enter HASTINGS *and* MISS NEVILLE

Mrs Hard. (*Aside.*) What, returned so soon! I begin not
to like it.

Hastings. (*To Hardcastle.*) For my late attempt to fly off with your niece, let my present confusion be my punishment. We are now come back to appeal from your justice to your humanity. By her father's consent, I first paid her my addresses, and our passions were first founded in duty.

Miss Neville. Since his death, I have been obliged to stoop to dissimulation to avoid oppression. In an hour of levity, I was ready even to give up my fortune to secure my choice. But I'm now recovered from the delusion, and hope from your tenderness what is denied me from a nearer connexion.

Mrs Hard. Pshaw, pshaw, this is all but the whining end of a modern novel.

Hard. Be it what it will, I'm glad they're come back to reclaim their due. Come hither, Tony boy. Do you refuse this lady's hand whom I now offer you?

Tony. What signifies my refusing? You know I can't refuse her till I'm of age, father.

Hard. While I thought concealing your age, boy, was likely to conduce to your improvement, I concurred with your mother's desire to keep it secret. But since I find she turns it to a wrong use, I must now declare, you have been of age these three months.

Tony. Of age! Am I of age, father?

Hard. Above three months.

Tony. Then you'll see the first use I'll make of my liberty. (*Taking Miss Neville's hand.*) Witness all men by these presents, that I, Anthony Lumpkin, Esquire, of BLANK place, refuse you, Constantia Neville, spinster, of no place at all, for my true and lawful wife. So Constance Neville may marry whom she pleases and Tony Lumpkin is his own man again!

Sir Charles. O brave 'squire!

Hastings. My worthy friend!

Mrs. Hard. My undutiful offspring!

Marlow. Joy, my dear George, I give you joy, sincerely.

And could I prevail upon my little tyrant here to be less arbitrary, I should be the happiest man alive, if you would return me the favour.

Hastings. (*To Miss Hardcastle.*) Come, madam, you are now driven to the very last scene of all your contrivances. I know you like him, I'm sure he loves you, and you must and shall have him.

Hard. (*Joining their hands.*) And I say so, too. And Mr Marlow, if she makes as good a wife as she has a daughter, I don't believe you'll ever repent your bargain. So now to supper. Tomorrow we shall gather all the poor of the parish about us, and the mistakes of the night shall be crowned with a merry morning; so boy, take her; and as you have been mistaken in the mistress, my wish is, that you may never be mistaken in the wife.

EPILOGUE

By Dr Goldsmith

WELL, having stooped to conquer with success,
And gained a husband without aid from dress,
Still as a barmaid, I could wish it too,
As I have conquered him to conquer you:
And let me say, for all your resolution,
That pretty barmaids have done execution.
Our life is all a play, composed to please,
'We have our exits and our entrances.'
The first act shows the simple country maid,
Harmless and young, of everything afraid;
Blushes when hired, and with unmeaning action,
'I hopes as how to give you satisfaction.'
Her second act displays a livelier scene, –
Th' unblushing barmaid of a country inn,
Who whisks about the house, at market caters,
Talks loud, coquets the guests, and scolds the waiters.
Next the scene shifts to town, and there she soars,
The chop-house toast of ogling connoisseurs.
On 'squires and cits she there displays her arts,
And on the gridiron broils her lovers' hearts –
And as she smiles, her triumphs to complete,
Even common councilmen forget to eat.
The fourth act shows her wedded to the 'squire,
And madam now begins to hold it higher;
Pretends to taste, at Operas cries caro,
And quits her Nancy Dawson, for Che Faro.
Doats upon dancing, and in all her pride,
Swims round the room, the Heinel of Cheapside:
Ogles and leers with artificial skill,
Till having lost in age the power to kill,
She sits all night at cards, and ogles at spadille.

Such, through our lives, the eventful history –
The fifth and last act still remains for me.
The barmaid now for your protection prays,
Turns female Barrister, and pleads for Bayes.

THE

SCHOOL FOR SCANDAL

By R. B. Sheridan

DRAMATIS PERSONAE

AS ORIGINALLY ACTED
AT DRURY LANE THEATRE IN 1777

SIR PETER TEAZLE	*Mr King*
SIR OLIVER SURFACE	*Mr Yates*
SIR TOBY BUMPER	*Mr Gaudry*
SIR BENJAMIN BACKBITE	*Mr Dodd*
JOSEPH SURFACE	*Mr Palmer*
CHARLES SURFACE	*Mr Smith*
CARELESS	*Mr Farren*
SNAKE	*Mr Packer*
CRABTREE	*Mr Parsons*
ROWLEY	*Mr Aickin*
MOSES	*Mr Baddeley*
TRIP	*Mr LaMash*
LADY TEAZLE	*Mrs Abingdon*
LADY SNEERWELL	*Miss Sherry*
MRS CANDOUR	*Miss Pope*
MARIA	*Miss P. Hopkins*

Gentlemen, Maid, and Servants

SCENE–LONDON

THE SCHOOL FOR SCANDAL

PROLOGUE

WRITTEN BY MR GARRICK

A SCHOOL for Scandal! tell me, I beseech you,
Needs there a school – this modish art to teach you?
No need of lessons now; – the knowing think –
We might as well be taught to eat and drink;
Caus'd by a dearth of scandal, should the vapours
Distress our fair ones – let 'em read the papers;
Their powerful mixtures such disorders hit;
Crave what you will – there's *quantum sufficit.*
'Lord!' cries my Lady *Wormwood* (who loves tattle,
And puts much salt and pepper in her prattle),
Just ris'n at noon, all night at cards, when threshing
Strong tea and scandal – 'Bless me, how refreshing!
Give me the papers, *Lisp* – how bold and free!   [*Sips.*
Last night Lord L. [*Sips.*] was caught with Lady D.
For aching heads what charming *sal volatile!*   [*Sips.*
If Mrs B. will still continue flirting,
We hope she'll *draw,* or we'll *undraw* the curtain.
Fine satire, poz – in public all abuse it,
But, by ourselves, [*Sips.*] our praise we can't refuse it.
Now, *Lisp,* read you – there, at that dash and star.'
'Yes, ma'am – A certain Lord had best beware,
Who lives not twenty miles from Grosv'nor Square;
For should he Lady W —— find willing, –
Wormwood is bitter' – 'Oh! that's me! the villain!
Throw it behind the fire, and never more
Let that vile paper *come within my door.*'
Thus at our friends we laugh, who feel the dart;
To reach *our* feelings, we ourselves must smart.
Is our young bard so young – to think that he
Can stop the full spring-tide of calumny?

Knows he the world so little, and its trade?
Alas! the devil's sooner *rais'd* than *laid*.
So strong, so swift, the monster there's no gagging:
Cut Scandal's head off, still the tongue is wagging.
Proud of your smiles once lavishly bestow'd,
Again our young Don Quixote takes the road;
To show his gratitude he draws his pen,
And seeks this Hydra, Scandal, in his den.
From his fell gripe the frighted fair to save –
Tho' he should fall th' attempt must please the brave.
For your applause all perils he would through –
He'll fight – that's write – a cavalero true,
Till every drop of blood – that's ink – is spilt for you.

ACT I, SCENE 1

Lady Sneerwell's House

LADY SNEERWELL *at the dressing-table.* MR SNAKE
drinking chocolate.

Lady Sneer. The paragraphs, you say, Mr Snake, were all
inserted?

Snake. They were, madam; and as I copied them myself
in a feigned hand, there can be no suspicion whence
they came.

Lady Sneer. Did you circulate the report of Lady Brittle's
intrigue with Captain Boastall?

Snake. That's in as fine a train as your ladyship could
wish. In the common course of things, I think it must
reach Mrs Clackit's ears within four-and-twenty hours;
and then, you know, the business is as good as done.

Lady Sneer. Why, truly, Mrs Clackit has a very pretty
talent, and a great deal of industry.

Snake. True, madam, and has been tolerably successful
in her day. To my knowledge she has been the cause
of six matches being broken off, and three sons disinherited; of four forced elopements, and as many close

confinements; nine separate maintenances, and two divorces. Nay, I have more than once traced her causing a *tête-à-tête* in the *Town and Country Magazine*, when the parties, perhaps, had never seen each other's face before in the course of their lives.

Lady Sneer. She certainly has talents, but her manner is gross.

Snake. 'Tis very true. – She generally designs well, has a free tongue and a bold invention; but her colouring is too dark, and her outlines often extravagant. She wants that delicacy of tint, and mellowness of sneer, which distinguish your ladyship's scandal.

Lady Sneer. You are partial, Snake.

Snake. Not in the least – everybody allows that Lady Sneerwell can do more with a word or look, than many can with the most laboured detail, even when they happen to have a little truth on their side to support it.

Lady Sneer. Yes, my dear Snake; and I am no hypocrite to deny the satisfaction I reap from the success of my efforts. Wounded myself, in the early part of my life, by the envenomed tongue of slander, I confess I have since known no pleasure equal to the reducing others to the level of my own injured reputation.

Snake. Nothing can be more natural. But, Lady Sneerwell, there is one affair in which you have lately employed me, wherein, I confess, I am at a loss to guess your motives.

Lady Sneer. I conceive you mean with respect to my neighbour, Sir Peter Teazle, and his family?

Snake. I do. Here are two young men, to whom Sir Peter has acted as a kind of guardian since their father's death; the eldest possessing the most amiable character, and universally well spoken of; the youngest, the most dissipated and extravagant young fellow in the kingdom, without friends or character: the former an avowed admirer of your ladyship's, and apparently your favourite; the latter attached to Maria, Sir Peter's ward, and confessedly beloved by her. Now,

on the face of these circumstances, it is utterly unaccountable to me, why you, the widow of a city
knight, with a good jointure, should not close with the
passion of a man of such character and expectations
as Mr Surface; and more so why you should be so un-
commonly earnest to destroy the mutual attachment
subsisting between his brother Charles and Maria.

Lady Sneer. Then at once to unravel this mystery, I must
inform you, that love has no share whatever in the
intercourse between Mr Surface and me.

Snake. No!

Lady Sneer. His real attachment is to Maria, or her
fortune; but finding in his brother a favoured rival,
he has been obliged to mask his pretensions, and
profit by my assistance.

Snake. Yet still I am more puzzled why you should interest yourself in his success.

Lady Sneer. How dull you are! Cannot you surmise the
weakness which I hitherto, through shame, have concealed even from you? Must I confess that Charles,
that libertine, that extravagant, that bankrupt in
fortune and reputation, that he it is for whom I'm
thus anxious and malicious, and to gain whom I
would sacrifice everything?

Snake. Now, indeed, your conduct appears consistent;
but how came you and Mr Surface so confidential?

Lady Sneer. For our mutual interest. I have found him
out a long time since. I know him to be artful, selfish,
and malicious – in short, a sentimental knave; while
with Sir Peter, and indeed with all his acquaintance,
he passes for a miracle of prudence, good sense, and
benevolence.

Snake. Yes; yet Sir Peter vows he has not his equal in
England, and above all, he praises him as a man of
sentiment.

Lady Sneer. True – and with the assistance of his sentiment and hypocrisy he has brought Sir Peter entirely

into his interest with regard to Maria, while poor
Charles has no friend in the house, though, I fear, he
has a powerful one in Maria's heart, against whom
we must direct our schemes.

Enter SERVANT

Ser. Mr Surface.
Lady Sneer. Show him up. [*Exit Servant.*] He generally
calls about this time. I don't wonder at people giving
him to me for a lover.

Enter JOSEPH SURFACE

Jos. Surface. My dear Lady Sneerwell, how do you do
today? Mr Snake, your most obedient.
Lady Sneer. Snake has just been rallying me on our
mutual attachment; but I have informed him of our
real views. You know how useful he has been to us,
and, believe me, the confidence is not ill-placed.
Jos. Surface. Madam, it is impossible for me to suspect a
man of Mr Snake's sensibility and discernment.
Lady Sneer. Well, well, no compliments now; but tell me
when you saw your mistress, Maria – or, what is more
material to me, your brother.
Jos. Surface. I have not seen either since I left you; but
I can inform you that they never meet. Some of your
stories have taken a good effect on Maria.
Lady Sneer. Ah! my dear Snake! the merit of this belongs
to you: but do your brother's distresses increase?
Jos. Surface. Every hour. I am told he has had another
execution in the house yesterday. In short, his dissipation and extravagance exceed anything I have ever
heard of.
Lady Sneer. Poor Charles!
Jos. Surface. True, madam; notwithstanding his vices,
one can't help feeling for him. Aye poor Charles,
indeed! I'm sure I wish it were in my power to be of
any essential service to him; for the man who does not

share in the distresses of a brother, even though merited
by his own misconduct, deserves –

Lady Sneer. O Lud! you are going to be moral, and forget
that you are among friends.

Jos. Surf. Egad, that's true! – I'll keep that sentiment
till I see Sir Peter; – however, it is certainly a charity
to rescue Maria from such a libertine, who, if he is to
be reclaimed, can be so only by a person of your
ladyship's superior accomplishments and understanding.

Snake. I believe, Lady Sneerwell, here's company
coming: I'll go and copy the letter I mentioned to
you. – Mr Surface, your most obedient. [*Exit Snake.*

Jos. Surf. Sir, your very devoted. – Lady Sneerwell, I am
very sorry you have put any further confidence in that
fellow.

Lady Sneer. Why so?

Jos. Surf. I have lately detected him in frequent conference with old Rowley, who was formerly my
father's steward, and has never, you know, been a
friend of mine.

Lady Sneer. And do you think he would betray us?

Jos. Surf. Nothing more likely: – take my word for't,
Lady Sneerwell, that fellow hasn't virtue enough to
be faithful even to his own villainy. – Ah! Maria!

Enter MARIA

Lady Sneer. Maria, my dear, how do you do? – What's
the matter?

Mar. O there's that disagreeable lover of mine, Sir
Benjamin Backbite, has just called at my guardian's,
with his odious uncle, Crabtree; so I slipped out, and
ran hither to avoid them.

Lady Sneer. Is that all?

Jos. Surf. If my brother Charles had been of the party,
madam, perhaps you would not have been so much
alarmed.

Lady Sneer. Nay, now you are severe; for I dare swear the truth of the matter is, Maria heard *you* were here. – But, my dear, what has Sir Benjamin done, that you would avoid him?

Mar. Oh, he has done nothing – but 'tis for what he has said: his conversation is a perpetual libel on all his acquaintance.

Jos. Surf. Ay, and the worst of it is, there is no advantage in not knowing him – for he'll abuse a stranger just as his best friend; and his uncle is as bad.

Lady Sneer. Nay, but we should make allowance – Sir Benjamin is a wit and a poet.

Mar. For my part, I confess, madam, wit loses its respect with me, when I see it in company with malice. – What do you think, Mr Surface?

Jos. Surf. Certainly, madam; to smile at the jest which plants a thorn in another's breast is to become a principal in the mischief.

Lady Sneer. Pshaw! – there's no possibility of being witty without a little ill nature: the malice of a good thing is the barb that makes it stick. – What's your opinion, Mr Surface?

Jos. Surf. To be sure, madam; that conversation, where the spirit of raillery is suppressed, will ever appear tedious and insipid.

Mar. Well, I'll not debate how far scandal may be allowable; but in a man, I am sure, it is always contemptible. We have pride, envy, rivalship, and a thousand motives to depreciate each other; but the male slanderer must have the cowardice of a woman before he can traduce one.

Enter SERVANT

Ser. Madam, Mrs Candour is below, and, if your ladyship's at leisure, will leave her carriage.

Lady Sneer. Beg her to walk in. – [*Exit Servant.*] Now, Maria, here is a character to your taste; for, though

Mrs Candour is a little talkative, everybody allows her to be the best-natured and best sort of woman.

Mar. Yet with a very gross affectation of good nature and benevolence, she does more mischief than the direct malice of old Crabtree.

Jos. Surf. I'faith 'tis true, Lady Sneerwell: whenever I hear the current running against the characters of my friends, I never think them in such danger as when Candour undertakes their defence.

Lady Sneer. Hush! – here she is! –

Enter MRS CANDOUR

Mrs Can. My dear Lady Sneerwell, how have you been this century? – Mr Surface, what news do you hear? – though indeed it is no matter, for I think one hears nothing else but scandal.

Jos. Surf. Just so, indeed, ma'am.

Mrs Can. Ah! Maria child, – what, is the whole affair off between you and Charles? – His extravagance, I presume – the town talks of nothing else.

Mar. I am very sorry, ma'am, the town has so little to do.

Mrs Can. True, true, child: but there's no stopping people's tongues. I own I was hurt to hear it, as I indeed was to learn, from the same quarter, that your guardian, Sir Peter, and Lady Teazle have not agreed lately as well as could be wished.

Mar. 'Tis strangely impertinent for people to busy themselves so.

Mrs Can. Very true, child; – but what's to be done? People will talk – there's no preventing it. Why, it was but yesterday I was told that Miss Gadabout had eloped with Sir Filagree Flirt. – But, Lord! there is no minding what one hears; though, to be sure, I had this from very good authority.

Mar. Such reports are highly scandalous.

Mrs Can. So they are, child – shameful! shameful! But the world is so censorious, no character escapes. –

Lord now! who would have suspected your friend, Miss Prim, of an indiscretion? Yet such is the ill-nature of people, that they say her uncle stopped her last week, just as she was stepping into the York diligence with her dancing-master.

Mar. I'll answer for't there are no grounds for the report.

Mrs Can. O no foundation in the world, I dare swear: no more, probably, than for the story circulated last month, of Mrs Festino's affair with Colonel Cassino; – though to be sure, that matter was never rightly cleared up.

Jos. Surf. The licence of invention some people take is monstrous indeed.

Mar. 'Tis so; but, in my opinion, those who report such things are equally culpable.

Mrs Can. To be sure they are; tale-bearers are as bad as the tale-makers – 'tis an old observation, and a very true one: but what's to be done, as I said before? How will you prevent people from talking? Today, Mrs Clackit assured me, Mr and Mrs Honeymoon were at last become mere man and wife, like the rest of their acquaintance. She likewise hinted that a certain widow, in the next street, had got rid of her dropsy and recovered her shape in a most surprising manner. And at the same time Miss Tattle, who was by, affirmed, that Lord Buffalo had discovered his lady at a house of no extraordinary fame; and that Sir Harry Bouquet and Tom Saunter were to measure swords on a similar provocation. But, Lord, do you think that I would report these things! No, no! tale-bearers, as I said before, are just as bad as the tale-makers.

Jos. Surf. Ah! Mrs Candour, if everybody had your forbearance and good nature!

Mrs Can. I confess, Mr Surface, I cannot bear to hear people attacked behind their backs; and when ugly circumstances come out against our acquaintance I own I always love to think the best. – By-the-by, I hope 'tis not true that your brother is absolutely ruined?

Jos. Surf. I am afraid his circumstances are very bad indeed, madam.

Mrs Can. Ah! I heard so – but you must tell him to keep up his spirits; everybody almost is in the same way – Lord Spindle, Sir Thomas Splint, Captain Quinze, and Mr Nickit – all up, I hear, within this week; so if Charles is undone, he'll find half his acquaintance ruined too, and that, you know, is a consolation.

Jos. Surf. Doubtless, ma'am – a very great one.

Enter SERVANT

Ser. Mr Crabtree and Sir Benjamin Backbite.

[*Exit Servant.*

Lady Sneer. So, Maria, you see your lover pursues you; positively you shan't escape.

Enter CRABTREE and SIR BENJAMIN BACKBITE

Crab. Lady Sneerwell, I kiss your hand – Mrs Candour, I don't believe you are acquainted with my nephew, Sir Benjamin Backbite? Egad! ma'am, he has a pretty wit, and is a pretty poet too; isn't he, Lady Sneerwell?

Sir Ben. Oh, fie, uncle!

Crab. Nay, egad it's true: I back him at a rebus or a charade against the best rhymer in the kingdom. – Has your ladyship heard the epigram he wrote last week on Lady Frizzle's feather catching fire? – Do Benjamin, repeat it, or the charade you made last night extempore at Mrs Drowzie's conversazione. Come now; – your first is the name of a fish, your second a great naval commander, and –

Sir Ben. Uncle, now – prythee –

Crab. I'faith, ma'am, 'twould surprise you to hear how ready he is at all these things.

Lady Sneer. I wonder, Sir Benjamin, you never publish anything.

Sir Ben. To say truth, ma'am, 'tis very vulgar to print;

and, as my little productions are mostly satires and lampoons on particular people, I find they circulate more by giving copies in confidence to the friends of the parties. However, I have some love elegies, which, when favoured with this lady's smiles, I mean to give the public.

Crab. 'Fore heaven, ma'am, they'll immortalize you! – you will be handed down to posterity, like Petrarch's Laura, or Waller's Sacharissa.

Sir Ben. Yes, madam, I think you will like them, when you shall see them on a beautiful quarto page, where a neat rivulet of text shall meander through a meadow of margin. 'Fore Gad, they will be the most elegant things of their kind!

Crab. But, ladies, that's true – have you heard the news?

Mrs Can. What, sir, do you mean the report of –

Crab. No, ma'am, that's not it. – Miss Nicely is going to be married to her own footman.

Mrs Can. Impossible!

Crab. Ask Sir Benjamin.

Sir Ben. 'Tis very true, ma'am: everything is fixed, and the wedding liveries bespoke.

Crab. Yes – and they do say there were pressing reasons for it.

Lady Sneer. Why, I have heard something of this before.

Mrs Can. It can't be – and I wonder any one should believe such a story, of so prudent a lady as Miss Nicely.

Sir Ben. O Lud! ma'am, that's the very reason 'twas believed at once. She has always been so cautious and so reserved, that everybody was sure there was some reason for it at bottom.

Mrs Can. Why, to be sure, a tale of scandal is as fatal to the credit of a prudent lady of her stamp as a fever is generally to those of the strongest constitutions. But there is a sort of puny sickly reputation, that is always ailing, yet will outlive the robuster characters of a hundred prudes.

Sir Ben. True, madam, – there are valetudinarians in reputation as well as constitution, who, being conscious of their weak part, avoid the least breath of air, and supply their want of stamina by care and circumspection.

Mrs Can. Well, but this may be all a mistake. You know, Sir Benjamin, very trifling circumstances often give rise to the most injurious tales.

Crab. That they do, I'll be sworn, ma'am. – Did you ever hear how Miss Piper came to lose her lover and her character last summer at Tunbridge? – Sir Benjamin, you remember it?

Sir Ben. Oh, to be sure! – the most whimsical circumstance.

Lady Sneer. How was it, pray?

Crab. Why, one evening, at Mrs Ponto's assembly, the conversation happened to turn on the difficulty of breeding Nova Scotia sheep in this country. Says a young lady in company, I have known instances of it; for Miss Letitia Piper, a first cousin of mine, had a Nova Scotia sheep that produced her twins. What! cries the Lady Dowager Dundizzy (who you know is as deaf as a post), has Miss Piper had twins? – This mistake, as you may imagine, threw the whole company into a fit of laughter. However, 'twas the next day everywhere reported, and in a few days believed by the whole town, that Miss Letitia Piper had actually been brought to bed of a fine boy and girl.

Lady Sneer. Strange, indeed!

Crab. Matter of fact, I assure you. – O Lud! Mr Surface, pray is it true that your uncle, Sir Oliver, is coming home?

Jos. Surf. Not that I know of, indeed, sir.

Crab. He has been in the East Indies a long time. You can scarcely remember him, I believe – Sad comfort, whenever he returns, to hear how your brother has gone on!

Jos. Surf. Charles has been imprudent, sir, to be sure; but I hope no busy people have already prejudiced Sir Oliver against him – he may reform.

Sir Ben. To be sure he may: for my part, I never believed him to be so utterly void of principle as people say; and though he has lost all his friends, I am told nobody is better spoken of by the Jews.

Crab. That's true, egad, nephew. If the Old Jewry was a ward, I believe Charles would be an alderman: – no man more popular there, 'fore Gad! I hear he pays as many annuities as the Irish tontine; and that, whenever he is sick, they have prayers for the recovery of his health in all the synagogues.

Sir Ben. Yet no man lives in greater splendour. They tell me, when he entertains his friends he will sit down to dinner with a dozen of his own securities; have a score of tradesmen waiting in the antechamber, and an officer behind every guest's chair.

Jos. Surf. This may be entertainment to you, gentlemen, but you pay very little regard to the feelings of a brother.

Mar. Their malice is intolerable! – Lady Sneerwell, I must wish you a good morning: I'm not very well.

[*Exit Maria.*

Mrs Can. O dear! she changes colour very much.

Lady Sneer. Do, Mrs Candour, follow her; she may want assistance.

Mrs Can. That I will, with all my soul, ma'am. – Poor dear creature, who knows what her situation may be!

[*Exit.*

Lady Sneer. 'Twas nothing but that she could not bear to hear Charles reflected on, notwithstanding their difference.

Sir Ben. The young lady's *penchant* is obvious.

Crab. But, Benjamin, you must not give up the pursuit for that: – follow her, and put her into good humour. Repeat her some of your own verses. Come, I'll assist you.

Sir Ben. Mr Surface, I did not mean to hurt you; but depend on't your brother is utterly undone.

Crab. O Lud, ay! undone as ever man was. Can't raise a guinea!

Sir Ben. Everything sold, I am told, that was movable.

Crab. I have seen one that was at his house. Not a thing left but some empty bottles that were overlooked, and the family pictures, which I believe are framed in the wainscot. –

Sir Ben. And I'm very sorry also to hear some bad stories against him.   [*Going.*

Crab. O! he has done many mean things, that's certain.

Sir Ben. But, however, as he's your brother –   [*Going.*

Crab. We'll tell you all another opportunity.   [*Exeunt.*

Lady Sneer. Ha! ha! 'tis very hard for them to leave a subject they have not quite run down.

Jos. Surf. And I believe the abuse was no more acceptable to your ladyship than to Maria.

Lady Sneer. I doubt her affections are further engaged than we imagine. But the family are to be here this evening, so you may as well dine where you are, and we shall have an opportunity of observing further; in the meantime, I'll go and plot mischief, and you shall study sentiment.   [*Exeunt.*

ACT I, SCENE 2

Sir Peter Teazle's House
Enter Sir Peter

Sir Pet. When an old bachelor marries a young wife, what is he to expect? 'Tis now six months since Lady Teazle made me the happiest of men – and I have been the most miserable dog ever since that ever committed wedlock! We tiffed a little going to church, and came to a quarrel before the bells had done ringing. I was more than once nearly choked with gall

during my honeymoon, and had lost all comfort in
life before my friends had done wishing me joy. Yet
I chose with caution — a girl bred wholly in the
country, who never knew luxury beyond one silk
gown, nor dissipation above the annual gala of a
race ball. Yet she now plays her part in all the
extravagant fopperies of the fashion and the town,
with as ready a grace as if she never had seen a bush
or a grass-plot out of Grosvenor Square! I am sneered
at by all my acquaintance, and paragraphed in the
newspapers. She dissipates my fortune, and contradicts all my humours; yet the worst of it is, I doubt I
love her, or I should never bear all this. However,
I'll never be weak enough to own it.

Enter ROWLEY

Row. O! Sir Peter, your servant; how is it with you,
sir?

Sir Pet. Very bad, Master Rowley, very bad. I meet
with nothing but crosses and vexations.

Row. What can have happened to trouble you since
yesterday?

Sir Pet. A good question to a married man!

Row. Nay, I'm sure, Sir Peter, your lady can't be the
cause of your uneasiness.

Sir Pet. Why, has anybody told you she was dead?

Row. Come, come, Sir Peter, you love her, notwithstanding your tempers don't exactly agree.

Sir Pet. But the fault is entirely hers, Master Rowley. I
am, myself, the sweetest-tempered man alive, and hate
a teasing temper; and so I tell her a hundred times a
day.

Row. Indeed!

Sir Pet. Ay; and what is very extraordinary, in all our
disputes she is always in the wrong! But Lady Sneerwell, and the set she meets at her house, encourage
the perverseness of her disposition. — Then, to complete

my vexation, Maria, my ward, whom I ought to have the power of a father over, is determined to turn rebel too, and absolutely refuses the man whom I have long resolved on for her husband; meaning, I suppose, to bestow herself on his profligate brother.

Row. You know, Sir Peter, I have always taken the liberty to differ with you on the subject of these two young gentlemen. I only wish you may not be deceived in your opinion of the elder. For Charles, my life on't! he will retrieve his errors yet. Their worthy father, once my honoured master, was, at his years, nearly as wild a spark; yet, when he died, he did not leave a more benevolent heart to lament his loss.

Sir Pet. You are wrong, Master Rowley. On their father's death, you know, I acted as a kind of guardian to them both, till their uncle Sir Oliver's eastern liberality gave them an early independence – of course, no person could have more opportunities of judging of their hearts, and I was never mistaken in my life. Joseph is indeed a model for the young men of the age. He is a man of sentiment, and acts up to the sentiments he professes; but, for the other, take my word for't, if he had any grain of virtue by descent, he has dissipated it with the rest of his inheritance. Ah! my old friend, Sir Oliver, will be deeply mortified when he finds how part of his bounty has been misapplied.

Row. I am sorry to find you so violent against the young man, because this may be the most critical period of his fortune. I came hither with news that will surprise you.

Sir Pet. What! let me hear.

Row. Sir Oliver is arrived, and at this moment in town.

Sir Pet. How! you astonish me! I thought you did not expect him this month.

Row. I did not: but his passage has been remarkably quick.

Sir Pet. Egad, I shall rejoice to see my old friend. 'Tis

sixteen years since we met. – We have had many a
day together: – but does he still enjoin us not to inform
his nephews of his arrival?

Row. Most strictly. He means, before it is known, to
make some trial of their dispositions.

Sir Pet. Ah! There needs no art to discover their merits –
he shall have his way; but, pray, does he know I am
married?

Row. Yes, and will soon wish you joy.

Sir Pet. What, as we drink health to a friend in a con-
sumption! Ah! Oliver will laugh at me. We used to
rail at matrimony together, but he has been steady to
his text. – Well, he must be soon at my house, though!
– I'll instantly give orders for his reception. But,
Master Rowley, don't drop a word that Lady Teazle
and I ever disagree.

Row. By no means.

Sir Pet. For I should never be able to stand Noll's jokes;
so I'll have him think, Lord forgive me! that we are
a very happy couple.

Row. I understand you: – but then you must be very
careful not to differ while he is in the house with you.

Sir Pet. Egad, and so we must – and that's impossible.
Ah! Master Rowley, when an old bachelor marries a
young wife, he deserves – no – the crime carries its
punishment along with it.   [*Exeunt.*

End of the First Act.

ACT II, SCENE 1

Sir Peter Teazle's House

Enter SIR PETER *and* LADY TEAZLE

Sir Pet. Lady Teazle, Lady Teazle, I'll not bear it!

Lady Teaz. Sir Peter, Sir Peter, you may bear it or not, as you please; but I ought to have my own way in everything, and what's more, I will too. What! though I was educated in the country, I know very well that women of fashion in London are accountable to nobody after they are married.

Sir Pet. Very well, ma'am, very well; – so a husband is to have no influence, no authority?

Lady Teaz. Authority! No, to be sure: – if you wanted authority over me, you should have adopted me, and not married me: I am sure you were old enough.

Sir Pet. Old enough! – aye, there it is! Well, well, Lady Teazle, though my life may be made unhappy by your temper, I'll not be ruined by your extravagance!

Lady Teaz. My extravagance! I'm sure I'm not more extravagant than a woman of fashion ought to be.

Sir Pet. No, no, madam, you shall throw away no more sums on such unmeaning luxury. 'Slife! to spend as much to furnish your dressing-room with flowers in winter as would suffice to turn the Pantheon into a greenhouse, and give a *fête champêtre* at Christmas.

Lady Teaz. Lord, Sir Peter, am I to blame, because flowers are dear in cold weather? You should find fault with the climate, and not with me. For my part, I'm sure, I wish it was spring all the year round, and that roses grew under one's feet!

Sir Pet. Oons! madam – if you had been born to this, I shouldn't wonder at your talking thus; but you forget what your situation was when I married you.

Lady Teaz. No, no, I don't; 'twas a very disagreeable one, or I should never have married you.

Sir Pet. Yes, yes, madam, you were then in somewhat an humbler style: – the daughter of a plain country squire. Recollect, Lady Teazle, when I saw you first, sitting at your tambour, in a pretty figured linen gown, with a bunch of keys at your side, your hair combed smooth over a roll, and your apartment hung round with fruits in worsted, of your own working.

Lady Teaz. Oh, yes! I remember it very well, and a curious life I led! my daily occupation to inspect the dairy, superintend the poultry, make extracts from the family receipt-book, and comb my Aunt Deborah's lapdog.

Sir Pet. Yes, yes, madam, 'twas so indeed.

Lady Teaz. And then, you know, my evening amusements! To draw patterns for ruffles, which I had not the materials to make up; to play Pope Joan with the curate; to read a sermon to my aunt; or to be stuck down to an old spinet to strum my father to sleep after a fox-chase.

Sir Pet. I am glad you have so good a memory. Yes, madam, these were the recreations I took you from; but now you must have your coach – *vis-à-vis* – and three powdered footmen before your chair; and, in the summer, a pair of white cats to draw you to Kensington Gardens. No recollection, I suppose, when you were content to ride double, behind the butler, on a dock'd coach-horse?

Lady Teaz. No – I swear I never did that; I deny the butler and the coach-horse.

Sir Pet. This, madam, was your situation; and what have I done for you? I have made you a woman of fashion, of fortune, of rank; – in short, I have made you *my wife*.

Lady Teaz. Well, then, – and there is but one thing more you can make me to add to the obligation, that is –

Sir Pet. My widow, I suppose?

Lady Teaz. Hem! hem!

Sir Pet. I thank you, madam – but don't flatter yourself; for, though your ill conduct may disturb my peace of mind, it shall never break my heart, I promise you: however, I am equally obliged to you for the hint.

Lady Teaz. Then why will you endeavour to make yourself so disagreeable to me, and thwart me in every little elegant expense?

Sir Pet. 'Slife, madam, I say, had you any of these little elegant expenses when you married me?

Lady Teaz. Lud, Sir Peter! would you have me be out of the fashion?

Sir Pet. The fashion, indeed! what had you to do with the fashion when you married me?

Lady Teaz. For my part, I should think you would like to have your wife thought a woman of taste.

Sir Pet. Aye – there again – taste – Zounds! madam, you had no taste when you married me!

Lady Teaz. That's very true, indeed, Sir Peter; and, after having married you, I am sure I should never pretend to taste again. But now, Sir Peter, since we have finished our daily jangle, I presume I may go to my engagement at Lady Sneerwell's?

Sir Pet. Aye, there's another precious circumstance – a charming set of acquaintance you have made there!

Lady Teaz. Nay, Sir Peter, they are all people of rank and fortune, and remarkably tenacious of reputation.

Sir Pet. Yes, egad, they are tenacious of reputation with a vengeance; for they don't choose anybody should have a character but themselves! – Such a crew! Ah! many a wretch has rid on a hurdle who has done less mischief than these utterers of forged tales, coiners of scandal, and clippers of reputation.

Lady Teaz. What, would you restrain the freedom of speech?

Sir Pet. Oh! they have made you just as bad as any one of the society.

Lady Teaz. Why, I believe I do bear a part with a tolerable grace. But I vow I bear no malice against the people I abuse. When I say an ill-natured thing, 'tis out of pure good humour; and I take it for granted, they deal exactly in the same manner with me. But, Sir Peter, you know you promised to come to Lady Sneerwell's too.

Sir Pet. Well, well, I'll call in just to look after my own character.

Lady Teaz. Then, indeed, you must make haste after me or you'll be too late. So good-bye to you.

[Exit Lady Teazle.

Sir Pet. So – I have gained much by my intended expostulation: yet with what a charming air she contradicts everything I say, and how pleasantly she shows her contempt for my authority! Well, though I can't make her love me, there is great satisfaction in quarrelling with her; and I think she never appears to such advantage as when she is doing everything in her power to plague me.   *[Exit.*

——

ACT II, SCENE 2

Lady Sneerwell's House

LADY SNEERWELL, MRS CANDOUR, CRABTREE, SIR BENJAMIN BACKBITE, *and* JOSEPH SURFACE *discovered*, SERVANTS *attending with tea*

Lady Sneer. Nay, positively, we will hear it.

Jos. Surf. Yes, yes, the epigram, by all means.

Sir Ben. Oh, plague on't, uncle! 'tis mere nonsense.

Crab. No, no; 'fore Gad, very clever for an extempore!

Sir Ben. But, ladies, you should be acquainted with the circumstances. You must know, that one day last week, as Lady Betty Curricle was taking the dust in Hyde

Park, in a sort of a duodecimo phaeton, she desired
me to write some verses on her ponies; upon which I
took out my pocket-book, and in one moment produced the following:

> Sure never were seen two such beautiful ponies;
> Other horses are clowns, but these macaronies:
> To give 'em this title I am sure isn't wrong.
> Their legs are so slim, and their tails are so long.

Crab. There, ladies, done in the smack of a whip, and
on horseback too.

Jos. Surf. A very Phoebus, mounted – indeed, Sir
Benjamin!

Sir Ben. Oh dear sir, – trifles – trifles.

Enter LADY TEAZLE *and* MARIA

Mrs Can. I must have a copy.

Lady Sneer. Lady Teazle, I hope we shall see Sir
Peter?

Lady Teaz. I believe he'll wait on your ladyship presently.

Lady Sneer. Maria, my love, you look grave. Come, you
shall sit down to cards with Mr Surface.

Mar. I take very little pleasure in cards – however, I'll
do as your ladyship pleases.

Lady Teaz. I am surprised Mr Surface should sit down
with her; I thought he would have embraced this
opportunity of speaking to me, before Sir Peter came.
[*Aside.*

Mrs Can. Now, I'll die, but you are so scandalous, I'll
forswear your society.

Lady Teaz. What's the matter, Mrs Candour?

Mrs Can. They'll not allow our friend Miss Vermillion
to be handsome.

Lady Sneer. Oh, surely she's a pretty woman.

Crab. I am very glad you think so, madam.

Mrs Can. She has a charming fresh colour.

Lady Teaz. Yes, when it is fresh put on.

Mrs Can. Oh, fie! I'll swear her colour is natural: I have seen it come and go!

Lady Teaz. I dare swear you have, ma'am: it goes off at night, and comes again in the morning.

Sir Ben. True, ma'am, it not only comes and goes, but, what's more – egad, her maid can fetch and carry it!

Mrs Can. Ha! ha! ha! how I hate to hear you talk so! But surely, now, her sister *is*, or *was*, very handsome.

Crab. Who? Mrs Evergreen? O Lord! she's six-and-fifty if she's an hour!

Mrs Can. Now positively you wrong her; fifty-two or fifty-three is the utmost – and I don't think she looks more.

Sir Ben. Ah! there's no judging by her looks, unless one could see her face.

Lady Sneer. Well, well, if Mrs Evergreen *does* take some pains to repair the ravages of time, you must allow she effects it with great ingenuity; and surely that's better than the careless manner in which the widow Ochre caulks her wrinkles.

Sir Ben. Nay, now, Lady Sneerwell, you are severe upon the widow. Come, come, 'tis not that she paints so ill – but, when she has finished her face, she joins it on so badly to her neck, that she looks like a mended statue, in which the connoisseur may see at once that the head's modern, though the trunk's antique!

Crab. Ha! ha! ha! Well said, nephew!

Mrs Can. Ha! ha! ha! Well, you make me laugh; but I vow I hate you for it. – What do you think of Miss Simper?

Sir Ben. Why, she has very pretty teeth.

Lady Teaz. Yes, and on that account, when she is neither speaking nor laughing (which very seldom happens), she never absolutely shuts her mouth, but leaves it always on a jar, as it were, thus –   [*Shows her teeth.*

Mrs Can. How can you be so ill-natured?

Lady Teaz. Nay, I'll allow even that's better than the

pains Mrs Prim takes to conceal her losses in front.
She draws her mouth till it positively resembles the
aperture of a poor's-box, and all her words appear to
slide out edgewise. As it were thus: *How do you do,
madam? Yes, madam.*

Lady Sneer. Very well, Lady Teazle; I see you can be
a little severe.

Lady Teaz. In defence of a friend it is but justice. – But
here comes Sir Peter to spoil our pleasantry.

Enter SIR PETER TEAZLE

Sir Pet. Ladies, your most obedient. – Mercy on me!
here is the whole set! a character dead at every word,
I suppose.   [*Aside.*

Mrs Can. I am rejoiced you are come, Sir Peter. They
have been so censorious – they will allow good
qualities to nobody; not even good nature to our
friend Mrs Pursy.

Lady Teaz. What, the fat dowager who was at Mrs
Codrille's last night?

Mrs Can. Nay, her bulk is her misfortune; and, when
she takes so much pains to get rid of it, you ought not
to reflect on her.

Lady Sneer. That's very true, indeed.

Lady Teaz. Yes, I know she almost lives on acids and
small whey; laces herself by pulleys; and often, in the
hottest noon in summer, you may see her on a little
squat pony, with her hair plaited up behind like a
drummer's, and puffing round the Ring on a full
trot.

Mrs Can. I thank you, Lady Teazle, for defending her.

Sir Pet. Yes, a good defence, truly.

Mrs Can. But Sir Benjamin is as censorious as Miss
Sallow.

Crab. Yes, and she is a curious being to pretend to be
censorious – an awkward gawky, without any one
good point under heaven.

Mrs Can. Positively you shall not be so very severe. Miss Sallow is a relation of mine by marriage, and as for her person, great allowance is to be made; for, let me tell you, a woman labours under many disadvantages who tries to pass for a girl of six-and-thirty.

Lady Sneer. Though, surely, she is handsome still – and for the weakness in her eyes, considering how much she reads by candle-light, it is not to be wondered at.

Mrs Can. True, and then as to her manner; upon my word I think it is particularly graceful, considering she never had the least education; for you know her mother was a Welch milliner, and her father a sugar-baker at Bristol.

Sir Ben. Ah! you are both of you too good-natured!

Sir Pet. Yes, damned good-natured! This their own relation! mercy on me!   [*Aside.*

Mrs Can. For my part, I own I cannot bear to hear a friend ill spoken of.

Sir Pet. No, to be sure!

Sir Ben. And Mrs Candour is of so moral a turn, she can sit for an hour and hear Lady Stucco talk sentiment.

Lady Teaz. Nay, I vow Lady Stucco is very well with the dessert after dinner; for she's just like the French fruit one cracks for mottoes – made up of paint and proverb.

Mrs Can. Well, I never will join in ridiculing a friend; and so I constantly tell my cousin Ogle, and you all know what pretensions she has to be critical on beauty.

Crab. Oh, to be sure! she has herself the oddest countenance that ever was seen; 'tis a collection of features from all the different countries of the globe.

Sir Ben. So she has, indeed – an Irish front –

Crab. Caledonian locks –

Sir Ben. Dutch nose –

Crab. Austrian lips –

Sir Ben. Complexion of a Spaniard –

Crab. And teeth *à la Chinoise* –

Sir Ben. In short, her face resembles a *table d'hôte* at Spa – where no two guests are of a nation –

Crab. Or a congress at the close of a general war – wherein all the members, even to her eyes, appear to have a different interest, and her nose and chin are the only parties likely to join issue.

Mrs Can. Ha! ha! ha!

Sir Pet. Mercy on my life! – a person they dine with twice a week!   [*Aside.*

Lady Sneer. Go, go; you are a couple of provoking toads.

Mrs Can. Nay, but I vow you shall not carry the laugh off so – for give me leave to say, that Mrs Ogle –

Sir Pet. Madam, madam, I beg your pardon – there's no stopping these good gentlemen's tongues. – But when I tell you, Mrs Candour, that the lady they are abusing is a particular friend of mine, I hope you'll not take her part.

Lady Sneer. Well said, Sir Peter! but you are a cruel creature – too phlegmatic yourself for a jest, and too peevish to allow wit in others.

Sir Pet. Ah! madam, true wit is more nearly allied to good-nature than your ladyship is aware of.

Lady Teaz. True, Sir Peter: I believe they are so near akin that they can never be united.

Sir Ben. Or rather, madam, suppose them to be man and wife, because one seldom sees them together.

Lady Teaz. But Sir Peter is such an enemy to scandal, I believe he would have it put down by Parliament.

Sir Pet. 'Fore heaven, madam, if they were to consider the sporting with reputation of as much importance as poaching on manors, and pass an Act for the Preservation of Fame, I believe there are many who would thank them for the bill.

Lady Sneer. O Lud! Sir Peter; would you deprive us of our privileges?

Sir Pet. Aye, madam; and then no person should be permitted to kill characters and run down reputations, but qualified old maids and disappointed widows.

Lady Sneer. Go, you monster.

Mrs Can. But, surely, you would not be quite so severe on those who only report what they hear?

Sir Pet. Yes, madam, I would have Law-Merchant for them too; and in all cases of slander currency, whenever the drawer of the lie was not to be found, the injured parties should have a right to come on any of the indorsers.

Crab. Well, for my part, I believe there never was a scandalous tale without some foundation.

Lady Sneer. Come, ladies, shall we sit down to cards in the next room?

Enter SERVANT, *who whispers Sir Peter*

Sir Pet. I'll be with them directly. I'll get away unperceived.   [*Apart.*

Lady Sneer. Sir Peter, you are not going to leave us?

Sir Pet. Your ladyship must excuse me; I'm called away by particular business. But I leave my character behind me.   [*Exit Sir Peter.*

Sir Ben. Well – certainly, Lady Teazle, that lord of yours is a strange being: I could tell you some stories of him would make you laugh heartily – if he were not your husband.

Lady Teaz. Oh, pray don't mind that; come, do let's hear them.   [*Lady T. joins the rest of the company, going into the next room.*

Jos. Surf. Maria, I see you have no satisfaction in this society.

Mar. How is it possible I should? If to raise malicious smiles at the infirmities or misfortunes of those who have never injured us be the province of wit or humour, Heaven grant me a double portion of dullness!

Jos. Surf. Yet they appear more ill-natured than they are – they have no malice at heart.

Mar. Then is their conduct still more contemptible; for, in my opinion, nothing could excuse the intemperance of their tongues, but a natural and uncontrollable bitterness of mind.

Jos. Surf. But can you, Maria, feel thus for others, and be unkind to me alone? Is hope to be denied the tenderest passion?

Mar. Why will you distress me by renewing the subject?

Jos. Surf. Ah! Maria! you would not treat me thus, and oppose your guardian, Sir Peter's will, but that I see that profligate Charles is still a favoured rival.

Mar. Ungenerously urged! – But whatever my sentiments are for that unfortunate young man, be assured I shall not feel more bound to give him up, because his distresses have lost him the regard even of a brother.

Enter LADY TEAZLE *and comes forward*

Jos. Surf. Nay, but Maria, do not leave me with a frown: by all that's honest, I swear – Gad's life, here's Lady Teazle. – [*Aside.*] – You must not – no, you shall not – for, though I have the greatest regard for Lady Teazle –

Mar. Lady Teazle!

Jos. Surf. Yet were Sir Peter once to suspect –

Lady Teaz. What is this, pray? Do you take her for me? – Child, you are wanted in the next room. – [*Exit Maria.*] – What is all this, pray?

Jos. Surf. O, the most unlucky circumstance in nature! Maria has somehow suspected the tender concern I have for your happiness, and threatened to acquaint Sir Peter with her suspicions, and I was just endeavouring to reason with her when you came in.

Lady Teaz. Indeed! but you seemed to adopt a very tender mode of reasoning – do you usually argue on your knees?

Jos. Surf. Oh, she's a child, and I thought a little
bombast. – But, Lady Teazle, when are you to give
me your judgement on my library, as you promised?

Lady Teaz. No, no; I begin to think it would be imprudent, and you know I admit you as a lover no
farther than fashion requires.

Jos. Surf. True – a mere platonic cicisbeo – what every
London wife is entitled to.

Lady Teaz. Certainly, one must not be out of the fashion.
However, I have so many of my country prejudices
left, that, though Sir Peter's ill-humour may vex me
ever so, it never shall provoke me to –

Jos. Surf. The only revenge in your power. Well – I
applaud your moderation.

Lady Teaz. Go – you are an insinuating wretch. – But
we shall be missed – let us join the company.

Jos. Surf. But we had best not return together.

Lady Teaz. Well – don't stay; for Maria shan't come to
hear any more of your reasoning, I promise you.

                              [*Exit Lady Teazle.*

Jos. Surf. A curious dilemma, truly, my politics have
run me into! I wanted, at first, only to ingratiate
myself with Lady Teazle, that she might not be my
enemy with Maria; and I have, I don't know how,
become her serious lover. Sincerely I begin to wish I
had never made such a point of gaining so very good
a character, for it has led me into so many cursed
rogueries that I doubt I shall be exposed at last.

                              [*Exit.*

————

ACT II, SCENE 3

Sir Peter Teazle's House

Enter ROWLEY *and* SIR OLIVER SURFACE

Sir Oliv. Ha! ha! ha! so my old friend is married, hey? –
a young wife out of the country. – Ha! ha! ha! that

he should have stood bluff to old bachelor so long, and sink into a husband at last!

Row. But you must not rally him on the subject, Sir Oliver: 'tis a tender point, I assure you, though he has been married only seven months.

Sir Oliv. Then he has been just half a year on the stool of repentance! – Poor Peter! – But you say he has entirely given up Charles, – never sees him, hey?

Row. His prejudice against him is astonishing, and I am sure greatly increased by a jealousy of him with Lady Teazle, which he had been industriously led into by a scandalous society in the neighbourhood, who have contributed not a little to Charles's ill name. Whereas the truth is, I believe, if the lady is partial to either of them, his brother is the favourite.

Sir Oliv. Aye, I know there are a set of malicious, prating, prudent gossips, both male and female, who murder characters to kill time; and will rob a young fellow of his good name, before he has years to know the value of it. – But I am not to be prejudiced against my nephew by such, I promise you. – No, no, – if Charles has done nothing false or mean, I shall compound for his extravagance.

Row. Then, my life on't, you will reclaim him. – Ah, sir, it gives me new life to find that *your* heart is not turned against him, and that the son of my good old master has one friend, however, left.

Sir Oliv. What, shall I forget, Master Rowley, when I was at his years myself? Egad, my brother and I were neither of us very prudent youths; and yet, I believe, you have not seen many better men than your old master was.

Row. Sir, 'tis this reflection gives me assurance that Charles may yet be a credit to his family. – But here comes Sir Peter.

Sir Oliv. Egad, so he does! – Mercy on me! – he's greatly

altered – and seems to have a settled married look!
One may read *husband* in his face at this distance!

Enter SIR PETER

Sir Pet. Ha! Sir Oliver – my old friend! Welcome to
England a thousand times!

Sir Oliv. Thank you – thank you, Sir Peter! and i'faith
I am glad to find you well, believe me!

Sir Pet. Oh! 'tis a long time since we met – sixteen years,
I doubt, Sir Oliver, and many a cross accident in the
time.

Sir Oliv. Aye. I have had my share. But what! I find
you are married, hey, my old boy? Well, well – it
can't be helped – and so – I wish you joy with all
my heart!

Sir Pet. Thank you, thank you, Sir Oliver. – Yes, I have
entered into – the happy state; – but we'll not talk of
that now.

Sir Oliv. True, true, Sir Peter; old friends should not
begin on grievances at first meeting – no, no, no.

Row. Take care, pray, sir.   [*To Sir Oliver.*

Sir Oliv. Well – so one of my nephews is a wild young
rogue, hey?

Sir Pet. Wild! – Ah! my old friend, I grieve for your
disappointment there; he's a lost young man, indeed.
However, his brother will make you amends; Joseph
is, indeed, what a youth should be. Everybody in the
world speaks well of him.

Sir Oliv. I am sorry to hear it; he has too good a character to be an honest fellow. Everybody speaks
well of him! – Pshaw! then he has bowed as low to
knaves and fools as to the honest dignity of genius
and virtue.

Sir Pet. What, Sir Oliver! do you blame him for not
making enemies?

Sir Oliv. Yes, if he has merit enough to deserve them.

Sir Pet. Well, well – you'll be convinced when you know

him. 'Tis edification to hear him converse; he professes the noblest sentiments.

Sir Oliv. Oh! plague of his sentiments! if he salutes me
with a scrap of morality in his mouth, I shall be sick
directly. – But, however, don't mistake me, Sir Peter;
I don't mean to defend Charles's errors: but, before I
form my judgement of either of them, I intend to make
a trial of their hearts; and my friend Rowley and I
have planned something for the purpose.

Row. And Sir Peter shall own he has been for once
mistaken.

Sir Pet. Oh, my life on Joseph's honour.

Sir Oliv. Well – come, give us a bottle of good wine, and
we'll drink your lady's health, and tell you our
scheme.

Sir Pet. Allons, then!

Sir Oliv. And don't, Sir Peter, be so severe against your
old friend's son. Odds my life! I am not sorry that he
has run out of the course a little: for my part, I hate
to see prudence clinging to the green suckers of youth;
'tis like ivy round a sapling, and spoils the growth of
the tree.   [*Exeunt.*

End of the Second Act

Sir Peter Teazle's House

Enter SIR PETER TEAZLE, SIR OLIVER, *and* ROWLEY

Sir Pet. Well, then, we will see this fellow first, and have our wine afterwards: – but how is this, Master Rowley? I don't see the jet of your scheme.

Row. Why, sir, this Mr Stanley, whom I was speaking of, is nearly related to them by their mother. He was once a merchant in Dublin, but has been ruined by a series of undeserved misfortunes. He has applied, by letter, since his confinement, both to Mr Surface and Charles: from the former he has received nothing but evasive promises of future service, while Charles has done all that his extravagance has left him power to do; and he is, at this time, endeavouring to raise a sum of money, part of which, in the midst of his own distresses, I know he intends for the service of poor Stanley.

Sir Oliv. Ah! – he is my brother's son.

Sir Pet. Well, but how is Sir Oliver personally to –

Row. Why, sir, I will inform Charles and his brother that Stanley has obtained permission to apply personally to his friends, and, as they have neither of them ever seen him, let Sir Oliver assume his character, and he will have a fair opportunity of judging, at least, of the benevolence of their dispositions: and believe me, sir, you will find in the youngest brother one who, in the midst of folly and dissipation, has still, as our immortal bard expresses it,

> *a heart to pity, and a hand*
> *Open as day, for melting charity.*

Sir Pet. Pshaw! What signifies his having an open hand or purse either, when he has nothing left to give? Well, well – make the trial, if you please. But where is the fellow whom you brought for Sir Oliver to examine, relative to Charles's affairs?

Row. Below, waiting his commands, and no one can give him better intelligence. This, Sir Oliver, is a friendly Jew, who, to do him justice, has done everything in his power to bring your nephew to a proper sense of his extravagance.

Sir Pet. Pray let us have him in.

Row. Desire Mr Moses to walk upstairs. [*Calls to Servant.*

Sir Pet. But, pray, why should you suppose he will speak the truth?

Row. Oh! I have convinced him that he has no chance of recovering certain sums advanced to Charles, but through the bounty of Sir Oliver, who he knows is arrived; so that you may depend on his fidelity to his own interests. I have also another evidence in my power, one Snake, whom I have detected in a matter little short of forgery, and shall shortly produce him to remove some of your prejudices, Sir Peter, relative to Charles and Lady Teazle.

Sir Pet. I have heard too much on that subject.

Row. Here comes the honest Israelite.

Enter MOSES

– This is Sir Oliver.

Sir Oliv. Sir, I understand you have lately had great dealings with my nephew, Charles.

Mos. Yes, Sir Oliver, I have done all I could for him; but he was ruined before he came to me for assistance.

Sir Oliv. That was unlucky, truly; for you have had no opportunity of showing your talents.

Mos. None at all; I hadn't the pleasure of knowing his distresses till he was some thousands worse than nothing.

Sir Oliv. Unfortunate, indeed! – But I suppose you have done all in your power for him, honest Moses?

Mos. Yes, he owns that: – this very evening I was to

have brought him a gentleman from the city, who does not know him, and will, I believe, advance him some money.

Sir Pet. What, – one Charles has never had money from before?

Mos. Yes, – Mr Premium, of Crutched Friars, formerly a broker.

Sir Pet. Egad, Sir Oliver, a thought strikes me! – Charles, you say, does not know Mr Premium?

Mos. Not at all.

Sir Pet. Now then, Sir Oliver, you may have a better opportunity of satisfying yourself than by an old romancing tale of a poor relation: go with my friend Moses, and represent Premium, and then, I'll answer for it, you'll see your nephew in all his glory.

Sir Oliv. Egad, I like this idea better than the other, and I may visit Joseph afterwards as Old Stanley.

Sir Pet. True – so you may.

Row. Well, this is taking Charles rather at a disadvantage, to be sure; – however, Moses, you understand Sir Peter, and will be faithful?

Mos. You may depend upon me. – This is near the time I was to have gone.

Sir Oliv. I'll accompany you as soon as you please, Moses. – But hold! I have forgot one thing – how the plague shall I be able to pass for a Jew?

Mos. There's no need – the principal is Christian.

Sir Oliv. Is he? I am very sorry to hear it. But, then again, an't I rather too smartly dressed to look like a money-lender?

Sir Pet. Not at all; 'twould not be out of character, if you went in your carriage – would it, Moses?

Mos. Not in the least.

Sir Oliv. Well – but how must I talk? – there's certainly some cant of usury and mode of treating that I ought to know.

Sir Pet. Oh! there's not much to learn. The great point,

as I take it, is to be exorbitant enough in your demands – hey, Moses?

Mos. Yes, that's a very great point.

Sir Oliv. I'll answer for't I'll not be wanting in that.
I'll ask him eight or ten per cent on the loan, at
least.

Mos. If you ask him no more than that, you'll be
discovered immediately.

Sir Oliv. Hey! – what, the plague! – how much then?

Mos. That depends upon circumstances. If he appears
not very anxious for the supply, you should require
only forty or fifty per cent; but if you find him in
great distress and want the moneys very bad, you
must ask double.

Sir Pet. A good honest trade you're learning, Sir Oliver!

Sir Oliv. Truly I think so – and not unprofitable.

Mos. Then, you know, you haven't the moneys yourself, but are forced to borrow them for him of a
friend.

Sir Oliv. Oh! I borrow it of a friend, do I?

Mos. And your friend is an unconscionable dog; but you
can't help it!

Sir Oliv. My friend an unconscionable dog, is he?

Mos. Yes, and he himself has not the moneys by him,
but is forced to sell stock at a great loss.

Sir Oliv. He is forced to sell stock at a great loss, is he?
Well, that's very kind of him.

Sir Pet. I'faith, Sir Oliver – Mr Premium, I mean,
you'll soon be master of the trade. But, Moses! would
not you have him run out a little against the Annuity
Bill? That would be in character, I should think.

Mos. Very much.

Row. And lament that a young man now must be at
years of discretion before he is suffered to ruin
himself?

Mos. Aye, great pity!

Sir Pet. And abuse the public for allowing merit to an

Act whose only object is to snatch misfortune and imprudence from the rapacious relief of usury, and give the minor the chance of inheriting his estate without being undone by coming into possession.

Sir Oliv. So – so – Moses shall give me further instructions as we go together.

Sir Pet. You will not have much time, for your nephew lives hard by.

Sir Oliv. Oh! never fear: my tutor appears so able, that though Charles lived in the next street, it must be my own fault if I am not a complete rogue before I turn the corner.   [*Exeunt Sir Oliver and Moses.*

Sir Pet. So, now, I think Sir Oliver will be convinced: you are partial, Rowley, and would have prepared Charles for the plot.

Row. No, upon my word, Sir Peter.

Sir Peter. Well, go bring me this Snake, and I'll hear what he has to say presently. – I see Maria, and want to speak with her. [*Exit Rowley.*] I should be glad to be convinced my suspicions of Lady Teazle and Charles were unjust. I have never yet opened my mind on this subject to my friend Joseph – I am determined I will do it – he will give me his opinion sincerely.

Enter MARIA

So, child, has Mr Surface returned with you?

Mar. No, sir; he was engaged.

Sir Pet. Well, Maria, do you not reflect, the more you converse with that amiable young man, what return his partiality for you deserves?

Mar. Indeed, Sir Peter, your frequent importunity on this subject distresses me extremely – you compel me to declare, that I know no man who has ever paid me a particular attention whom I would not prefer to Mr Surface.

Sir Pet. So – here's perverseness! No, no, Maria, 'tis

Charles only whom you would prefer. 'Tis evident his vices and follies have won your heart.

Mar. This is unkind, sir. You know I have obeyed you in neither seeing nor corresponding with him: I have heard enough to convince me that he is unworthy my regard. Yet I cannot think it culpable, if, while my understanding severely condemns his vices, my heart suggests pity for his distresses.

Sir Pet. Well, well, pity him as much as you please; but give your heart and hand to a worthier object.

Mar. Never to his brother!

Sir Pet. Go – perverse and obstinate! but take care, madam; you have never known what the authority of a guardian is: don't compel me to inform you of it.

Mar. I can only say, you shall not have a just reason. 'Tis true, by my father's will, I am for a short period bound to regard you as his substitute; but must cease to think you so when you would compel me to be miserable.   [*Exit Maria.*

Sir Pet. Was ever man so crossed as I am? everything conspiring to fret me! I had not been involved in matrimony a fortnight, before her father, a hale and hearty man, died, on purpose, I believe, for the pleasure of plaguing me with the care of his daughter. But here comes my helpmate – she appears in great good humour. How happy I should be if I could tease her into loving me, though but a little!

Enter LADY TEAZLE

Lady Teaz. Lud! Sir Peter, I hope you haven't been quarrelling with Maria? It is not using me well to be ill-humoured when I am not by.

Sir Pet. Ah, Lady Teazle, you might have the power to make me good-humoured at all times.

Lady Teaz. I am sure I wish I had; for I want you to be in a charming sweet temper at this moment. Do be

good-humoured now, and let me have two hundred
pounds, will you?

Sir Pet. Two hundred pounds; what, an't I to be in a
good humour without paying for it? But speak to me
thus, and i'faith there's nothing I could refuse you.
You shall have it; but seal me a bond for the repay-
ment.

Lady Teaz. Oh, no – there – my note of hand will do
as well.   [*Offering her hand.*

Sir Pet. And you shall no longer reproach me with not
giving you an independent settlement. I mean shortly
to surprise you; – but shall we always live thus, hey?

Lady Teaz. If you please. I'm sure I don't care how soon
we leave off quarrelling, provided you'll own you were
tired first.

Sir Pet. Well – then let your future contest be, who shall
be most obliging.

Lady Teaz. I assure you, Sir Peter, good nature becomes
you. You look now as you did before we were married,
when you used to walk with me under the elms, and
tell me stories of what a gallant you were in your
youth, and chuck me under the chin, you would; and
ask me if I thought I could love an old fellow, who
would deny me nothing – didn't you?

Sir Pet. Yes, yes, and you were as kind and attentive –

Lady Teaz. Ay, so I was, and would always take your
part, when my acquaintance used to abuse you, and
turn you into ridicule.

Sir Pet. Indeed!

Lady Teaz. Ay, and when my cousin Sophy has called
you a stiff, peevish old bachelor, and laughed at me
for thinking of marrying one who might be my father,
I have always defended you, and said, I didn't think
you so ugly by any means.

Sir Pet. Thank you.

Lady Teaz. And I dared say you'd make a very good
sort of a husband.

Sir Pet. And you prophesied right; and we shall certainly now be the happiest couple –

Lady Teaz. And never differ again?

Sir Pet. No, never – though at the same time, indeed, my dear Lady Teazle, you must watch your temper very narrowly; for in all our little quarrels, my dear, if you recollect, my love, you always began first.

Lady Teaz. I beg your pardon, my dear Sir Peter: indeed, you always gave the provocation.

Sir Pet. Now, see, my angel! take care – contradicting isn't the way to keep friends.

Lady Teaz. Then, don't you begin it, my love!

Sir Pet. There, now! you – you are going on. You don't perceive, my life, that you are just doing the very thing which you know always makes me angry.

Lady Teaz. Nay, you know if you will be angry without any reason – my dear –

Sir Pet. There! now you want to quarrel again.

Lady Teaz. No, I am sure I don't: but if you will be so peevish –

Sir Pet. There now, who begins first?

Lady Teaz. Why, you, to be sure. I said nothing – but there's no bearing your temper.

Sir Pet. No, no, madam; the fault's in your own temper.

Lady Teaz. Aye, you are just what my Cousin Sophy said you would be.

Sir Pet. Your Cousin Sophy is a forward, impertinent gipsy.

Lady Teaz. You are a great bear, I am sure, to abuse my relations. How dare you abuse my relations?

Sir Pet. Now may all the plagues of marriage be doubled on me, if ever I try to be friends with you any more!

Lady Teaz. So much the better.

Sir Pet. No, no, madam: 'tis evident you never cared a pin for me, and I was a madman to marry you – a pert, rural coquette, that had refused half the honest 'squires in the neighbourhood!

Lady Teaz. And I am sure I was a fool to marry you – an old dangling bachelor, who was single at fifty, only because he never could meet with anyone who would have him.

Sir Pet. Aye, aye, madam; but you were pleased enough to listen to me: you never had such an offer before.

Lady Teaz. No! didn't I refuse Sir Tivy Terrier, who everybody said would have been a better match? for his estate is just as good as yours, and he has broke his neck since we have been married.

Sir Pet. I have done with you, madam! You are an unfeeling, ungrateful – but there's an end of everything. I believe you capable of everything that is bad. Yes, madam, I now believe the reports relative to you and Charles, madam. – Yes, madam, you and Charles are – not without grounds –

Lady Teaz. Take care, Sir Peter! you had better not insinuate any such thing! I'll not be suspected without cause, I promise you.

Sir Pet. Very well, madam, very well! a separate maintenance as soon as you please. Yes, madam, or a divorce! I'll make an example of myself for the benefit of all old bachelors. – Let us separate, madam.

Lady Teaz. Agreed! agreed! – And now, my dear Sir Peter, we are of a mind once more, we may be the happiest couple – and never differ again, you know – ha! ha! ha! Well, you are going to be in a passion, I see, and I shall only interrupt you – so, bye! bye!
                                                        [*Exit.*

Sir Pet. Plagues and tortures! Can't I make her angry either! Oh, I am the miserablest fellow! But I'll not bear her presuming to keep her temper: no! she may break my heart, but she shan't keep her temper.
                                                        [*Exit.*

ACT III, SCENE 2

At Charles's house, a chamber

Enter TRIP, MOSES, *and* SIR OLIVER

Trip. Here, Master Moses! if you'll stay a moment I'll try whether Mr— what's the gentleman's name?

Sir Oliv. Mr— [*Apart.*] Moses, what is my name?

Mos. Mr Premium.

Trip. Premium – very well.   [*Exit, taking snuff.*

Sir Oliv. To judge by the servants, one wouldn't believe the master was ruined. But what! – sure, this was my brother's house?

Mos. Yes, sir; Mr Charles bought it of Mr Joseph, with the furniture, pictures, etc., just as the old gentleman left it. Sir Peter thought it a piece of extravagance in him.

Sir Oliv. In my mind, the other's economy in selling it to him was more reprehensible by half.

Enter TRIP

Trip. My master says you must wait, gentlemen: he has company, and can't speak with you yet.

Sir Oliv. If he knew who it was wanted to see him, perhaps he would not have sent such a message?

Trip. Yes, yes, sir; he knows you are here – I did not forget little Premium: no, no, no –

Sir Oliv. Very well; and I pray, sir, what may be your name?

Trip. Trip, sir; my name is Trip, at your service.

Sir Oliv. Well, then, Mr Trip, you have a pleasant sort of place here, I guess?

Trip. Why, yes – here are three or four of us pass our time agreeably enough; but then our wages are sometimes a little in arrear – and not very great either – but fifty pounds a year, and find our own bags and bouquets.

Sir Oliv. Bags and bouquets! halters and bastinadoes!
[*Aside.*

Trip. And *à propos*, Moses, have you been able to get me that little bill discounted?

Sir Oliv. Wants to raise money, too! — mercy on me! Has his distresses too, I warrant, like a lord, and affects creditors and duns.   [*Aside.*

Mos. 'Twas not to be done, indeed, Mr Trip.

Trip. Good lack, you surprise me! My friend Brush has endorsed it, and I thought when he put his name at the back of a bill 'twas as good as cash.

Mos. No! 'twouldn't do.

Trip. A small sum — but twenty pounds. Hark'ee, Moses, do you think you couldn't get it me by way of annuity?

Sir Oliv. An annuity! ha! ha! a footman raise money by way of annuity! Well done, luxury, egad!   [*Aside.*

Mos. Well, but you must insure your place.

Trip. Oh, with all my heart! I'll insure my place, and my life too, if you please.

Sir Oliv. It's more than I would your neck.   [*Aside.*

Trip. But then, Moses, it must be done before this d—d Register takes place; one wouldn't like to have one's name made public, you know.

Mos. No, certainly. But is there nothing you could deposit?

Trip. Why, nothing capital of my master's wardrobe has dropped lately; but I could give you a mortgage on some of his winter clothes, with equity of re-demption before November — or you shall have the reversion of the French velvet, or a post-obit on the blue and silver: — these, I should think, Moses, with a few pair of point ruffles, as a collaterial security — hey, my little fellow?

Mos. Well, well.   [*Bell rings.*

Trip. Egad, I heard the bell! I believe, gentlemen, I can now introduce you. Don't forget the annuity,

little Moses! This way, gentlemen: insure my place,
you know.

Sir Oliv. If the man be a shadow of the master, this is the
temple of dissipation indeed!   [*Exeunt.*

———

ACT III, SCENE 3

CHARLES SURFACE, CARELESS, SIR TOBY BUMPER,
etc., discovered at a table, drinking wine

Chas. Surf. 'Fore heaven, 'tis true! – there's the great
degeneracy of the age. Many of our acquaintance
have taste, spirit, and politeness; but, plague on't,
they won't drink.

Care. It is so, indeed, Charles! they give in to all the
substantial luxuries of the table, and abstain from
nothing but wine and wit.

Chas. Surf. Oh, certainly society suffers by it intolerably;
for now, instead of the social spirit of raillery that
used to mantel over a glass of bright Burgundy, their
conversation is become just like the Spa water they
drink, which has all the pertness and flatulence of
champagne without its spirit or flavour.

First Gent. But what are they to do who love play better
than wine?

Care. True! there's Harry diets himself for gaming, and
is now under a hazard regimen.

Chas. Surf. Then he'll have the worst of it. What! you
wouldn't train a horse for the course by keeping him
from corn? For my part, egad, I'm never so successful
as when I am a little merry; let me throw on a bottle
of champagne, and I never lose – at least I never feel
my losses, which is exactly the same thing.

Second Gent. Ay, that I believe.

Chas. Surf. And, then, what man can pretend to be a
believer in love, who is an abjurer of wine? 'Tis the
test by which the lover knows his own heart. Fill a

dozen bumpers to a dozen beauties, and she that
floats to the top is the maid that has bewitched you.

Care. Now then, Charles, be honest, and give us your
real favourite.

Chas. Surf. Why, I have withheld her only in compassion
to you. If I toast her, you must give a round of her
peers, which is impossible – on earth.

Care. Oh! then we'll find some canonized vestals or
heathen goddesses that will do, I warrant!

Chas. Surf. Here then, bumpers, you rogues! bumpers!
Maria! Maria –

First Gent. Maria who?

Chas. Surf. Oh, damn the surname! – 'tis too formal to
be registered in Love's calendar – but now, Sir Toby,
beware, we must have beauty superlative.

Care. Nay, never study, Sir Toby: we'll stand to the
toast, though your mistress should want an eye, and
you know you have a song will excuse you.

Sir Tob. Egad, so I have! and I'll give him the song
instead of the lady.

Song

Here's to the maiden of bashful fifteen;
 Here's to the widow of fifty;
Here's to the flaunting extravagant quean,
 And here's to the housewife that's thrifty.

Chorus.   Let the toast pass, –
   Drink to the lass,
I'll warrant she'll prove an excuse for a glass.

Here's to the charmer whose dimples we prize;
 Now to the maid who has none, sir;
Here's to the girl with a pair of blue eyes,
 And here's to the nymph with but *one,* sir.

Chorus.   Let the toast pass, –
   Drink to the lass,
I'll warrant she'll prove an excuse for a glass.

Here's to the maid with a bosom of snow:
 Now to her that's as brown as a berry:

Here's to the wife with her face full of woe,
    And now to the damsel that's merry.

Chorus.   Let the toast pass, –
               Drink to the lass,
I'll warrant she'll prove an excuse for a glass.

For let 'em be clumsy, or let 'em be slim,
    Young or ancient, I care not a feather;
So fill a pint bumper quite up to the brim,
    And let us e'en toast them together.

Chorus.   Let the toast pass, –
               Drink to the lass,
I'll warrant she'll prove an excuse for a glass.

All. Bravo! Bravo!

Enter TRIP *and whispers to Charles*

Chas. Surf. Gentlemen, you must excuse me a little. Careless, take the chair, will you?

Care. Nay, prithee, Charles, what now? This is one of your peerless beauties, I suppose, has dropt in by chance?

Chas. Surf. No, faith! To tell you the truth, 'tis a Jew and a broker, who are come by appointment.

Care. Oh, damn it! let's have the Jew in.

First Gent. Ay, and the broker too, by all means.

Second Gent. Yes, yes, the Jew and the broker.

Chas. Surf. Egad, with all my heart! – Trip, bid the gentlemen walk in. – [*Exit Trip.*] Though there's one of them a stranger, I can tell you.

Care. Charles, let us give them some generous Burgundy, and perhaps they'll grow conscientious.

Chas. Surf. Oh, hang 'em, no! wine does but draw forth a man's natural qualities; and to make them drink would only be to whet their knavery.

Enter TRIP, SIR OLIVER, *and* MOSES

Chas. Surf. So, honest Moses, walk in: walk in, pray, Mr

Premium – that's the gentleman's name, isn't it, Moses?

Mos. Yes, sir.

Chas. Surf. Set chairs, Trip – sit down, Mr Premium – glasses, Trip. – Sit down, Moses. Come, Mr Premium, I'll give you a sentiment; here's *Success to usury* – Moses, fill the gentleman a bumper.

Mos. Success to usury!

Care. Right, Moses – usury is prudence and industry, and deserves to succeed.

Sir Oliv. Then – *here's all the success it deserves!*

Care. No, no, that won't do, Mr Premium; you have demurred to the toast, and must drink it in a pint bumper.

First Gent. A pint bumper, at least.

Mos. Oh, pray, sir, consider – Mr Premium's a gentleman.

Care. And therefore loves good wine.

Second Gent. Give Moses a quart glass – this is mutiny, and a high contempt for the chair.

Care. Here, now for't! I'll see justice done, to the last drop of my bottle.

Sir Oliv. Nay, pray, gentlemen – I did not expect this usage.

Chas. Surf. No, hang it, you shan't! Mr Premium's a stranger.

Sir Oliv. Odd! I wish I was well out of their company. [*Aside.*

Care. Plague on 'em then! if they won't drink, we'll not sit down with them. Come, Harry, the dice are in the next room – Charles, you'll join us when you have finished your business with these gentlemen?

Chas. Surf. I will! I will! – [*Exeunt Gentlemen.*] Careless!

Care. [*Returning*] Well!

Chas. Surf. Perhaps I may want you.

Care. Oh, you know I am always ready: word, note, or bond, 'tis all the same to me. [*Exit.*

Mos. Sir, this is Mr Premium, a gentleman of the strictest honour and secrecy; and always performs what he undertakes. Mr Premium, this is –

Chas. Surf. Pshaw! have done. – Sir, my friend Moses is a very honest fellow, but a little slow at expression: he'll be an hour giving us our titles. Mr Premium, the plain state of the matter is this: I am an extravagant young fellow who wants to borrow money – you I take to be a prudent old fellow, who has got money to lend. I am blockhead enough to give fifty per cent sooner than not have it; and you, I presume, are rogue enough to take an hundred if you can get it. Now, sir, you see we are acquainted at once, and may proceed to business without further ceremony.

Sir Oliv. Exceeding frank, upon my word. – I see, sir, you are not a man of many compliments.

Chas. Surf. Oh, no, sir! plain dealing in business I always think best.

Sir Oliv. Sir, I like you the better for it – however, you are mistaken in one thing; I have no money to lend, but I believe I could procure some of a friend; but then he's an unconscionable dog. Isn't he, Moses? And must sell stock to accommodate you, mustn't he, Moses?

Mos. Yes, indeed! You know I always speak the truth, and scorn to tell a lie!

Chas. Surf. Right. People that speak truth generally do: but these are trifles, Mr Premium. What! I know money isn't to be bought without paying for't!

Sir Oliv. Well – but what security could you give? You have no land, I suppose?

Chas. Surf. Not a mole-hill, nor a twig, but what's in beau-pots out of the window!

Sir Oliv. Nor any stock, I presume?

Chas. Surf. Nothing but live stock – and that's only a few pointers and ponies. But pray, Mr Premium, are you acquainted at all with any of my connexions?

Sir Oliv. Why, to say the truth, I am.

Chas. Surf. Then you must know that I have a dev'lish rich uncle in the East Indies, Sir Oliver Surface, from whom I have the greatest expectations?

Sir Oliv. That you have a wealthy uncle, I have heard; but how your expectations will turn out is more, I believe, than you can tell.

Chas. Surf. Oh, no! – there can be no doubt. They tell me I'm a prodigious favourite, and that he talks of leaving me everything.

Sir Oliv. Indeed! this is the first I've heard of it.

Chas. Surf. Yes, yes, 'tis just so. Moses knows 'tis true; don't you, Moses?

Mos. Oh, yes! I'll swear to't.

Sir Oliv. Egad, they'll persuade me presently I'm at Bengal.   [*Aside.*

Chas. Surf. Now I propose, Mr Premium, if it's agreeable to you, a post-obit on Sir Oliver's life: though at the same time the old fellow has been so liberal to me, that I give you my word, I should be very sorry to hear that anything had happened to him.

Sir Oliv. Not more than I should, I assure you. But the bond you mention happens to be just the worst security you could offer me – for I might live to a hundred and never recover the principal.

Chas. Surf. Oh, yes, you would – the moment Sir Oliver dies, you know, you would come on me for the money.

Sir Oliv. Then I believe I should be the most unwelcome dun you ever had in your life.

Chas. Surf. What! I suppose you're afraid that Sir Oliver is too good a life?

Sir Oliv. No, indeed I am not; though I have heard he is as hale and healthy as any man of his years in Christendom.

Chas. Surf. There again, now, you are misinformed. No, no, the climate has hurt him considerably, poor uncle Oliver. Yes, yes, he breaks apace, I am told – and is so much altered lately that his nearest relations wouldn't know him.

Sir Oliv. No! ha! ha! ha! so much altered lately that his nearest relations wouldn't know him! That's droll! egad – ha! ha! ha!

Chas. Surf. Ha! ha! – you're glad to hear that, little Premium?

Sir Oliv. No, no, I'm not.

Chas. Surf. Yes, yes, you are – ha! ha! ha! – you know that mends your chance.

Sir Oliv. But I'm told Sir Oliver is coming over; nay, some say he is actually arrived.

Chas. Surf. Pshaw! Sure I must know better than you whether he's come or not. No, no, rely on't he's at this moment at Calcutta – isn't he, Moses?

Mos. Yes, certainly.

Sir Oliv. Very true, as you say, you must know better than I, though I have it from pretty good authority – haven't I, Moses?

Mos. Yes, most undoubted!

Sir Oliv. But, sir, as I understand you want a few hundreds immediately – is there nothing you could dispose of?

Chas. Surf. How do you mean?

Sir Oliv. For instance, now, I have heard that your father left behind him a great quantity of massy old plate.

Chas. Surf. O Lud! – that's gone long ago. – Moses can tell you how better than I can.

Sir Oliv. Good lack! all the family race-cups and corporation bowls! – [*Aside*] Then it was also supposed that his library was one of the most valuable and complete –

Chas. Surf. Yes, yes, so it was – vastly too much so for a private gentleman. For my part, I was always of a communicative disposition, so I thought it a shame to keep so much knowledge to myself.

Sir Oliv. Mercy upon me! Learning that had run in the

family like an heirloom! – [*Aside*] Pray, what are
become of the books?

Chas. Surf. You must inquire of the auctioneer, master
Premium, for I don't believe even Moses can direct
you.

Mos. I never meddle with books.

Sir. Oliv. So, so, nothing of the family property left, I
suppose?

Chas. Surf. Not much, indeed; unless you have a mind
to the family pictures. I have got a room full of ancestors above, and if you have a taste for old paintings,
egad, you shall have them a bargain!

Sir Oliv. Hey! what the devil! sure, you wouldn't sell
your forefathers, would you?

Chas. Surf. Every man of 'em, to the best bidder.

Sir Oliv. What! your great-uncles and aunts?

Chas. Surf. Aye, and my grandfathers and grandmothers too.

Sir Oliv. Now I give him up! [*Aside*] – What the plague,
have you no bowels for your own kindred? Odd's life,
do you take me for Shylock in the play, that you would
raise money of me on your own flesh and blood?

Chas. Surf. Nay, my little broker, don't be angry: what
need you care, if you have your money's worth?

Sir Oliv. Well, I'll be the purchaser: I think I can dispose
of the family canvas. – Oh, I'll never forgive him
this! never! [*Aside*]

Enter CARELESS

Care. Come, Charles, what keeps you?

Chas. Surf. I can't come yet; i'faith, we are going to have
a sale above stairs; here's little Premium will buy all
my ancestors!

Care. Oh, burn your ancestors!

Chas. Surf. No, he may do that afterwards, if he pleases.
Stay, Careless, we want you: egad, you shall be
auctioneer: so come along with us.

Care. Oh, have with you, if that's the case. I can handle a hammer as well as a dice-box – a-going – a-going.

Sir Oliv. Oh, the profligates! [*Aside.*

Chas. Surf. Come, Moses, you shall be appraiser, if we want one. Gad's life, little Premium, you don't seem to like the business?

Sir Oliv. Oh, yes, I do, vastly! Ha! ha! ha! yes, yes, I think it a rare joke to sell one's family by auction – ha! ha! – Oh, the prodigal! [*Aside.*

Chas. Surf. To be sure! when a man wants money, where the plague should he get assistance, if he can't make free with his own relations? [*Exeunt.*

End of the Third Act

ACT IV, SCENE 1

Picture Room at Charles's House

Enter CHARLES, SIR OLIVER, MOSES, *and* CARELESS

Chas. Surf. Walk in, gentlemen, pray walk in; – here they
are, the family of the Surfaces, up to the Conquest.

Sir Oliv. And, in my opinion, a goodly collection.

Chas. Surf. Ay, ay, these are done in the true spirit of
portrait-painting; no *volunteer grace* or expression. Not
like the works of your modern Raphaels, who give you
the strongest resemblance, yet contrive to make your
portrait independent of you; so that you may sink
the original and not hurt the picture. No, no; the merit
of these is the inveterate likeness – all stiff and awkward as the originals, and like nothing in human
nature besides.

Sir Oliv. Ah! we shall never see such figures of men again.

Chas. Surf. I hope not. – Well, you see, Master Premium,
what a domestic character I am; here I sit of an evening surrounded by my family. – But come, get to your
pulpit, Mr Auctioneer; here's an old gouty chair of
my grandfather's will answer the purpose.

Care. Ay, ay, this will do. But, Charles, I haven't a
hammer; and what's an auctioneer without his
hammer?

Chas. Surf. Egad, that's true. What parchment have we
here? *Richard heir to Thomas.* Oh, our genealogy in full.
Here, Careless – you shall have no common bit of
mahogany, here's the family tree for you, you rogue, –
this shall be your hammer, and now you may knock
down my ancestors with their own pedigree.

Sir Oliv. What an unnatural rogue! – an *ex post facto*
parricide!   [*Aside.*

Care. Yes, yes, here's a list of your generation indeed;
– faith, Charles, this is the most convenient thing you

could have found for the business, for 'twill not only
serve as a hammer, but a catalogue into the bargain.
But come, begin. – A-going, a-going, a-going!

Chas. Surf. Bravo, Careless! Well, here's my great-uncle,
Sir Richard Raveline, a marvellous good general in
his day, I assure you. He served in all the Duke of
Marlborough's wars, and got that cut over his eye at
the battle of Malplaquet. – What say you, Mr Premium? – look at him – there's a hero for you, not cut
out of his feathers, as your modern clipt captains are,
but enveloped in wig and regimentals, as a general
should be. – What do you bid?

Sir Oliv. Bid him speak.   [*Aside to Moses.*

Mos. Mr Premium would have *you* speak.

Chas. Surf. Why, then, he shall have him for ten pounds,
and I'm sure that's not dear for a staff-officer.

Sir Oliv. Heaven deliver me! his famous Uncle Richard
for ten pounds! – [*Aside*]. Very well, sir, I take him at
that.

Chas. Surf. Careless, knock down my Uncle Richard.
– Here, now, is a maiden sister of his, my great-aunt
Deborah, done by Kneller, in his best manner, and
esteemed a very formidable likeness. – There she is,
you see, a shepherdess feeding her flock. – You shall
have her for five pounds ten – the sheep are worth the
money.

Sir Oliv. Ah! poor Deborah! a woman who set such value
on herself! [*Aside.*] – Five pounds ten – she's mine.

Chas. Surf. Knock down my Aunt Deborah! – Here,
now, are two that were a sort of cousins of theirs. –
You see, Moses, these pictures were done some time
ago, when beaux wore wigs, and the ladies their
own hair.

Sir Oliv. Yes, truly, head-dresses appear to have been a
little lower in those days.

Chas. Surf. Well, take this couple for the same.

Mos. 'Tis a good bargain.

Chas. Surf. This, now, is a grandfather of my mother's, a learned judge, well known on the western circuit. – What do you rate him at, Moses?

Mos. Four guineas.

Chas. Surf. Four guineas! – Gad's life, you don't bid me the price of his wig. – Mr Premium, you have more respect for the woolsack; do let us knock his lordship down at fifteen.

Sir Oliv. By all means.

Care. Gone!

Chas. Surf. And there are two brothers of his, William and Walter Blunt, Esquires, both members of Parliament, and noted speakers, and what's very extraordinary, I believe, this is the first time they were ever bought or sold.

Sir Oliv. That is very extraordinary, indeed! I'll take them at your own price, for the honour of Parliament.

Care. Well said, little Premium! – I'll knock them down at forty.

Chas. Surf. Here's a jolly fellow – I don't know what relation, but he was mayor of Norwich: take him at eight pounds.

Sir Oliv. No, no; six will do for the mayor.

Chas. Surf. Come, make it guineas, and I'll throw you the two aldermen there into the bargain.

Sir Oliv. They're mine.

Chas. Surf. Careless, knock down the mayor and aldermen. – But, plague on't, we shall be all day retailing in this manner; do let us deal wholesale: what say you, little Premium? Give me three hundred pounds for the rest of the family in the lump.

Care. Aye, aye, that will be the best way.

Sir Oliv. Well, well, anything to accommodate you; – they are mine. But there is one portrait which you have always passed over.

Care. What, that ill-looking little fellow over the settee?

Sir Oliv. Yes, sir, I mean that; though I don't think him so ill-looking a little fellow, by any means.

Chas. Surf. What, that? – Oh; that's my uncle Oliver; 'twas done before he went to India.

Care. Your uncle Oliver! Gad, then you'll never be friends, Charles. That, now, to me, is as stern a looking rogue as ever I saw; an unforgiving eye, and a damned disinheriting countenance! an inveterate knave, depend on't. Don't you think so, little Premium?

Sir Oliv. Upon my soul sir, I do not; I think it is as honest a looking face as any in the room, dead or alive; – but I suppose Uncle Oliver goes with the rest of the lumber?

Chas. Surf. No, hang it! I'll not part with poor Noll. The old fellow has been very good to me, and, egad, I'll keep his picture while I've a room to put it in.

Sir Oliv. The rogue's my nephew after all! [*Aside.*] – But, sir, I have somehow taken a fancy to that picture.

Chas. Surf. I'm sorry for't, for you certainly will not have it. Oons, haven't you got enough of them?

Sir Oliv. I forgive him everything! [*Aside.*] – But sir, when I take a whim in my head, I don't value money, I'll give you as much for that as for all the rest.

Chas. Surf. Don't tease me, master broker; I tell you I'll not part with it, and there's an end of it.

Sir Oliv. How like his father the dog is. – Well, well, I have done. – I did not perceive it before, but I think I never saw such a striking resemblance. – [*Aside.*] – Here is a draft for your sum.

Chas. Surf. Why, 'tis for eight hundred pounds!

Sir Oliv. You will not let Sir Oliver go?

Chas. Surf. Zounds! no! – I tell you, once more.

Sir Oliv. Then never mind the difference, we'll balance that another time – but give me your hand on the bargain; you are an honest fellow, Charles – I beg pardon, sir, for being so free. – Come, Moses.

Chas. Surf. Egad, this is a whimsical old fellow! But

hark'ee, Premium, you'll prepare lodgings for these gentlemen.

Sir Oliv. Yes, yes, I'll send for them in a day or two.

Chas. Surf. But hold; do now send a genteel conveyance for them, for I assure you, they were most of them used to ride in their own carriages.

Sir Oliv. I will, I will – for all but Oliver.

Chas. Surf. Aye, all but the little nabob.

Sir Oliv. You're fixed on that?

Chas. Surf. Peremptorily.

Sir Oliv. A dear extravagant rogue! [*Aside.*] – Good-day! – Come, Moses. – Let me hear now who dares call him profligate!

[*Exeunt Sir Oliver Surface and Moses.*

Care. Why, this is the oddest genius of the sort I ever met with!

Chas. Surf. Egad, he's the prince of brokers, I think. I wonder how the devil Moses got acquainted with so honest a fellow. – Ha! here's Rowley; do, Careless, say I'll join the company in a moment.

Care. I will – but don't let that old blockhead persuade you to squander any of that money on old musty debts, or any such nonsense; for tradesmen, Charles, are the most exorbitant fellows.

Chas. Surf. Very true, and paying them is only encouraging them.

Care. Nothing else.

Chas. Surf. Aye, aye, never fear. [*Exit Careless.*] So! this was an odd old fellow, indeed. – Let me see, two-thirds of this is mine by right, – five hundred and thirty odd pounds. 'Fore Heaven! I find one's ancestors are more valuable relations than I took them for! – Ladies and gentlemen, your most obedient and very grateful servant.

Enter ROWLEY

Ha! old Rowley! egad, you are just come in time to take leave of your old acquaintance.

Row. Yes, I heard they were a-going. But I wonder you can have such spirits under so many distresses.

Chas. Surf. Why, there's the point! my distresses are so many, that I can't afford to part with my spirits; but I shall be rich and splenetic, all in good time. However, I suppose you are surprised that I am not more sorrowful at parting with so many near relations; to be sure, 'tis very affecting; but rot 'em, you see they never move a muscle, so why should I?

Row. There's no making you serious a moment.

Chas. Surf. Yes, faith, I am so now. Here, my honest Rowley, here, get me this changed directly, and take a hundred pounds of it immediately, to old Stanley.

Row. A hundred pounds! Consider only –

Chas. Surf. Gad's life, don't talk about it: poor Stanley's wants are pressing, and, if you don't make haste, we shall have someone call that has a better right to the money.

Row. Ah! there's the point! I never will cease dunning you with the old proverb –

Chas. Surf. 'Be just before you're generous.' – Why, so I would if I could; but Justice is an old hobbling beldame, and I can't get her to keep pace with Generosity for the soul of me.

Row. Yet, Charles, believe me, one hour's reflection –

Chas. Surf. Aye, aye, it's all very true; but, hark'ee, Rowley, while I have, by Heaven I'll give; so, damn your economy, and now for hazard. [*Exeunt.*

ACT IV, SCENE 2

The Parlour
Enter Sir Oliver *and* Moses

Mos. Well, sir, I think, as Sir Peter said, you have seen Mr Charles in high glory; 'tis great pity he's so extravagant.

Sir Oliv. True, but he would not sell my picture.

Mos. And loves wine and women so much.

Sir Oliv. But he would not sell my picture.

Mos. And games so deep.

Sir Oliv. But he would not sell my picture. – Oh, here's Rowley.

Enter ROWLEY

Row. So, Sir Oliver, I find you have made a purchase –

Sir Oliv. Yes, yes, our young rake has parted with his ancestors like old tapestry.

Row. And here has he commissioned me to re-deliver you part of the purchase-money – I mean, though, in your necessitous character of old Stanley.

Mos. Ah! there is the pity of all: he is so damned charitable.

Row. And I left a hosier and two tailors in the hall, who, I'm sure, won't be paid, and this hundred would satisfy them.

Sir Oliv. Well, well, I'll pay his debts, and his benevolence too. – But now I am no more a broker, and you shall introduce me to the elder brother as old Stanley.

Row. Not yet awhile; Sir Peter, I know, means to call there about this time.

Enter TRIP

Trip. Oh, gentlemen, I beg pardon for not showing you out; this way – Moses, a word.

[*Exeunt Trip and Moses.*

Sir Oliv. There's a fellow for you – would you believe it, that puppy intercepted the Jew on our coming, and wanted to raise money before he got to his master!

Row. Indeed!

Sir Oliv. Yes, they are now planning an annuity business. – Ah, Master Rowley, in my days servants were content with the follies of their masters, when they were worn a little threadbare; but now, they have

their vices, like their birthday clothes, with the gloss
on. [*Exeunt.*

———

ACT IV, SCENE 3

A Library

JOSEPH SURFACE *and a* SERVANT

Jos. Surf. No letter from Lady Teazle?

Ser. No, sir.

Jos. Surf. I am surprised she has not sent, if she is prevented from coming. Sir Peter certainly does not
suspect me. Yet I wish I may not lose the heiress,
through the scrape I have drawn myself into with the
wife; however, Charles's imprudence and bad character are great points in my favour. [*Knock without.*

Ser. Sir, I believe that must be Lady Teazle.

Jos. Surf. Hold! – See whether it is or not, before you go
to the door: I have a particular message for you if it
should be my brother.

Ser. 'Tis her ladyship, sir; she always leaves the chair at
the milliner's in the next street.

Jos. Surf. Stay, stay: draw that screen before the window
– that will do; – my opposite neighbour is a maiden
lady of so curious a temper. – [*Servant draws the screen,
and exit.*] I have a difficult hand to play in this affair.
Lady Teazle has lately suspected my views on Maria;
but she must by no means be let into that secret, –
at least, till I have her more in my power.

Enter LADY TEAZLE

Lady Teaz. What, sentiment in soliloquy? Have you been
very impatient now? – O Lud! don't pretend to look
grave – I vow I couldn't come before.

Jos. Surf. Oh, Madam, punctuality is a species of constancy very unfashionable in a lady of quality.

Lady Teaz. Upon my word, you ought to pity me. Do

you know Sir Peter is grown so ill-tempered to me of
late, and so jealous of Charles, too; that's the best of
the story, isn't it?

Jos. Surf. I am glad my scandalous friends keep that up.

[*Aside.*

Lady Teaz. I am sure I wish he would let Maria marry
him, and then perhaps he would be convinced; don't
you, Mr Surface?

Jos. Surf. Indeed I do not. [*Aside.*] – Oh, certainly I do!
for then my dear Lady Teazle would also be convinced
how wrong her suspicions were of my having any
design on the silly girl.

Lady Teaz. Well, well, I'm inclined to believe you. But
isn't it provoking, to have the most ill-natured things
said of one? – And there's my friend Lady Sneerwell
has circulated I don't know how many scandalous
tales of me, and all without any foundation, too –
that's what vexes me.

Jos. Surf. Aye madam, to be sure, that is the provoking
circumstance – without foundation; yes, yes, there's
the mortification, indeed; for, when a scandalous
story is believed against one, there certainly is no
comfort like the consciousness of having deserved it.

Lady Teaz. No, to be sure, then I'd forgive their malice;
but to attack me, who am really so innocent, and who
never say an ill-natured thing of anybody – that is,
of my friends; and then Sir Peter, too, to have him so
peevish, and so suspicious, when I know the integrity
of my own heart – indeed 'tis monstrous!

Jos. Surf. But, my dear Lady Teazle, 'tis your own fault
if you suffer it. When a husband entertains a groundless suspicion of his wife, and withdraws his confidence
from her, the original compact is broke, and she owes
it to the honour of her sex to endeavour to outwit him.

Lady Teaz. Indeed! – So that, if he suspects me without
cause, it follows, that the best way of curing his
jealousy is to give him reason for't?

Jos. Surf. Undoubtedly – for your husband should never be deceived in you, – and in that case it becomes you to be frail in compliment to his discernment.

Lady Teaz. To be sure, what you say is very reasonable, and when the consciousness of my innocence –

Jos. Surf. Ah! my dear madam, there is the great mistake; 'tis this very conscious innocence that is of the greatest prejudice to you. What is it makes you negligent of forms, and careless of the world's opinion? – why, the consciousness of your own innocence. What makes you thoughtless in your conduct, and apt to run into a thousand little imprudences? – why, the consciousness of your own innocence. What makes you impatient of Sir Peter's temper, and outrageous at his suspicions? – why, the consciousness of your innocence.

Lady Teaz. 'Tis very true!

Jos. Surf. Now, my dear Lady Teazle, if you would but once make a trifling *faux pas*, you can't conceive how cautious you would grow, and how ready to humour and agree with your husband.

Lady Teaz. Do you think so?

Jos. Surf. Oh, I'm sure on't; and then you would find all scandal would cease at once, for, in short, your character at present is like a person in a plethora, absolutely dying from too much health.

Lady Teaz. So, so; then I perceive your prescription is, that I must sin in my own defence, and part with my virtue to preserve my reputation?

Jos. Surf. Exactly so, upon my credit, ma'am.

Lady Teaz. Well, certainly this is the oddest doctrine, and the newest receipt for avoiding calumny!

Jos. Surf. An infallible one, believe me. Prudence, like experience, must be paid for.

Lady Teaz. Why, if my understanding were once convinced –

Jos. Surf. Oh, certainly, madam, your understanding should be convinced. – Yes, yes – Heaven forbid I should persuade you to do anything you thought wrong. No, no, I have too much honour to desire it.

Lady Teaz. Don't you think we may as well leave *honour* out of the argument?

Jos. Surf. Ah, the ill effects of your country education, I see, still remain with you.

Lady Teaz. I doubt they do indeed; and I will fairly own to you, that if I could be persuaded to do wrong, it would be by Sir Peter's ill usage sooner than your *honourable logic*, after all.

Jos. Surf. Then, by this hand, which he is unworthy of –
[*Taking her hand.*

Enter SERVANT

'Sdeath, you blockhead – what do you want?

Ser. I beg pardon, sir, but I thought you would not choose Sir Peter to come up without announcing him.

Jos. Surf. Sir Peter! – Oons and the devil!

Lady Teaz. Sir Peter! O Lud – I'm ruined – I'm ruined!

Ser. Sir, 'twasn't I let him in.

Lady Teaz. Oh! I'm quite undone! What will become of me now, Mr Logic? Oh! he's on the stairs – I'll get behind here – and if ever I'm so imprudent again –
[*Goes behind the screen.*

Jos. Surf. Give me that book.
[*Sits down, servant pretends to adjust his chair.*

Enter SIR PETER TEAZLE

Sir Pet. Aye, ever improving himself. Mr Surface, Mr Surface –

Jos. Surf. Oh, my dear Sir Peter, I beg your pardon. [*Gaping, throws away the book.*] I have been dozing over a stupid book. – Well, I am much obliged to you for this call. You haven't been here, I believe, since I fitted up this room. – Books, you know, are the only things I am a coxcomb in.

Sir Pet. 'Tis very neat indeed. – Well, well, that's proper; and you can make even your screen a source of knowledge – hung, I perceive, with maps.

Jos. Surf. Oh, yes, I find great use in that screen.

Sir Pet. I dare say you must, certainly, when you want to find anything in a hurry.

Jos. Surf. Aye, or to hide anything in a hurry either. [*Aside.*

Sir Pet. Well, I have a little private business –

Jos. Surf. You need not stay. [*To Servant*

Ser. No, sir. [*Exit.*

Jos. Surf. Here's a chair, Sir Peter – I beg –

Sir Pet. Well, now we are alone, there is a subject, my dear friend, on which I wish to unburthen my mind to you – a point of the greatest moment to my peace; in short, my good friend, Lady Teazle's conduct of late has made me very unhappy.

Jos. Surf. Indeed! I am very sorry to hear it.

Sir Pet. Aye, 'tis but too plain she has not the least regard for me; but, what's worse, I have pretty good authority to suspect she has formed an attachment to another.

Jos. Surf. You astonish me!

Sir Pet. Yes; and, between ourselves, I think I've discovered the person.

Jos. Surf. How! you alarm me exceedingly.

Sir Pet. Ah, my dear friend, I knew you would sympathize with me!

Jos. Surf. Yes – believe me, Sir Peter, such a discovery would hurt me just as much as it would you.

Sir Pet. I am convinced of it. – Ah! it is a happiness to have a friend whom we can trust even with one's family secrets. But have you no guess who I mean?

Jos. Surf. I haven't the most distant idea. It can't be Sir Benjamin Backbite!

Sir Pet. Oh no! What say you to Charles?

Jos. Surf. My brother! impossible! O no, Sir Peter, you must not credit the scandalous insinuations you may hear. No, no, Charles to be sure has been charged with many things of this kind, but I can never think he would meditate so gross an injury.

Sir Pet. Ah, my dear friend, the goodness of your own heart misleads you. You judge of others by yourself.

Jos. Surf. Certainly, Sir Peter, the heart that is conscious of its own integrity is ever slow to credit another's treachery.

Sir Pet. True; but your brother has no sentiment – you never hear him talk so.

Jos. Surf. Yet I can't but think Lady Teazle herself has too much principle.

Sir Pet. Aye, but what is principle against the flattery of a handsome, lively young fellow?

Jos. Surf. That's very true.

Sir Pet. And then, you know, the difference of our ages makes it very improbable that she should have any great affection for me; and if she were to be frail, and I were to make it public, why the town would only laugh at me – the foolish old bachelor, who had married a girl.

Jos. Surf. That's true, to be sure – they *would* laugh.

Sir Pet. Laugh – aye, and make ballads, and paragraphs, and the devil knows what of me.

Jos. Surf. No – you must never make it public.

Sir Pet. But then again – that the nephew of my old friend, Sir Oliver, should be the person to attempt such a wrong, hurts me more nearly.

Jos. Surf. Aye, there's the point. – When ingratitude barbs the dart of injury, the wound has double danger in it.

Sir Pet. Aye – I, that was, in a manner, left his guardian: in whose house he had been so often entertained; who never in my life denied him – my advice!

Jos. Surf. Oh, 'tis not to be credited! There may be a man capable of such baseness, to be sure; but, for my part, till you can give me positive proofs, I cannot

but doubt it. However, if it should be proved on him,
he is no longer a brother of mine – I disclaim kindred
with him: for the man who can break the laws of
hospitality, and attempt the wife of his friend, deserves to be branded as the pest of society.

Sir Pet. What a difference there is between you! What
noble sentiments!

Jos. Surf. Yet, I cannot suspect Lady Teazle's honour.

Sir Pet. I am sure I wish to think well of her, and to remove all ground of quarrel between us. She has
lately reproached me more than once with having
made no settlement on her; and, in our last quarrel,
she almost hinted that she should not break her heart
if I was dead. Now, as we seem to differ in our ideas
of expense, I have resolved she shall have her own
way, and be her own mistress in that respect for the
future; and, if I were to die, she will find I have not
been inattentive to her interest while living. Here, my
friend, are the drafts of two deeds, which I wish to
have your opinion on. – By one, she will enjoy eight
hundred a year independent while I live; and, by the
other, the bulk of my fortune at my death.

Jos. Surf. This conduct, Sir Peter, is indeed truly generous. – I wish it may not corrupt my pupil.   [*Aside.*

Sir Pet. Yes, I am determined she shall have no cause to
complain, though I would not have her acquainted
with the latter instance of my affection yet awhile.

Jos. Surf. Nor I, if I could help it.   [*Aside.*

Sir Pet. And now, my dear friend, if you please, we will
talk over the situation of your hopes with Maria.

Jos. Surf. Oh, no, Sir Peter; another time, if you please.

Sir Pet. I am sensibly chagrined at the little progress you
seem to make in her affections.

Jos. Surf. I beg you will not mention it. What are my
disappointments when your happiness is in debate! –
[*Softly*] 'Sdeath, I shall be ruined every way!   [*Aside.*

Sir Pet. And though you are averse to my acquainting

Lady Teazle with *your* passion, I'm sure she's not your enemy in the affair.

Jos. Surf. Pray, Sir Peter, now, oblige me. I am really too much affected by the subject we have been speaking of, to bestow a thought on my own concerns. The man who is entrusted with his friend's distresses can never —

Enter SERVANT

Well, sir?

Ser. Your brother, sir, is speaking to a gentleman in the street, and says he knows you are within.

Jos. Surf. 'Sdeath, blockhead, I'm not within — I'm out for the day.

Sir Pet. Stay — hold — a thought has struck me: — you shall be at home.

Jos. Surf. Well, well, let him up. — [*Exit Servant.*] He'll interrupt Sir Peter, however.   [*Aside.*

Sir Pet. Now, my good friend, oblige me, I entreat you. Before Charles comes, let me conceal myself somewhere — then do you tax him on the point we have been talking on, and his answer may satisfy me at once.

Jos. Surf. Oh, fie, Sir Peter! would you have me join in so mean a trick? — to trepan my brother too?

Sir Pet. Nay, you tell me you are *sure* he is innocent; if so, you do him the greatest service by giving him an opportunity to clear himself, and you will set my heart at rest. Come, you shall not refuse me: here, behind the screen will be — hey! what the devil! there seems to be one listener here already — I'll swear I saw a petticoat!

Jos. Surf. Ha! ha! ha! Well, this is ridiculous enough. I'll tell you, Sir Peter, though I hold a man of intrigue to be a most despicable character, yet you know, it does not follow that one is to be an absolute Joseph either! Hark'ee, 'tis a little French milliner, — a silly rogue that plagues me, — and having some character to lose, on your coming, sir, she ran behind the screen.

Sir Pet. Ah! you rogue! But, egad, she has overheard all I have been saying of my wife.

Jos. Surf. Oh, 'twill never go any farther, you may depend upon it!

Sir Pet. No! then, faith, let her hear it out. – Here's a closet will do as well.

Jos. Surf. Well, go in there.

Sir Pet. Sly rogue! sly rogue.   [*Goes into the closet.*

Jos. Surf. A narrow escape, indeed! and a curious situation I'm in, to part man and wife in this manner.

Lady Teaz. [*Peeping.*] Couldn't I steal off?

Jos. Surf. Keep close, my angel!

Sir Pet. [*Peeping.*] Joseph, tax him home.

Jos. Surf. Back, my dear friend!

Lady Teaz. Couldn't you lock Sir Peter in?

Jos. Surf. Be still, my life!

Sir Pet. [*Peeping.*] You're sure the little milliner won't blab?

Jos. Surf. In, in, my dear Sir Peter! – 'Fore Gad, I wish I had a key to the door.

Enter CHARLES SURFACE

Chas. Surf. Holla! brother, what has been the matter? Your fellow would not let me up at first. What! have you had a Jew or a wench with you?

Jos. Surf. Neither, brother, I assure you.

Chas. Surf. But what has made Sir Peter steal off? I thought he had been with you.

Jos. Surf. He *was*, brother; but, hearing you were coming, he did not choose to stay.

Chas. Surf. What! was the old gentleman afraid I wanted to borrow money of him!

Jos. Surf. No, sir; but I am sorry to find, Charles, you have lately given that worthy man grounds for great uneasiness.

Chas. Surf. Yes, yes, yes, they tell me I do that to a great many worthy men. – But how so, pray?

Jos. Surf. To be plain with you, brother – he thinks you are
   endeavouring to gain Lady Teazle's affections from him.

Chas. Surf. Who, I? O Lud! not I, upon my word. Ha!
   ha! ha! ha! so the old fellow has found out that he
   has got a young wife, has he? – or, what is worse, has
   her ladyship discovered she has an old husband?

Jos. Surf. This is no subject to jest upon, brother. He who
   can laugh –

Chas. Surf. True, true, as you were going to say – then,
   seriously, I never had the least idea of what you charge
   me with, upon my honour.

Jos. Surf. Well, it will give Sir Peter great satisfaction to
   hear this.   [*Aloud.*

Chas. Surf. To be sure, I once thought the lady seemed to
   have taken a fancy to me; but, upon my soul, I never
   gave her the least encouragement: – besides, you know
   my attachment to Maria.

Jos. Surf. But sure, brother, even if Lady Teazle had
   betrayed the fondest partiality for you –

Chas. Surf. Why, look'ee, Joseph, I hope I shall never
   deliberately do a dishonourable action; but if a pretty
   woman was purposely to throw herself in my way –
   and that pretty woman married to a man old enough
   to be her father –

Jos. Surf. Well –

Chas. Surf. Why, I believe I should be obliged to borrow
   a little of your morality, that's all. – But, brother, do
   you know now that you surprise me exceedingly, by
   naming *me* with Lady Teazle; for i'faith, I always
   understood *you* were her favourite.

Jos. Surf. Oh, for shame, Charles! This retort is foolish.

Chas. Surf. Nay, I swear I have seen you exchange such
   significant glances –

Jos. Surf. Nay, nay, sir, this is no jest.

Chas. Surf. Egad, I'm serious. Don't you remember one
   day, when I called here –

Jos. Surf. Nay, prithee, Charles –

Chas. Surf. And found you together –

Jos. Surf. Zounds, sir, I insist –

Chas. Surf. And another time, when your servant –

Jos. Surf. Brother, brother, a word with you! – Gad, I
    must stop him.   [*Aside.*

Chas. Surf. Informed, I say, that –

Jos. Surf. Hush! I beg your pardon, but Sir Peter has
    overheard all we have been saying. I knew you would
    clear yourself, or I should not have consented.

Chas. Surf. How, Sir Peter! Where is he?

Jos. Surf. Softly; there!   [*Points to the closet.*

Chas. Surf. Oh, 'fore Heaven, I'll have him out. Sir Peter,
    come forth!

Jos. Surf. No, no –

Chas. Surf. I say, Sir Peter, come into court. – [*Pulls in Sir
    Peter.*] What! my old guardian! – What! turn in-
    quisitor, and take evidence, incog?

Sir Pet. Give me your hand, Charles – I believe I have
    suspected you wrongfully; but you mustn't be angry
    with Joseph – 'twas my plan!

Chas. Surf. Indeed!

Sir Pet. But I acquit you. I promise you I don't think near
    so ill of you as I did: what I have heard has given me
    great satisfaction.

Chas. Surf. Egad, then, 'twas lucky you didn't hear any
    more. Wasn't it, Joseph?

Sir Pet. Ah! you would have retorted on him.

Chas. Surf. Aye, aye, that was a joke.

Sir Pet. Yes, yes, I know his honour too well.

Chas. Surf. But you might as well have suspected *him* as
    me in this matter, for all that. Mightn't he, Joseph?

Sir Pet. Well, well, I believe you.

Jos. Surf. Would they were both out of the room!

    Enter SERVANT, *and whispers* JOSEPH SURFACE

Sir Pet. And in future, perhaps, we may not be such
    strangers.

Ser. Lady Sneerwell is below, and says she will come up.

Jos. Surf. [*to the Servant.*] Lady Sneerwell! Gad's life, she mustn't come here. Gentlemen, I beg pardon – I must wait on you downstairs; here's a person come on particular business.

Chas. Surf. Well, you can see him in another room. Sir Peter and I have not met a long time, and I have something to say to him.

Jos. Surf. [*Aside.*] They must not be left together. – [*to Charles*] I'll send this man away, and return directly. – Sir Peter, not a word of the French milliner.

Sir Pet. Oh, not for the world! – [*Exit Joseph.*] Ah, Charles, if you associated more with your brother, one might indeed hope for your reformation. He is a man of sentiment. – Well, there is nothing in the world so noble as a man of sentiment.

Chas. Surf. Pshaw! he is too moral by half; – and so apprehensive of his good name, as he calls it, that I suppose he would as soon let a priest into his house as a girl.

Sir Pet. No, no, – come, come, – you wrong him. No, no, Joseph is no rake, but he is no such saint in that respect either. – I have a great mind to tell him – we should have a laugh.   [*Aside.*

Chas. Surf. Oh, hang him! he's a very anchorite, a young hermit!

Sir Pet. Hark'ee – you must not abuse him: he may chance to hear of it again, I promise you.

Chas. Surf. Why, you won't tell him?

Sir Pet. No – but – this way. – Egad, I'll tell him. – [*Aside.*] Hark'ee, have you a mind to have a good laugh at Joseph?

Chas. Surf. I should like it of all things.

Sir Pet. Then, i'faith, we will! – I'll be quit with him for discovering me. He had a girl with him when I called.
                                                [*Whispers.*

Chas. Surf. What! Joseph? you jest.

Sir Pet. Hush! – a little French milliner – and the best of the jest is – she's in the room now.

Chas. Surf. The devil she is!   [*Looking at the closet.*

Sir Pet. Hush! I tell you.   [*Points to the screen.*

Chas. Surf. Behind the screen! Odds life, let's unveil her!

Sir Pet. No, no – he's coming – you shan't, indeed!

Chas. Surf. Oh, egad, we'll have a peep at the little milliner!

Sir Pet. Not for the world! – Joseph will never forgive me.

Chas. Surf. I'll stand by you –

Sir Pet. Odds, here he is!

JOSEPH SURFACE *enters just as* CHARLES SURFACE *throws down the screen*

Chas. Surf. Lady Teazle, by all that's wonderful!

Sir Pet. Lady Teazle, by all that's damnable!

Chas. Surf. Sir Peter, this is one of the smartest French milliners I ever saw. Egad, you seem all to have been diverting yourselves here at hide and seek, and I don't see who is out of the secret. Shall I beg your ladyship to inform me? Not a word! – Brother, will you be pleased to explain this matter? What! is Morality dumb too? – Sir Peter, though I found you in the dark, perhaps you are not so now! All mute! Well – though I can make nothing of the affair, I suppose you perfectly understand one another – so I'll leave you to yourselves. – [*Going.*] Brother, I'm sorry to find you have given that worthy man grounds for so much uneasiness. – Sir Peter! there's nothing in the world so noble as a man of sentiment!

[*Exit Charles. They stand for some time looking at each other.*]

Jos. Surf. Sir Peter – notwithstanding – I confess – that appearances are against me – if you will afford me your patience – I make no doubt – but I shall explain everything to your satisfaction.

Sir Pet. If you please, sir.

Jos. Surf. The fact is, sir – that Lady Teazle, knowing
my pretensions to your ward, Maria – I say, sir, Lady
Teazle, being apprehensive of the jealousy of your
temper – and knowing my friendship to the family –
she, sir, I say – called here – in order that – I might
explain these pretensions – but on your coming –
being apprehensive – as I said – of your jealousy –
she withdrew – and this, you may depend on it, is the
whole truth of the matter.

Sir Pet. A very clear account, upon my word; and I dare
swear the lady will vouch for every article of it.

Lady Teaz. For not one word of it, Sir Peter!

Sir Pet. How! don't you think it worth while to agree in
the lie?

Lady Teaz. There is not one syllable of truth in what that
gentleman has told you.

Sir Pet. I believe you, upon my soul, ma'am!

Jos. Surf. [*Aside.*] 'Sdeath, madam, will you betray me?

Lady Teaz. Good Mr Hypocrite, by your leave, I'll speak
for myself.

Sir Pet. Aye, let her alone, sir; you'll find she'll make
out a better story than you, without prompting.

Lady Teaz. Hear me, Sir Peter! – I came here on no
matter relating to your ward, and even ignorant of
this gentleman's pretensions to her. But I came,
seduced by his insidious arguments, at least to listen
to his pretended passion, if not to sacrifice your honour
to his baseness.

Sir Pet. Now, I believe, the truth is coming out indeed!

Jos. Surf. The woman's mad!

Lady Teaz. No, sir – she has recovered her senses, and
your own arts have furnished her with the means. –
Sir Peter, I do not expect you to credit me – but the
tenderness you expressed for me, when I am sure
you could not think I was a witness to it, has pene-
trated so to my heart, that had I left the place without
the shame of this discovery, my future life should have

spoken the sincerity of my gratitude. As for that smooth-tongued hypocrite, who would have seduced the wife of his too credulous friend, while he affected honourable addresses to his ward – I behold him now in a light so truly despicable, that I shall never again respect myself for having listened to him.   [*Exit.*

Jos. Surf. Notwithstanding all this, Sir Peter, Heaven knows –

Sir Pet. That you are a villain! and so I leave you to your conscience.

Jos. Surf. You are too rash, Sir Peter; you *shall* hear me. The man who shuts out conviction by refusing to –

Sir Pet. O damn your sentiments.

        [*Exeunt, Surface following and speaking.*

End of the Fourth Act

ACT V, SCENE 1

The Library

Enter JOSEPH SURFACE *and* SERVANT

Jos. Surf. Mr Stanley! – and why should you think I would see him? you must know he comes to ask something.

Ser. Sir, I should not have let him in, but that Mr Rowley came to the door with him.

Jos. Surf. Pshaw! blockhead! to suppose that I should now be in a temper to receive visits from poor relations! – Well, why don't you show the fellow up?

Ser. I will, sir. – Why, sir, it was not my fault that Sir Peter discovered my lady –

Jos. Surf. Go, fool! – [*Exit Servant.*] Sure Fortune never played a man of my policy such a trick before! My character with Sir Peter, my hopes with Maria, destroyed in a moment! I'm in a rare humour to listen to other people's distresses! I shan't be able to bestow even a benevolent sentiment on Stanley. – So! here he comes, and Rowley with him. I must try to recover myself, and put a little charity into my face, however.   [*Exit.*

Enter SIR OLIVER *and* ROWLEY

Sir Oliv. What! does he avoid us? – That was he, was it not?

Row. It was, sir. But I doubt you are come a little too abruptly. His nerves are so weak, that the sight of a poor relation may be too much for him. I should have gone first to break it to him.

Sir Oliv. Oh, plague of his nerves! Yet this is he whom Sir Peter extols as a man of the most benevolent way of thinking!

Row. As to his way of thinking, I cannot pretend to decide, for, to do him justice, he appears to have as

much speculative benevolence as any private gentleman in the kingdom, though he is seldom so sensual
as to indulge himself in the exercise of it.

Sir Oliv. Yet he has a string of charitable sentiments,
I suppose, at his fingers' ends.

Row. Or, rather, at his tongue's end, Sir Oliver; for
I believe there is no sentiment he has more faith in
than that 'Charity begins at home.'

Sir Oliv. And his, I presume, is of that domestic sort;
it never stirs abroad at all.

Row. I doubt you'll find it so; – but he's coming. I
mustn't seem to interrupt you; and you know, immediately as you leave him, I come in to announce
your arrival in your real character.

Sir Oliv. True; and afterwards you'll meet me at Sir
Peter's.

Row. Without losing a moment. [*Exit.*

Sir Oliv. I don't like the complaisance of his features.

Enter JOSEPH SURFACE

Jos. Surf. Sir, I beg you ten thousand pardons for keeping
you a moment waiting. – Mr Stanley, I presume.

Sir Oliv. At your service.

Jos. Surf. Sir, I beg you will do me the honour to sit
down – I entreat you, sir.

Sir Oliv. Dear sir – there's no occasion. – Too civil by
half. [*Aside.*

Jos. Surf. I have not the pleasure of knowing you, Mr
Stanley; but I am extremely happy to see you look
so well. You were nearly related to my mother, I
think, Mr Stanley?

Sir Oliv. I was sir; – so nearly that my present poverty,
I fear, may do discredit to her wealthy children, else
I should not have presumed to trouble you.

Jos. Surf. Dear sir, there needs no apology: – He that is
in distress, though a stranger, has a right to claim
kindred with the wealthy. I am sure I wish I was one

of that class, and had it in my power to offer you even a small relief.

Sir Oliv. If your uncle, Sir Oliver, were here, I should have a friend.

Jos. Surf. I wish he was, sir, with all my heart: you should not want an advocate with him, believe me, sir.

Sir Oliv. I should not need one – my distresses would recommend me. But I imagined his bounty had enabled you to become the agent of his charity.

Jos. Surf. My dear sir, you were strangely misinformed. Sir Oliver is a worthy man, a very worthy sort of man; but avarice, Mr Stanley, is the vice of age. I will tell you, my good sir, in confidence, what he has done for me has been a mere nothing; though people, I know, have thought otherwise, and, for my part, I never chose to contradict the report.

Sir Oliv. What! has he never transmitted you bullion – rupees – pagodas?

Jos. Surf. Oh, dear sir, nothing of the kind! – No, no – a few presents now and then – china, shawls, congou tea, avadavats, and Indian crackers – little more, believe me.

Sir Oliv. Here's gratitude for twelve thousand pounds! – Avadavats and Indian crackers!   [*Aside.*

Jos. Surf. Then, my dear sir, you have heard, I doubt not, of the extravagance of my brother; there are very few would credit what I have done for that unfortunate young man.

Sir Oliv. Not I, for one!   [*Aside.*

Jos. Surf. The sums I have lent him! – Indeed I have been exceedingly to blame; it was an amiable weakness – however – I don't pretend to defend it – and now I feel it doubly culpable, since it has deprived me of the pleasure of serving *you*, Mr Stanley, as my heart dictates.

Sir Oliv. Dissembler! – [*Aside.*] Then, sir, you can't assist me?

Jos. Surf. At present, it grieves me to say, I cannot; but, whenever I have the ability, you may depend upon hearing from me.

Sir Oliv. I am extremely sorry –

Jos. Surf. Not more than I, believe me; – to pity, without the power to relieve, is still more painful than to ask and be denied.

Sir Oliv. Kind sir, your most obedient humble servant.

Jos. Surf. You leave me deeply affected, Mr Stanley. – William, be ready to open the door.

Sir Oliv. O, dear sir, no ceremony.

Jos. Surf. Your very obedient.

Sir Oliv. Your most obsequious.

Jos. Surf. You may depend upon hearing from me, whenever I can be of service.

Sir Oliv. Sweet sir, you are too good.

Jos. Surf. In the meantime I wish you health and spirits.

Sir Oliv. Your ever grateful and perpetual humble servant.

Jos. Surf. Sir, yours as sincerely.

Sir Oliv. Charles! – you are my heir.   [*Aside. Exit.*

Jos. Surf. This is one bad effect of a good character; it invites application from the unfortunate, and there needs no small degree of address to gain the reputation of benevolence without incurring the expense. The silver ore of pure charity is an expensive article in the catalogue of a man's good qualities; whereas the sentimental French plate I use instead of it makes just as good a show, and pays no tax.

Enter ROWLEY

Row. Mr Surface, your servant: I was apprehensive of interrupting you, though my business demands immediate attention, as this note will inform you.

Jos. Surf. Always happy to see Mr Rowley. – How! – [*Reads the letter.*] Oliver Surface! – My uncle arrived!

Row. He is, indeed: we have just parted – quite well,

after a speedy voyage, and impatient to embrace his worthy nephew.

Jos. Surf. I am astonished! – William! stop Mr Stanley, if he's not gone.

Row. Oh! he's out of reach, I believe.

Jos. Surf. Why did you not let me know this when you came in together?

Row. I thought you had particular business; – but I must be gone to inform your brother, and appoint him here to meet his uncle. He will be with you in a quarter of an hour.

Jos. Surf. So he says. Well, I am strangely overjoyed at his coming. – Never, to be sure, was anything so damned unlucky!   [*Aside.*

Row. You will be delighted to see how well he looks.

Jos. Surf. Oh! I'm rejoiced to hear it. – Just at this time!
                                                       [*Aside.*

Row. I'll tell him how impatiently you expect him.

Jos. Surf. Do, do; pray give my best duty and affection. Indeed, I cannot express the sensations I feel at the thought of seeing him. – [*Exit Rowley.*] Certainly his coming just at this time is the cruellest piece of ill fortune.   [*Exit.*

———

ACT V, SCENE 2

Sir Peter Teazle's
Enter MRS CANDOUR *and* MAID

Maid. Indeed, ma'am, my lady will see nobody at present.

Mrs Can. Did you tell her it was her friend Mrs Candour?

Maid. Yes, ma'am; but she begs you will excuse her.

Mrs Can. Do go again. – I shall be glad to see her, if it be only for a moment, for I am sure she must be in great distress. – [*Exit Maid.*] Dear heart, how provoking! I'm not mistress of half the circumstances!

We shall have the whole affair in the newspapers, with the names of the parties at full length, before I have dropped the story at a dozen houses.

Enter SIR BENJAMIN BACKBITE

Oh, Sir Benjamin! you have heard, I suppose –

Sir Ben. Of Lady Teazle and Mr Surface –

Mrs Can. And Sir Peter's discovery –

Sir Ben. Oh, the strangest piece of business, to be sure!

Mrs Can. Well, I never was so surprised in my life. I am so sorry for all parties, indeed.

Sir Ben. Now, I don't pity Sir Peter at all: he was so extravagantly partial to Mr Surface.

Mrs Can. Mr Surface! Why, 'twas with Charles Lady Teazle was detected.

Sir Ben. No such thing! – Mr Surface is the gallant.

Mrs Can. No, no! Charles is the man. 'Twas Mr Surface brought Sir Peter on purpose to discover them.

Sir Ben. I tell you I had it from one –

Mrs Can. And I have it from one –

Sir Ben. Who had it from one, who had it –

Mrs Can. From one immediately – but here comes Lady Sneerwell; perhaps she knows the whole affair.

Enter LADY SNEERWELL

Lady Sneer. So, my dear Mrs Candour, here's a sad affair of our friend Teazle!

Mrs Can. Aye, my dear friend, who could have thought it?

Lady Sneer. Well, there is no trusting to appearances; though indeed, she was always too lively for me.

Mrs Can. To be sure, her manners were a little too free; but then she was very young!

Lady Sneer. And had, indeed, some good qualities.

Mrs Can. So she had, indeed. But have you heard the particulars?

Lady Sneer. No; but everybody says that Mr Surface –

Sir Ben. Aye, there; I told you Mr Surface was the man.

Mrs Can. No, no, indeed, the assignation was with Charles.

Lady Sneer. With Charles! You alarm me, Mrs Candour!

Mrs Can. Yes, yes, he was the lover. Mr Surface, to do him justice, was only the informer.

Sir Ben. Well, I'll not dispute with you, Mrs Candour; but, be it which it may, I hope that Sir Peter's wound will not –

Mrs Can. Sir Peter's wound! Oh, mercy! I didn't hear a word of their fighting.

Lady Sneer. Nor I, a syllable.

Sir Ben. No! what, no mention of the duel?

Mrs Can. Not a word.

Sir Ben. Oh Lord, yes, yes: they fought before they left the room.

Lady Sneer. Pray let us hear.

Mrs Can. Aye, do oblige us with the duel.

Sir Ben. 'Sir,' says Sir Peter, immediately after the discovery, 'you are a most ungrateful fellow.'

Mrs Can. Aye, to Charles –

Sir Ben. No, no – to Mr Surface – 'a most ungrateful fellow; and old as I am, sir,' says he, 'I insist on immediate satisfaction.'

Mrs Can. Aye, that must have been to Charles; for 'tis very unlikely Mr Surface should go fight in his own house.

Sir Ben. 'Gad's life, ma'am, not at all – 'giving me immediate satisfaction,' – On this, ma'am, Lady Teazle, seeing Sir Peter in such danger, ran out of the room in strong hysterics, and Charles after her, calling out for hartshorn and water; then, madam, they began to fight with swords –

Enter CRABTREE

Crab. With pistols, nephew – pistols: I have it from undoubted authority.

Mrs Can. Oh, Mr Crabtree, then it is all true!

Crab. Too true, indeed, madam, and Sir Peter dangerously wounded –

Sir Ben. By a thrust in *seconde* quite through his left
side –

Crab. By a bullet lodged in the thorax.

Mrs Can. Mercy on me! Poor Sir Peter!

Crab. Yes, madam; though Charles would have avoided
the matter, if he could.

Mrs Can. I knew Charles was the person.

Sir Ben. My uncle, I see, knows nothing of the matter.

Crab. But Sir Peter taxed him with the basest ingratitude –

Sir Ben. That I told you, you know –

Crab. Do, nephew, let me speak! and insisted on immediate –

Sir Ben. Just as I said –

Crab. Odds life, nephew, allow others to know something too! A pair of pistols lay on the bureau (for
Mr Surface, it seems, had come home the night before
late from Salthill, where he had been to see the
Montem with a friend, who has a son at Eton), so,
unluckily, the pistols were left charged.

Sir Ben. I heard nothing of this.

Crab. Sir Peter forced Charles to take one, and they
fired, it seems, pretty nearly together. Charles's shot
took effect, as I tell you, and Sir Peter's missed; but,
what is very extraordinary, the ball struck against a
little bronze Shakespeare that stood over the fire-
place, grazed out of the window at a right angle,
and wounded the postman, who was just coming to
the door with a double letter from Northamptonshire.

Sir Ben. My uncle's account is more circumstantial, I
confess; but I believe mine is the true one, for all that.

Lady Sneer. I am more interested in this affair than they
imagine, and must have better information.

[*Aside. Exit.*

Sir Ben. [*After a pause, looking at each other.*] Ah! Lady Sneerwell's alarm is very easily accounted for.

Crab. Yes, yes, they certainly *do* say – but that's neither here nor there.

Mrs Can. But, pray, where is Sir Peter at present?

Crab. Oh! they brought him home, and he is now in the house, though the servants are ordered to deny him.

Mrs Can. I believe so, and Lady Teazle, I suppose, attending him.

Crab. Yes, yes; and I saw one of the faculty enter just before me.

Sir Ben. Hey! who comes here?

Crab. Oh, this is he: the physician, depend on't.

Mrs Can. Oh, certainly! it must be the physician; and now we shall know.

Enter SIR OLIVER

Crab. Well, doctor, what hopes?

Mrs Can. Aye, doctor, how's your patient?

Sir Ben. Now, doctor, isn't it a wound with a small-sword?

Crab. A bullet lodged in the thorax, for a hundred.

Sir Oliv. Doctor! a wound with a small-sword! and a bullet in the thorax? What! are you mad, good people?

Sir Ben. Perhaps, sir, you are not a doctor?

Sir Oliv. Truly, I am to thank you for my degree, if I am.

Crab. Only a friend of Sir Peter's, then, I presume. But, sir, you must have heard of his accident?

Sir Oliv. Not a word!

Crab. Not of his being dangerously wounded?

Sir Oliv. The devil he is!

Sir Ben. Run through the body –

Crab. Shot in the breast –

Sir Ben. By one Mr Surface –

Crab. Aye, the younger.

Sir Oliv. Hey! what the plague! you seem to differ

strangely in your accounts: however, you agree that Sir Peter is dangerously wounded.

Sir Ben. Oh, yes, we agree there.

Crab. Yes, yes, I believe there can be no doubt in that.

Sir Oliv. Then, upon my word, for a person in that situation, he is the most imprudent man alive; for here he comes, walking as if nothing at all was the matter.

Enter SIR PETER

Odds heart, Sir Peter, you are come in good time, I promise you; for we had just given you over!

Sir Ben. Egad, uncle, this is the most sudden recovery!

Sir Oliv. Why, man, what do you do out of bed with a small-sword through your body, and a bullet lodged in your thorax?

Sir Pet. A small-sword and a bullet!

Sir Oliv. Aye, these gentlemen would have killed you without law or physic, and wanted to dub me a doctor, to make me an accomplice.

Sir Pet. Why, what is all this?

Sir Ben. We rejoice, Sir Peter, that the story of the duel is not true, and are sincerely sorry for your other misfortune.

Sir Pet. So, so; all over the town already. [*Aside.*

Crab. Though, Sir Peter, you were certainly vastly to blame to marry at all at your years.

Sir Pet. Sir, what business is that of yours?

Mrs Can. Though, indeed, as Sir Peter made so good a husband, he's very much to be pitied.

Sir Pet. Plague on your pity, ma'am! I desire none of it.

Sir Ben. However, Sir Peter, you must not mind the laughing and jests you will meet with on the occasion.

Sir Pet. Sir, sir, I desire to be master in my own house.

Crab. 'Tis no uncommon case, that's one comfort.

Sir Pet. I insist on being left to myself: without ceremony – I insist on your leaving my house directly!

Mrs Can. Well, well, we are going; and depend on't, we'll make the best report of you we can. [*Exit.*

Sir Pet. Leave my house!

Crab. And tell how hardly you've been treated.   [*Exit.*

Sir Pet. Leave my house!

Sir Ben. And how patiently you bear it.   [*Exit.*

Sir Pet. Fiends! vipers! furies! Oh! that their own venom would choke them!

Sir Oliv. They are very provoking indeed, Sir Peter.

Enter ROWLEY

Row. I heard high words: what has ruffled you, sir?

Sir Pet. Pshaw! what signifies asking? Do I ever pass a day without my vexations?

Sir Oliv. Well, I'm not inquisitive. I come only to tell you, that I have seen both my nephews in the manner we proposed.

Sir Pet. A precious couple they are!

Row. Yes, and Sir Oliver is convinced that your judgement was right, Sir Peter.

Sir Oliv. Yes, I find Joseph is indeed the man, after all.

Row. Aye, as Sir Peter says, he is a man of sentiment.

Sir Oliv. And acts up to the sentiments he professes.

Row. It certainly is edification to hear him talk.

Sir Oliv. Oh, he's a model for the young men of the age! – But how's this, Sir Peter? you don't join us in your friend Joseph's praise, as I expected.

Sir Pet. Sir Oliver, we live in a damned wicked world, and the fewer we praise the better.

Row. What! do you say so, Sir Peter, who were never mistaken in your life?

Sir Pet. Pshaw! plague on you both! I see by your sneering you have heard the whole affair. I shall go mad among you!

Row. Then, to fret you no longer, Sir Peter, we are indeed acquainted with it all. I met Lady Teazle coming from Mr Surface's so humbled, that she deigned to request me to be her advocate with you.

Sir Pet. And does Sir Oliver know all too?

Sir Oliv. Every circumstance.

Sir Pet. What, of the closet – and the screen, hey?

Sir Oliv. Yes, yes, and the little French milliner. Oh, I
. have been vastly diverted with the story! Ha! ha! ha!

Sir Pet. 'Twas very pleasant.

Sir Oliv. I never laughed more in my life, I assure you:
ha! ha! ha!

Sir Pet. Oh, vastly diverting! ha! ha! ha!

Row. To be sure, Joseph with his sentiments! ha! ha!
ha!

Sir Pet. Yes, his sentiments! Ha! ha! ha! Hypocritical
villain!

Sir Oliv. Aye, and that rogue Charles to pull Sir Peter
out of the closet: ha! ha! ha!

Sir Pet. Ha! ha! 'twas devilish entertaining, to be sure!

Sir Oliv. Ha! ha! ha! Egad, Sir Peter, I should like to
have seen your face when the screen was thrown down:
ha! ha!

Sir Pet. Yes, my face when the screen was thrown down:
ha! ha! ha! Oh, I must never show my head again!

Sir Oliv. But come, come, it isn't fair to laugh at you
neither, my old friend; though, upon my soul, I can't
help it.

Sir Pet. Oh, pray don't restrain your mirth on my
account: it does not hurt me at all! I laugh at the
whole affair myself. Yes, yes, I think being a standing
jest for all one's acquaintance a very happy situation.
Oh, yes, and then of a morning to read the paragraphs
about Mr S—, Lady T—, and Sir P—, will be so
diverting! I shall certainly leave town tomorrow and
never look mankind in the face again.

Row. Without affectation, Sir Peter, you may despise
the ridicule of fools: but I see Lady Teazle going
towards the next room; I am sure you must desire a
reconciliation as earnestly as she does.

Sir Oliv. Perhaps my being here prevents her coming
to you. Well, I'll leave honest Rowley to mediate

between you; but he must bring you all presently to Mr Surface's, where I am now returning, if not to reclaim a libertine, at least to expose hypocrisy.

Sir Pet. Ah, I'll be present at your discovering yourself there with all my heart; though 'tis a vile unlucky place for discoveries.

Row. We'll follow.   [*Exit Sir Oliver.*

Sir Pet. She is not coming here, you see, Rowley.

Row. No, but she has left the door of that room open, you perceive. See, she is in tears.

Sir Pet. Certainly a little mortification appears very becoming in a wife. Don't you think it will do her good to let her pine a little?

Row. Oh, this is ungenerous in you!

Sir Pet. Well, I know not what to think. You remember the letter I found of hers evidently intended for Charles!

Row. A mere forgery, Sir Peter, laid in your way on purpose. This is one of the points which I intend Snake shall give you conviction of.

Sir Pet. I wish I were once satisfied of that. She looks this way. What a remarkably elegant turn of the head she has! Rowley, I'll go to her.

Row. Certainly.

Sir Pet. Though, when it is known that we are reconciled people will laugh at me ten times more.

Row. Let them laugh, and retort their malice only by showing them you are happy in spite of it.

Sir Pet. I'faith, so I will! and, if I'm not mistaken, we may yet be the happiest couple in the country.

Row. Nay, Sir Peter, he who once lays aside suspicion –

Sir Pet. Hold, Master Rowley! if you have any regard for me, never let me hear you utter anything like a sentiment: I have had enough of them to serve me the rest of my life.   [*Exeunt.*

ACT V, SCENE 3

The Library

Enter JOSEPH SURFACE *and* LADY SNEERWELL

Lady Sneer. Impossible! Will not Sir Peter immediately be reconciled to Charles, and of consequence no longer oppose his union with Maria? The thought is distraction to me.

Jos. Surf. Can passion furnish a remedy?

Lady Sneer. No, nor cunning either. Oh! I was a fool, an idiot, to league with such a blunderer!

Jos. Surf. Surely, Lady Sneerwell, I am the greatest sufferer; yet you see I bear the accident with calmness.

Lady Sneer. Because the disappointment doesn't reach your heart; your interest only attached you to Maria. Had you felt for her what I have for that ungrateful libertine, neither your temper nor hypocrisy could prevent your showing the sharpness of your vexation.

Jos. Surf. But why should your reproaches fall on me for this disappointment?

Lady Sneer. Are you not the cause of it? What had you to bate in your pursuit of Maria to pervert Lady Teazle by the way? Had you not a sufficient field for your roguery in blinding Sir Peter, and supplanting your brother, but you must endeavour to seduce his wife? I hate such an avarice of crimes; 'tis an unfair monopoly, and never prospers.

Jos. Surf. Well, I admit I have been to blame. I confess I deviated from the direct road of wrong, but I don't think we're so totally defeated neither.

Lady Sneer. No!

Jos. Surf. You tell me you have made a trial of Snake since we met, and that you still believe him faithful to us?

Lady Sneer. I do believe so.

Jos. Surf. And that he has undertaken, should it be
necessary, to swear and prove, that Charles is at this
time contracted by vows and honour to your ladyship,
which some of his former letters to you will serve to
support?

Lady Sneer. This, indeed, might have assisted.

Jos. Surf. Come, come; it is not too late yet. [*Knocking at
the door.*] But hark! this is probably my uncle, Sir
Oliver: retire to that room; we'll consult further when
he's gone.

Lady Sneer. Well, but if *he* should find you out too?

Jos. Surf. Oh, I have no fear of that. Sir Peter will hold
his tongue for his own credit's sake – and you may
depend on it I shall soon discover Sir Oliver's weak
side!

Lady Sneer. I have no diffidence of your abilities: only
be constant to one roguery at a time.

　　　　　　　　　　　　　　[*Exit Lady Sneerwell.*

Jos. Surf. I will, I will! – So! 'tis confounded hard, after
such bad fortune, to be baited by one's confederate
in evil. Well, at all events, my character is so much
better than Charles's, that I certainly – hey! – what –
this is not Sir Oliver, but old Stanley again. Plague
on't that he should return to tease me just now
– I shall have Sir Oliver come and find him here
– and –

Enter SIR OLIVER

Gad's life, Mr Stanley, why have you come back to
plague me at this time? You must not stay now, upon
my word.

Sir Oliv. Sir, I hear your uncle Oliver is expected here,
and though he has been so penurious to you, I'll try
what he'll do for me.

Jos. Surf. Sir, 'tis impossible for you to stay now, so I
must beg. – Come any other time, and I promise you,
you shall be assisted.

Sir Oliv. No: Sir Oliver and I must be acquainted.

Jos. Surf. Zounds, sir! then I insist on your quitting the room directly.

Sir Oliv. Nay, sir –

Jos. Surf. Sir, I insist on't: – here, William! show this gentleman out. Since you compel me, sir, not one moment – this is such insolence.

Enter CHARLES

Chas. Surf. Heyday! what's the matter now? What the devil, have you got hold of my little broker here? Zounds, brother, don't hurt little Premium. What's the matter, my little fellow?

Jos. Surf. So! he has been with you, too, has he?

Chas. Surf. To be sure he has. Why, he's as honest a little – But sure, Joseph, you have not been borrowing money too, have you?

Jos. Surf. Borrowing! no! But, brother, you know we expect Sir Oliver here every –

Chas. Surf. O Gad, that's true! Noll mustn't find the little broker here, to be sure.

Jos. Surf. Yet, Mr Stanley insists –

Chas. Surf. Stanley! why his name's Premium.

Jos. Surf. No, no, Stanley.

Chas. Surf. No, no, Premium.

Jos. Surf. Well, no matter which – but –

Chas. Surf. Aye, aye, Stanley or Premium, 'tis the same thing, as you say; for I suppose he goes by half a hundred names, besides A. B. at the coffee-house.

[*Knocking.*

Jos. Surf. 'Sdeath! here's Sir Oliver at the door. Now I beg, Mr Stanley –

Chas. Surf. Aye, aye, and I beg, Mr Premium –

Sir Oliv. Gentlemen –

Jos. Surf. Sir, by heaven you shall go!

Chas. Surf. Aye, out with him, certainly.

Sir Oliv. This violence –

Jos. Surf. 'Tis your own fault.

Chas. Surf. Out with him, to be sure.

> [*Both forcing Sir Oliver out.*

Enter SIR PETER *and* LADY TEAZLE, MARIA,
and ROWLEY

Sir Pet. My old friend, Sir Oliver – hey! What in the
name of wonder! – here are dutiful nephews – assault
their uncle at his first visit!

Lady Teaz. Indeed, Sir Oliver, 'twas well we came in
to release you.

Row. Truly, it was; for I perceive, Sir Oliver, the
character of old Stanley was not a protection to you.

Sir Oliv. Nor of Premium either: the necessities of the
former could not extort a shilling from that benevolent
gentleman; and with the other I stood a chance of
faring worse than my ancestors, and being knocked
down without being bid for.

Jos. Surf. Charles!

Chas. Surf. Joseph!

Jos. Surf. 'Tis now complete!

Chas. Surf. Very.

Sir Oliv. Sir Peter, my friend, and Rowley too, look on
that elder nephew of mine. You know what he has
already received from my bounty; and you also know
how gladly I would have regarded half my fortune as
held in trust for him: judge, then, my disappointment
in discovering him to be destitute of truth, charity,
and gratitude!

Sir Pet. Sir Oliver, I should be more surprised at this
declaration, if I had not myself found him to be
selfish, treacherous, and hypocritical.

Lady Teaz. And if the gentleman pleads not guilty to
these, pray let him call *me* to his character.

Sir Pet. Then, I believe, we need add no more: if he
knows himself, he will consider it as the most perfect
punishment that he is known to the world.

Chas. Surf. If they talk this way to Honesty, what will they say to me, by-and-by? [*Aside.*

Sir Oliv. As for that prodigal, his brother, there –

Chas. Surf. Aye, now comes my turn: the damned family pictures will ruin me. [*Aside.*

Jos. Surf. Sir Oliver – uncle, will you honour me with a hearing?

Chas. Surf. Now, if Joseph would make one of his long speeches, I might recollect myself a little. [*Aside.*

Sir Oliv. I suppose you would undertake to justify yourself? [*To Joseph.*

Jos. Surf. I trust I could.

Sir Oliv. Pshaw! – nay, if you desert your roguery in this distress and try to be justified, you have even less principle than I thought you had. [*Turns from him in contempt.*] Well, sir! [*to Charles.*] – and you would justify yourself too, I suppose?

Chas. Surf. Not that I know of, Sir Oliver.

Sir Oliv. What! – Little Premium has been let too much into the secret, I suppose?

Chas. Surf. True, sir; but they were *family* secrets, and should not be mentioned again, you know.

Row. Come, Sir Oliver, I know you cannot speak of Charles's follies with anger.

Sir Oliv. Odd's heart, no more I can; nor with gravity either. – Sir Peter, do you know the rogue bargained with me for all his ancestors; sold me judges and generals by the foot, and maiden aunts as cheap as broken china.

Chas. Surf. To be sure, Sir Oliver, I did make a little free with the family canvas, that's the truth on't. My ancestors may rise in judgement against me, there's no denying it; but believe me sincere when I tell you – and upon my soul I would not say so if I was not – that if I do not appear mortified at the exposure of my follies, it is because I feel at this moment the warmest satisfaction at seeing you, my liberal benefactor.

Sir Oliv. Charles, I believe you. Give me your hand again: the ill-looking little fellow over the settee has made your peace.

Chas. Surf. Then, sir, my gratitude to the original is still increased.

Lady Teaz. Yet, I believe, Sir Oliver, here is one whom Charles is still more anxious to be reconciled to.

Sir Oliv. Oh, I have heard of his attachment there; and with the young lady's pardon, if I construe right – that blush –

Sir Pet. Well, child, speak your sentiments.

Mar. Sir, I have little to say, but that I shall rejoice to hear that he is happy; for me, – whatever claim I had to his attention, I willingly resign to one who has a better title.

Chas. Surf. How, Maria!

Sir Pet. Heyday! what's the mystery now? – While he appeared an incorrigible rake, you would give your hand to no one else; and now that he is likely to reform I'll warrant you won't have him.

Mar. His own heart and Lady Sneerwell know the cause.

Chas. Surf. Lady Sneerwell!

Jos. Surf. Brother, it is with great concern I am obliged to speak on this point, but my regard to justice compels me, and Lady Sneerwell's injuries can no longer be concealed.   [*Goes to door.*

Enter LADY SNEERWELL

All. Lady Sneerwell!

Sir Pet. So! another French milliner! Egad, he has one in every room in the house, I suppose!

Lady Sneer. Ungrateful Charles! Well may you be surprised, and feel for the indelicate situation your perfidy has forced me into.

Chas. Surf. Pray, uncle, is this another plot of yours? For, as I have life, I don't understand it.

Jos. Surf. I believe, sir, there is but the evidence of one person more necessary to make it extremely clear.

Sir Pet. And that person, I imagine, is Mr Snake. – Rowley, you were perfectly right to bring him with you, and pray let him appear.

Row. Walk in, Mr Snake.

Enter SNAKE

I thought his testimony might be wanted; however, it happens unluckily, that he comes to confront Lady Sneerwell, not to support her.

Lady Sneer. A villain! Treacherous to me at last! – Speak, fellow, have you too conspired against me?

Snake. I beg your ladyship ten thousand pardons: you paid me extremely liberally for the lie in question; but I unfortunately have been offered double to speak the truth.

Lady Sneer. The torments of shame and disappointment on you all!   [*Going.*

Lady Teaz. Hold, Lady Sneerwell – before you go, let me thank you for the trouble you and that gentleman have taken, in writing letters from me to Charles, and answering them yourself; and let me also request you to make my respects to the Scandalous College, of which you are president, and inform them, that Lady Teazle, licentiate, begs leave to return the diploma they granted her, as she leaves off practice, and kills characters no longer.

Lady Sneer. You too, madam – provoking – insolent – May your husband live these fifty years!   [*Exit.*

Sir Pet. Oons! what a fury!

Lady Teaz. A malicious creature it is.

Sir Pet. Hey! not for her last wish?

Lady Teaz. Oh, no!

Sir Oliv. Well, sir, and what have you to say now?

Jos. Surf. Sir, I am so confounded, to find that Lady Sneerwell could be guilty of suborning Mr Snake in this manner, to impose on us all, that I know not

what to say: however, lest her revengeful spirit should
prompt her to injure my brother, I had certainly
better follow her directly.   [*Exit.*

Sir Pet. Moral to the last drop!

Sir Oliv. Ay, and marry her, Joseph, if you can. Oil and
vinegar, egad! you'll do very well together.

Row. I believe we have no more occasion for Mr Snake
at present?

Snake. Before I go, I beg pardon once for all, for whatever
uneasiness I have been the humble instrument of
causing to the parties present.

Sir Pet. Well, well, you have made atonement by a good
deed at last.

Snake. But I must request of the company that it shall
never be known.

Sir Pet. Hey! – what the plague! – Are you ashamed of
having done a right thing once in your life?

Snake. Ah, sir, consider, – I live by the badness of my
character; and, if it were once known that I had been
betrayed into an honest action, I should lose every
friend I have in the world.

Sir Pet. Here's a precious rogue!

Sir Oliv. Well, well – we'll not traduce you by saying
anything in your praise, never fear.   [*Exit Snake.*

Lady Teaz. See, Sir Oliver, there needs no persuasion
now to reconcile your nephew and Maria.

Sir Oliv. Aye, aye, that's as it should be, and, egad, we'll
have the wedding to-morrow morning.

Chas. Surf. Thank you, my dear uncle.

Sir Pet. What, you rogue! don't you ask the girl's consent
first?

Chas. Surf. Oh, I have done that a long time – a minute
ago – and she has looked *yes*.

Mar. For shame, Charles! – I protest, Sir Peter, there
has not been a word.

Sir Oliv. Well, then, the fewer the better: – may your
love for each other never know abatement.

Sir Pet. And may you live as happily together as Lady
  Teazle and I – intend to do.

Chas. Surf. Rowley, my old friend, I am sure you congratulate me; and I suspect that I owe you much.

Sir Oliv. You do, indeed, Charles.

Row. If my efforts to serve you had not succeeded you
  would have been in my debt for the attempt; but
  deserve to be happy, and you overpay me.

Sir Pet. Aye, honest Rowley always said you would
  reform.

Chas. Surf. Why, as to reforming, Sir Peter, I'll make no
  promises, and that I take to be a proof that I intend
  to set about it. But here shall be my monitor – my
  gentle guide. – Ah! can I leave the virtuous path those
  eyes illumine?

Though thou, dear maid, shouldst waive thy beauty's
    sway,
Thou still must rule, because I will obey:
An humble fugitive from Folly view,
No sanctuary near but Love [*To the audience*] and you:
You can, indeed, each anxious fear remove,
For even Scandal dies if you approve.

End of the Fifth Act

EPILOGUE
By Mr Colman
Spoken by Mrs Abington in the character of Lady Teazle

  I, who was late so volatile and gay,
Like a trade wind must now blow all one way,
Bend all my cares, my studies, and my vows,
To one dull rusty weathercock – my spouse!
So wills our virtuous bard – the pye-ball'd Bayes
Of crying epilogues and laughing plays!
Old bachelors, who marry smart young wives,
Learn from our play to regulate your lives:
Each bring his dear to town, all faults upon her –
London will prove the very source of honour.
Plung'd fairly in, like a cold bath it serves,
When principles relax, – to brace the nerves:
Such is my case – and yet I must deplore
That the gay dream of dissipation's o'er:
And say, ye fair, was ever lively wife,
Born with a genius for the highest life,
Like me untimely blasted in her bloom,
Like me condemn'd to such a dismal doom?
Save money – when I just knew how to *waste* it!
Leave London – just as I began to taste it!

Must I then watch the early crowing cock,
The melancholy ticking of a clock;
In a lone rustic hall for ever pounded,
With dogs, cats, rats, and squalling brats surrounded?
With humble curate can I now retire
(While good Sir Peter boozes with the squire),
And at backgammon mortify my soul,
That pants for loo, or flutters at a vole.
Seven's the main! Dear sound! that must expire,
Lost at hot cockles round a Christmas fire;

The transient hour of fashion too soon spent,
Farewell the tranquil mind, farewell content!
Farewell the *plumèd* head, the cushion'd *tête*,
That takes the cushion from its proper seat!
That spirit-stirring drum! – card-drums I mean,
Spadille – odd trick – pam – basto – king and queen!
And you, ye knockers, that, with brazen throat,
The welcome visitors' approach denote;
Farewell! – all quality of high renown,
Pride, pomp, and circumstance of glorious Town!
Farewell! your revels I partake no more,
And Lady Teazle's occupation's o'er!
And this I told our bard; he smiled, and said 'twas clear,
I ought to play deep tragedy next year.
Meanwhile he drew wise morals from his play,
And in these solemn periods stalk'd away: –
'Blest were the fair like you; her faults who stopt,
And closed her follies when the curtain dropt!
No more in vice or error to engage,
Or play the fool at large on life's great stage.'

MORE ABOUT PENGUINS

Penguinews, which appears every month, contains details of all the new books issued by Penguins as they are published. From time to time it is supplemented by *Penguins in Print*, which is a complete list of all books published by Penguins which are in print. (There are some five thousand of these.)

A specimen copy of *Penguinews* will be sent to you free on request, and you can become a subscriber for the price of the postage – 50p for a year's issues (including the complete lists) if you live in the United Kingdom, or 75p if you live elsewhere. Just write to Dept EP, Penguin Books Ltd, Harmondsworth, Middlesex, enclosing a cheque or postal order, and your name will be added to the mailing list.

Some other books published by Penguins are described on the following page.

Note: *Penguinews* and *Penguins in Print*
are not available in the U.S.A. or Canada

Two volumes in the Penguin English Library

THREE RESTORATION COMEDIES

The Man of Mode – ETHEREGE
The Country Wife – WYCHERLEY
Love for Love – CONGREVE

Artificial, irreverent, and bawdy, the Restoration theatre came as a violent reaction to the strict ordinance of the Commonwealth. Played before the most cliquish and cynical audience in the history of the theatre, consciously trailing its coat at the puritan citizenry, it has delighted and offended over the centuries in about equal measure. Yet, take it or leave it, it offers a morality of its own, in which elegance and wit are the chief virtues, and folly, meanness, and hypocrisy the butts of its genial satire. At its best, as in the three plays included here, it produced some of the greatest comedy of all time, holding up to its age a mirror whose image, however partial, is 'bright, sharp and pertinent, un-dimmed with the breath of years'.

Ben Jonson

THREE COMEDIES

As Shakespeare's nearest rival on the English stage, Ben Jonson has both gained and suffered. Productions of recent years have, as it were, rediscovered him as a comic dramatist of genius and a master of language. This volume contains his best-known comedies.

Volpone, which is perhaps his greatest, and *The Alchemist* are both *tours de force* of brilliant knavery, unflagging in wit and and comic invention. *Bartholomew Fair*, an earthier work, portrays Jonson's fellow Londoners in festive mood – bawdy, energetic, and never at a loss for words.